Muriel Duckworth
A Very Active Pacifist

For Naomi

With best wishes

Marion D. Kerans

Muriel Duckworth

Muriel at a labour demonstration, 1974.

Muriel Duckworth
A Very Active Pacifist

A Biography

Marion Douglas Kerans

Fernwood Publishing • Halifax

Editing: Anne Webb
Design and production: Beverley Rach
Cover photos: Pat Kipping (right), Beverley Rach (bottom left)
Photography: Effort has been made to credit the photographers whose photos are
included in this book however many came from personal collections where sources
were unknown.
Printed and bound in Canada by: Hignell Printing Limited

A publication of:
Fernwood Publishing
Box 9409, Station A
Halifax, Nova Scotia
B3K 5S3

Fernwood Publishing Company Limited gratefully acknowledges the financial support
of The Ministry of Canadian Heritage and the Nova Scotia Department of Education
and Culture.

Canadian Cataloguing in Publication Data

Kerans, Marion Douglas

      Muriel Duckworth

      Includes bibliographical references.
      ISBN 1-8956686-68-7

1. Duckworth, Muriel, 1908– 2. Pacifists -- Canada -- Biography.
I. Title.

JX1962.D82K47 1996   303.6'6'092   C96-950167-6

Contents

To Danielle, Mariel, Heather, Lyn, Margaret and Mary Anne
who represent for me the hope of the future.

My heart is moved by all I cannot save:
so much has been destroyed

I have to cast my lot with those
who age after age, perversely,

with no extraordinary power,
reconstitute the world.

Adrienne Rich, "Natural Resources,"
in *The Dream of a Common Language, Poems, 1974–77*
New York: Norton 1978

Events in the Life of Muriel Duckworth

1908, Oct. 31	Born Muriel Helena Ball at East Bolton (now Austin) Quebec.
1917, Dec.	Family moved to Magog, Quebec.
1925	Senior matriculation, Ontario Ladies College, Whitby, Ontario.
1929	B.A. and teaching diploma, McGill University, Montreal.
1929, June	Married Jack Duckworth.
1929–30	Attended Union Theological Seminary, New York City, with her husband.
1930	Returned to Montreal.
1930–32	Part-time secretary to Student Christian Movement, McGill University.
1933	Birth of son, Martin Duckworth.
1935	Birth of daughter, Eleanor Duckworth.
1938	Birth of son, John Duckworth.
1944	Death of brother, Norman, RCAF, returning from air raid over Germany.
1947	Death of mother.
1947	Move to Halifax, Nova Scotia. Jack Duckworth becomes executive director of Halifax YMCA.
1948–62	Part-time parent education advisor, Department of Education, Province of Nova Scotia.
1950	Founding member of Halifax Branch, Canadian Mental Health Association. Board member during the 1950s.
1954–55	President of Nova Scotia Federation of Home and School.
1958	Founding member of the Canadian Conference on Education.
1959	Founding member of the Nova Scotia Education Association.
1960	Founding member of Voice of Women (VOW), Halifax.
1960-75	Board member of VOW, Canada.

1962–67	Full-time program advisor, Adult Education Division, Department of Education, Province of Nova Scotia.
1965	Founding member of the Canadian Council for International Cooperation.
1965	Honorary Vice Chair, Canadian International Cooperation Year Committee.
1965	Honorary Life Member, Nova Scotia Federation of Home and School Associations.
1965–66	Board member of Canada's Centennial International Development Program.
1967	Honorary Life Member, Canadian Association for Adult Education.
1967	VOW delegate to International Conference of Women for Peace, Moscow.
1967–71	National President of VOW, Canada.
1971	Founding member of the Movement for Citizens Voice and Action Halifax.
1974	NDP candidate for Halifax-Cornwallis provincial constituency.
1975	May 17, death of husband, Jack Duckworth.
1975	VOW delegate to UN International Women's Year Tribune, Mexico City.
1975	Joined the Religious Society of Friends (Quakers).
1975–78	Member of the National Board of Oxfam.
1976	Founding member of the Canadian Research Institute for the Advancement of Women (CRIAW).
1977–79	Member of the Federal Policy Review Committee, NDP.
1978	NDP candidate for Halifax-Cornwallis provincial constituency.
1978	Honorary Doctor of Humane Letters, Mount Saint Vincent University, Halifax.
1979–80	President of CRIAW.
1980	Delegate representing CRIAW and VOW to United Nations Mid-decade Conference on Women, Copenhagen.
1980–81	Member of the International Affairs Committee, NDP, Canada.

1981	Delegate to Federal NDP Convention.
1981	Persons' Award, presented by Governor General.
1981	Muriel Duckworth Award established by CRIAW.
1981	Halifax YWCA Award for Contributions to the Community and to the Advancement of Women.
1981	Founding member of the Canadian Association for the Advancement of Women and Sport.
1981	Honorary Life Member of CRIAW.
1981	Honorary Life member, Nova Scotia Women's Health Network.
1982	Chair presenting Women's Petition for Peace to Canadian Ambassador at UN Special Session on Disarmament II, New York.
1983	Honorary Doctor of Laws, Concordia University, Montreal.
1983	Companion of the Order of Canada.
1983	Trip to Japan to World Conference Against Atomic and Hydrogen Bombs, Tokyo and Hiroshima.
1984	Honorary Doctor of Laws, McGill University, Montreal.
1984	Trip to Soviet Union to film *Speaking our Peace.*
1985	Chair, Program Committee, International Conference of Women for Peace, Mount Saint Vincent University, Halifax.
1985	Member of Mission for Peace in Central America.
1986	Honorary Doctor of Laws, University of Prince Edward Island, Charlottetown.
1987	Honorary Doctor of Laws, Dalhousie University, Halifax.
1987	Founding member of Nova Scotia Women's Action Coalition.
1989	Honorary Doctor of Laws, Simon Fraser University, Burnaby.
1989	Goes to court over non-payment of taxes which support the military.
1993	Honorary Doctor of Laws, Acadia University, Wolfville.

Author's Note

I could never have written this biography about Muriel Duckworth without the help of the persons I interviewed. The following women and men told me stories of Muriel, of how they saw her and how they were affected by her: Michael Bradfield, Suellen Bradfield, Linda Christiansen-Ruffman, Claire Culhane, Mary Cutler, Eleanor Duckworth, John Duckworth, Martin Duckworth, Doris Dyke, Margrit Eichler, Ursula Franklin, Margaret Fulton, Ann Gertler, Kay Inglis, Rocky Jones, Kay Macpherson, Alexa McDonough, Betty Murray (deceased), Gwen Norman, Mary O'Brien, Johanna Oosterveld (deceased), Marguerite Overington, Betty Peterson, Lydia Sayle, Norma Scott, Donna Smyth, Gillian Thomas, Maureen Vine and Olive White.

I thank all of them, not only for their time and for their willingness to let me tape record their impressions and memories, but for the inspiration each of them provided me. Theirs are wonderful memories. To the many friends and relatives of Muriel whom I did not reach, I hope you find that these stories evoke your own.

I thank E. Bruce Copland, Margaret Kidd, Kay Macpherson, Gwen Norman, Ernest Stabler and Norah Toole (deceased) for the letters they wrote to me about Muriel.

Although writing this book was a labour of love, I might never have finished it without the support of my family and friends (many of whom are Muriel's friends too). Particularly I wish to thank my son Patrick Kellerman, and John Kirk for their encouragement at crucial moments. Special thanks go to Maureen Kellerman, Pat Kerans and Margaret Tucz for copy editing which, in my view, is the biggest chore of all. To my husband Pat I am forever grateful for his sustaining support.

I would like to thank the courteous staff of the National Archives, Canada, and the Public Archives of Nova Scotia for their help and most particularly Rosemary Barbour, who catalogued Muriel's papers, for her ready and cheerful assistance. I am grateful to Jane Buss of the Writers Federation of Nova Scotia for her helpful advice. I would also like to thank Betty Peterson for providing a wonderful selection of photographs.

I thank Errol Sharpe, the publisher at Fernwood for his faith in me, Beverley Rach, the production co-ordinator and designer for the meticulous care she took, Brenda Conroy for her enormous promotion effort, Donna Davis for her proofreading and Chauna James for her typing. I am very grateful to Anne Webb both for her careful editing and encouraging remarks.

Finally Muriel Duckworth herself deserves my biggest vote of thanks for the many interesting hours I spent interviewing her. I did not always grasp the significance of what she told me the first time round. I thank her for her gentle and kind corrections and for being such a patient adult educator. I appreciate greatly the help she gave me with the research and the time she put into going over the text. Any errors are my own.

A Note About Sources

In the early chapters of the book, my sources are interviews with Muriel. As her life becomes more public, it becomes increasingly documented; thus, in later chapters the sources are interviews, the National Archives of Canada (NAC), the Public Archives of Nova Scotia (PANS) and Dalhousie University Archives (DUA). The source of quotations from interviews is made plain in the text; the archival source for other quotations is specified in notes at the end of each chapter. Gendered language in the quotations has not been altered.

Introduction

In the summer of 1982 my friend Muriel Duckworth became ill with Guillain-Barré syndrome. She was hospitalized in Sherbrooke, Quebec, the nearest city to her summer cottage. When she recovered sufficiently she was flown home to Halifax. When I met her at the airport I was shocked to see such a vibrant person so frail. A few days later in conversation with Muriel's son, Martin, and her friend Linda Christiansen-Ruffman, we admitted to one another how sad it would be to lose Muriel and how much each of us wanted to have a record of her life. I determined then that I would write about her history in the women's peace movement.

Muriel continued to make a marvellous recovery during the autumn and winter of 1982-83. When I raised with her the subject of recording her stories she very nearly dismissed me saying that she was just an ordinary woman and not a luminary in the peace movement like Alva Myrdal, the renowned Swedish United Nations diplomat. I persuaded her that it was precisely because ordinary women could identify with her and she with them that her life story should be told.

The following May, when she had returned to her summer cottage on the hilly shores of Lake Memphremagog at Austin, Quebec, I visited her to tape a series of interviews. Her cottage occupies land beside the lake and next door to the farm where she was born. This is where she spends every

The Duckworth cottage, Austin, Quebec, in autumn.

spring and summer. As I walked down the road to the cottage I saw an old orchard with its apple trees in full bloom. Gazing at the clouds of pink blossoms against the brilliant blue sky, I thought how much Muriel reminded me of these ancient trees that are so firmly rooted and yet continue to throw out tender new shoots each spring. With her creative energy and her deep wisdom, she inspires many of us who have known her. It is not only her record of accomplishments which deserves acknowledgement, as her ability to make lasting friendships is legendary. Her compassion and her good humour are infectious.

I was curious to learn what influences had shaped and sustained her as a peace activist for over sixty years. And I wanted to uncover something of her effect on others. After talking with a number of Muriel's friends, I decided to expand this project into a biography about her remarkable achievements in organizations concerned with human rights, international peace and development, and women's equality.

Some of the people I interviewed see Muriel primarily as a gifted adult educator, others see her as a pioneer Canadian feminist, as a radical pacifist or as a great community developer and social change activist. Nearly everyone sees her as the best friend they will ever have.

Muriel Duckworth has been associated with a great many organizations. She is one of the founders of seventeen at the national and provincial levels. I have focussed on her activity in four: the Voice of Women, the Movement for Citizens Voice and Action, the New Democratic Party and the Canadian Research Institute for the Advancement of Women. I tell her story partly from her own words, partly from conversations with many who know her and from my own observations of her as a friend during these past twenty years.

When I began interviewing Muriel in 1983 she was seventy-four. We discussed then the possibility of her going to Japan that August to observe Hiroshima Day at the Peace Park in Hiroshima. I encouraged her to make the trip, thinking that such a scene would make a fitting conclusion to her biography. Little did I anticipate that in the ensuing years she would return to the Soviet Union for the filming of "Speaking Our Peace," help organize the Women's International Peace Conference in Halifax, go as a delegate on a Peace Mission to Central America, help organize the Women's Action Coalition in Nova Scotia as well as a series of peace coalitions in that province, travel unaccompanied through New Zealand following her eightieth birthday, defend in a federal court her non-payment of taxes which support the military, be present at countless peace demonstrations and continue to remain accessible to the press and to teachers and young people who call upon her to address their classes.

Although I have known Muriel Duckworth only in the latter part of her life, our lives very nearly touched more than fifty years ago. Her husband

Jack directed the YMCA, a family community centre, in Notre Dame de Grace, Montreal, from 1930 to 1947. I lived in that neighbourhood in the forties. During those years Muriel was often around the Y, working with high school girls in their Hi Y Program, going to gym and swim classes and helping to start a play school for the children of women exercising in the gym. I lived just a few streets away from the Family Y and the activities that I attended there, as a teenager, were the Y's famous twice-weekly Bonfire Nights in summertime and the lively Friday night "moccasin dances" at their outdoor rinks in the winter. However, outdoor events were as far as a young Catholic student ventured in those days. Even though I was active in Montreal student organizations, I would never have stepped inside the Y. That was for Protestants. And so it would be another thirty years before I met Muriel Duckworth, who became for me a model and a mentor.

Muriel and Marion Kerans. Muriel holding Marion's granddaughter,
Mariel Kellerman Angus, named for both of them, 1985.

Chapter 1

"A Farmer's Daughter"
Memories of Growing up in Quebec

*M*uriel was born October 31, 1908 on her parents' farm in Austin, a village in the Eastern Townships of Quebec known then as East Bolton but renamed in the fifties. Christened Muriel Helena Ball in the small local Methodist church, she was the third of Anna Westover and Ezra Ball's five children and the second of their three daughters. Evelyn was four years older and Mildred three years younger. Gordon, the eldest, was seven years older than Muriel and Norman, the youngest, was ten years her junior. Both of Muriel's parents' families grew up in Brome County, Quebec, where they lived all their lives and now lie buried in local church graveyards.

Top, left: Abbie, Ezra, George. Middle row: Emily Sargent Ball, Jerome Green Ball. Lower, left: Whiting Reaford, Annis Ball Brock, Wm. Sargent, 1887.

Her native village was founded in 1792 by an ancestor, Nicholas Austin, a Quaker from New Hampshire. During the American Revolution he helped the governor of New Hampshire find carpenters in response to a request from the British to build barracks in Boston for British soldiers. For this he was obliged to apologize on his knees in 1774 to a judicial committee in Rochester, New Hampshire. Nevertheless, after the war he was elected and served in the New Hampshire legislature and voted for New Hampshire to join the US. It is not clear why he decided to move his family to Canada. After making eighteen trips by horse and boat to Quebec City to get permission to immigrate, Nicholas Austin eventually led a company of fifty-four families, four of whom were Quakers, from New Hampshire to the shores of Lake Memphremagog.

There they were finally notified in 1793 that their grant of 100 square miles was approved. It was wild, uncultivated land and included most of the present town of Magog at the north end of the lake. Each family received approximately 1200 acres, much of which was to be returned to Austin for his costs related to surveying and road building. However, this never happened and he died a poor man.[1] Nicholas and his wife Phoebe and their family settled in picturesque Austin Bay, a small bay within Sargent's Bay. Muriel identifies Nicholas Austin to children and grandchildren by saying, "my grandmother was Nicholas Austin's great granddaughter."

In 1913, when Muriel was five, Muriel's aunt, her mother's eldest sister, and uncle from Boston built a cottage on the lake, next door to the Ball farm. They remained childless and even-

Wedding photo of
Anna Westover and Ezra Ball, 1900.

tually Muriel inherited this cottage. It became a favourite rendezvous for the extended family and is a place to which Muriel returns almost every summer to renew her energies and to touch base with her origins.

Magog is only 80 miles from Montreal. The surrounding countryside is so beautiful that the area, even in Muriel's childhood, was a favourite summer community. Lake Memphremagog, which is 30 miles long, bisects the steep rolling hills and Muriel's parents' farm lies in a valley between the hills and alongside the lake. Although the scenery was spectacular the farmland was not fertile. To supplement the farm income her mother ran a boarding home for summer visitors and her father sold lightning rods.

House where Muriel was born.

As a very young child Muriel was taught the alphabet by her Grandmother Westover who lived with the family. The chalk and slate, hanging on the kitchen wall, were in frequent use and by the time she was four her proud grandmother used to encourage her to pick out words in newspapers and magazines. When Muriel turned five, the following autumn, the family felt she was ready for school. But when away from home and with strangers, Muriel was shy and timid. There were few children close to her age in the one-room country school she attended. Living in the country encouraged Muriel to be reflective. She remembers herself as a solitary child with an early love for nature.

> Certainly nature had a fantastic influence and I do remember the wonderful feeling of walking through a field of daisies and buttercups and looking up at the sky. We had three tall pine trees in front of the house and I remember thinking that the tops of the trees touched the sky. What I thought the sky was I don't know, but the trees touched the sky. And then at the foot of the hill was the lake. So there you were between the lake and the sky. It was really lovely.
>
> I remember sitting on the veranda. The house was long and low with a veranda almost around three sides of it. And you could sit on the veranda and see the weather absolutely clearly. When you saw a thunderstorm coming down the lake you would bring blankets out and sit on the veranda. That's a really good memory! Part of it is that we weren't afraid of thunderstorms. We couldn't be afraid because our father sold lightning rods—that was one of his little sidelines. We had complete faith in lightning rods! Our neighbours who didn't have them used to come and stay at our house if they were scared of thunderstorms. I remember feeling so fearless and just being able to enjoy the thunderstorms.

When she started school Muriel felt very lonely and thought nobody liked her. She would sit alone and eat her lunch. But gradually Muriel overcame her isolation from the other school children and joined in their games.

> In the wintertime a favourite game was "Fox and Geese." You make a big circle in the snow and tracks across it as if you were cutting it into a pie. We'd all be the geese chasing the fox and try to corner it. That was a good game for kids to play—all marked out in the snow without any equipment at all, just the snow. And then in the spring we played in the brook behind the school. The brook was especially beautiful in the spring when the ice formed beautiful designs along the shores. You would be able to break off these delicate pieces of ice and hold them in your hand for a while before they would melt away. Then of course in the summer it was the lake and the lakeshore. We taught ourselves to swim. There was nobody around to teach us. For quite a while I pretended to swim, while I kept one foot on the ground.

Muriel experienced a lot of freedom on the farm. Her parents never warned her to "watch out!" Being one of the younger ones she was not given indoor chores but had outdoor ones like feeding the chickens and collecting eggs. From early on her parents encouraged a sense of responsibility:

> I remember too riding on the back of an enormous Clydesdale horse. My father used to let me ride from the barn to the watering trough. It was almost like riding a camel. If you fell off, you'd have a terrific fall but they were so slow and solid and safe and that was a good experience. And we always had a dog and a bunch of cats and cows and hens. One of my jobs as I got to be near eight, was to go and get the cows with the dog. We had a collie dog who could have done it by himself, I'm sure, but I was allowed to think that I was getting the cows with the dog and we would go up the lane behind the barn and bring the cows home at the end of the day and let them go at the beginning of the day.

Besides a sense of beauty, security and adventure, early childhood brought a measure of loneliness and occasionally of fear. Like many young children, Muriel was very afraid of the dark.

When she was seven, Muriel's parents decided to send her to school in Magog along with Evelyn and Gordon who were too old for the one room school house and who had already been boarding in the town during the school year. Muriel's aunt, Eva Westover, had planned to take a year out from her work as a public health nurse on Cape Cod, Massachusetts, and agreed to look after the children in town. They lived in a rented house across from the school. Because Muriel could already read and do figures the teachers placed her in Grade 3. That year she did not make any friends and was quite miserable. Being a year younger than her classmates she reverted to her shy ways. Her rather strict aunt was not the type Muriel could confide in about her fears of going outside at night to use the outhouse. She lived for the weekends when her father came to fetch them by horse and buggy to take them back to the farm. Always on Friday nights her mother would have Washington Pie for dessert smothered in whipped cream and on Saturday nights they would have Boston baked beans and steamed brown bread.

Summertime was much better. But even then Muriel felt that grown-ups lived in a world apart. She loved the wild flowers that grew in the fields and by the water's edge but, to a farmer trying to grow crops, all wild flowers were weeds. Whenever she asked their names her father would say impatiently, "they are just weeds." And her mother was always busy. She ran a boarding house during the summer, had a staff, boarded the teacher, did the meals for "hired men" as well as the family and boarders and was active in the church. This did not leave her much time for joining the children outside. Muriel remembered affectionate moments with her father were rare occurrences. And she recalled some early traumatic experiences.

> I remember my adenoids being removed on the kitchen table with my feet on the wood box. And another time when I was about seven, on a rainy Sunday afternoon when my father was sleeping and we were supposed to be sitting quietly in the parlour, I went to play in a neighbour's barn and I stepped on a rusty nail. At first my father was angry. He needed his Sunday nap and we shouldn't have been in the barn. We had to take the steamer to Magog where the doctor came to the boat and cleaned out the wound with a gilt wire as there was no anti-tetanus in those days. I was sick from the chloroform and I remember how my father took very good care of me that night. He held me in his arms on the way home in the boat. Mother was in Montreal where her own mother was dying.

One of the strong memories Muriel retained from these early years on the farm was the consciousness of seasonal plenty. It left her with a lifelong sense of appreciation for each season's pleasures.

> A very clear memory—and maybe why I love maple syrup so much—is the maple sugar bush and the sugar house that had evergreen trees around it, where we used to go to play "house" while the men were making maple syrup. And the gorgeous smell of the sap cooking! We would take our dolls and whatever we had to keep house with. I remember the trunk of the trees came out in such a way that you could pretend that you had four different rooms in a house. It was one of the great favourite places to play in the spring.

Muriel came to associate autumn with the smell of smoking hams, a cellar full of canned fruit and dried apples and vegetables in the root cellar. Spring meant dandelion greens and rhubarb and, even before that, their much-loved maple syrup morning, noon and night—on their porridge, for dessert or on pancakes. With summer came wild strawberries and asparagus. For the rest of her life, Muriel would prize foods that were in season.

Reflecting on her early life, Muriel recognized that these formative experiences were crucial in giving her a sense of security, of where she belonged in her world. She was brought up in a strong Methodist home with religious practices that were as predictable as the seasons:

> Church every Sunday, a Christmas concert every year, a new hat and dress for Easter, regular Sunday School classes with Bible

verses to memorize, hymn sings around our piano with family and friends on Sunday evenings, Sunday School picnics, with games and races—these are all a part of my childhood. When the Psalms were read responsively in church, my father didn't even glance at the bible. He knew all the Psalms by heart. He read from the bible and led us in family prayers, on our knees, by our chairs, after breakfast, for many years.

Living in Magog, 1917-24

Near the end of the First World World War, when Muriel was nine, her father sold his farm to a man in Magog who had two sons of military age. The man was eager to buy because his sons would be exempt from conscription if they farmed. For his part, Ezra Ball was only too glad to sell the land because it had never been good for crops, although the scenery was beautiful. He had never really liked farming. His three brothers had left home to become a lawyer, a postmaster and a railway worker while he stayed to work with his own aging father. Now, seventeen years after his marriage, his parents were dead and he had four children. He finally had this chance to sell out and start a business in town. He bought a grocery and feed store and dealt largely with the farmers he had known before moving into town.

Magog is also on the shore of the lovely Lake Memphremagog. It was a textile town. The factory, located at the other end of town, was run with French-Canadian workers and bosses brought over from England. Muriel retained romantic memories of the move to town.

> We moved on New Year's Eve, 1917 . . . by sleigh drawn by a horse down the lake over the ice from the farm to Magog. It's about seven miles directly over the ice and nine miles by road. I remember as a child knowing it was much shorter if you went on the ice. And it was cold! It was forty degrees below zero that day. We were all so bundled up in buffalo robes, I'm sure I wasn't the slightest bit cold. We had warmed up bricks that were placed at our feet and we wore all the warm clothes we had. That was quite an adventure.

But the days ahead brought difficult adjustments. Again Muriel had to make new friends. Her sister Evelyn, being almost five years older, was less a playmate than a junior mother in the family. So Muriel turned to her little sister Mildred and her sister's friends for play and friendship.

> In my new home I wasn't very happy. The boys at school teased me about being a farmer's daughter. I wore clothes that one of my aunts had made that looked like miniature adult clothes. I was a mousy, timid child, between two very attractive sisters—healthy and bouncy

and good-looking. Anyway I got my kicks out of being good in
school. Also I was good at piano and I had a very good piano
teacher. So I learned to play the piano and I always got good marks
in school, but I really felt quite isolated.

It took me quite a while to make friends and to feel comfortable.
I think it was partly because I was about two years ahead of my age
group that I didn't find friends quickly and I played with my little
sister Mildred and her friends. We used to cut out paper dolls from
the Eaton's catalogue and put them in shoe boxes. All the ones that
had dark hair went in one box with their clothes and the ones with
blond hair in another box. And we had romances for them. A few
paper men models were thrown into these boxes with much glee. I
thought it was wonderful. You had to cut them out and you had to
invent names for them. They had all these clothes, endless clothes!
And you cut out the furniture—the old catalogues were great
sources of play things.

Their new home in town was on a large lot with a vegetable garden and
fruit trees so the family still retained some sense of space and of the
outdoors. Next door was the playground of a Catholic boys school. Muriel,
as a good Protestant child, was nervous about the priests in charge of this
school even though they were friendly. Maybe they would try to convert her.
But that thought did not stop her from tearing through the school yard as it
was a short cut to her own school. Once one of the priests gave Muriel a
medallion of one of the saints and a very gaudy religious picture. She sensed
this made her mother a little bit nervous too.

Muriel had two encounters with death during her childhood that filled
her with terror. During the summer when she was ten years old a little girl
of her age drowned off the docks by the lake near Muriel's home. The child
had been playing in one of the boat houses and slipped into the water. Muriel
saw her body being retrieved and was badly frightened by the thought that
someone her age was dead.

Then, within a couple of years, Muriel's great uncle dropped dead on
the street. She was playing nearby and was drawn by the crowd of people
who surrounded him. Muriel hardly recognized him as her uncle, his
appearance was so altered. To her he looked grotesque. That night she could
not sleep and finally got up and went to her parents' room. Realizing how
afraid she was, her mother and father took her into bed with them—
something she could not recall her parents ever doing before.

The move to town was a difficult adjustment for Muriel's mother. Anna
Ball had become pregnant just before leaving the farm. Seven years had
passed since her last child. She had had a difficult time delivering babies and
her sisters, one a public health nurse, were quite impatient with her for being

pregnant again. But to an active person like Muriel's mother, the immediate future probably looked quite empty with all the children now settled in school and no summer boarders to look after. She hoped for another son. In her memories Muriel associated her infant brother with the end of the First World War.

> My brother was born in August of 1918. Of course the baby was born at home and we were all very excited when it was a boy. And I remember going from that house down to the main street to be with the crowd celebrating the end of the war. That was so exciting! I remember the feeling about it, with everybody on the street. Everybody happy. Everybody talking to everybody else. Flags and bunting. What I remember most was my pushing this little baby boy downtown in his carriage. He would have been less than three months old the day the war ended.

The following year, after Muriel's father bought his business, her parents decided to buy a large house just two houses up from the store, immediately around the corner from the main highway that went through the town. This would allow her mother to go into business too. With larger quarters, Anna Ball saw the possibility of having a whole new set of customers enjoy her home cooking and stay as summer boarders. The steamer that travelled up and down the lake every day tied up at a landing at the foot of their street and people came trooping past their door. The house was also a block away from the railway station, another site of much coming and going. And so Anna moved the family into their new home in the fall of 1918 only to encounter a major disappointment not many months later. As Muriel recounted it:

> One Saturday morning the following spring my mother and I walked as usual to the farmers' market at the other end of the town when, as we were coming home laden with fresh vegetables, the fire engines passed us. My mother had a really sensitive something in her soul and she sensed that this was our house that was on fire. We walked as fast as we could to get there and it was! The fire engines were there. Mildred had taken baby Norman out of the house. Our great uncle and aunt who lived two streets away took us in.
>
> Early that evening my mother sent me back into the house to get a bottle of aspirin or something. That was one of the most scary things I ever did in my life! It was getting dark and it was all charred inside. I have never forgotten the smell of smoke and how scared I was. Of course the electricity was off and I had to find a chair and climb up into the cupboard. I don't even remember whether I found

it or not but I ran fast out of the house, up the street, away from the charred house. It was absolutely too scary to do, but I had to do it, because my mother was in no state to think about how I would feel about going into our burned-out home in the dark. The fire was a set back in other ways. Of course we lost all our clothes and a lot of furniture. People were very good to us. I remember them giving us clothes.

Undaunted, Muriel's parents made plans to have their home rebuilt while the family took up other quarters in a house next door to the store that belonged to her father's uncle. He had been readying it for his son and his British war bride but offered it to the Balls while they rebuilt, using fire insurance money.

The original house was enlarged according to Anna's design. The downstairs porch became the tea room which she called the "Korneryn Tea Room." The upstairs addition became the sleeping quarters for the family in the summertime. Then the regular bedrooms could be filled with paying guests. She completely redesigned the kitchen and had a built-in refrigerator between the house and the shed. Unfortunately it did not work too well because she planned it with the ice blocks underneath instead of on top of the food, and things were always going bad.

Muriel and her sisters were very much a part of their mother's enterprise. As they grew older they helped by cleaning, cooking, changing beds, polishing silver and waiting on tables. The tea room meant that Muriel learned to deal with the public by meeting tourists as well as local people; this helped her to overcome some of her shyness. She also came to admire her mother's ability to manage people, run her business and be such an excellent cook. Anna Ball was a friendly, gregarious woman with tremendous energy and Muriel loved her sense of humour.

Mildred, 15 and Muriel, 18, wearing waitress costumes.

The tea room opened on July 1st. We all helped out and Mother managed the whole kitchen. She had all the recipes in her head. She

would have two or three people doing different things, telling us
what to put in and how long to beat it, how long to cook it and so
on. We all worked. When I was fifteen and graduated from high
school I became a summertime waitress. Mother paid us $5.00 a
week. Then there were tips and that was what made life exciting,
not knowing whether you were going to get a nice fat tip. It was a
busy life. I think what was most fun were the people. You could like
them or you could get furious with them when they were rude or you
could think they were great and really enjoy them.

Any time of the day people could come in and Mother served
them meals. The stove could be all cleaned and everything put away
and when they arrived late needing dinner everything would come
out again and she would start over. We used to get mad about that
sometimes because it would interfere with our lives very much. I
had to be ready to wait tables at any hour of the day or night.
Nevertheless, we often jumped into our bathing suits, grabbed a
towel and dashed down to the lake for a swim.

My mother also cooked for church bake sales. I remember
feeling resentful about that because she was such a good cook and
when she took her baking to the church bake sales she would feel
she had to buy something too, and she would bring home food that
was not nearly as good as her own cooking. This left me with a
lifelong passionate determination that I would not cook for bake
sales. I always preferred potluck suppers where you get everybody's best cooking and get to enjoy the leftovers.

Although the tea room clearly added to the family's income, Muriel's
impression was that there was never much money. Profits were slim in her
father's business despite his attempts to branch out into other enterprises.
Besides the store he also kept a woodlot and sold wood. He brought in oil
by the tank load by train and sold it all through the countryside. Muriel was
pleased when she was sometimes allowed to accompany her father and ride
high alongside him in the oil wagon. Still, she remained aware that business
was not all fun and that money was hard to come by. If her parents'
thriftiness was not lost on her, neither was their generosity.

My parents never talked money with us. They were very strict about
spending. That is one of the really harsh memories I have, that we
never had money to spend, and if we wasted money or if we broke
something we never heard the end of it. It was just too much that
this hard-earned money would be wasted by one of the children.
There couldn't have been a very big income. But they were always
very generous. They always gave a lot of money to the church and
they always welcomed people coming to Magog to shop from the

farming community where they had lived. It was taken for granted that they would come for a meal. And being so close to the railway station, men riding the rails learned that this was a place you could always get fed. They would come to the back door and come in and sit down in that little family dining room. There was a lot of generosity towards the people who needed it more that we did.

Anna Ball was an energetic force in her community and provided a powerful model for Muriel. When Muriel herself was past eighty, she was once asked by a CBC interviewer why she had been a social activist all her life. She replied that she was influenced by her mother who cared passionately about what she did, believed she could have some effect and did have some effect. Anna was a woman of determination. On the farm she refused to do any of the outdoor work that farm wives traditionally undertook in those days, including milking, feeding the chickens and helping at harvest time. Instead she ran her own business, operating a summer boarding house and having complete control over the kitchen.

Besides inheriting her social conscience and independent nature, Muriel traced her feminist roots to a mother who read Nellie McClung, who turned her china cabinet into a bookcase to start a community lending library, and who helped to earn money for her children to go to university. Muriel's mother was a great admirer of Nellie McClung and Agnes Macphail and she would laughingly called herself a "suffragette." Anna was also active in her church and in the Women's Christian Temperance Union. She was fully immersed in responding to her community's needs. She not only fed hungry men off the trains, but she raised money to establish an elderly people's home. Travellers Aid asked her to be their representative and she was often called upon by the town station master to offer shelter to young women who stepped off the trains as homeless strangers. Living at a time when the people of Quebec were divided according to their different faiths, Muriel remembered her mother as a person lacking racial and religious prejudice. She was remarkably open to those of religions other than her own.

> I remember my mother writing about the Catholic Bishop of Quebec when he died that he was a fine man who would be hard to replace. She also admired a wonderful Catholic priest in Magog, Father Bourassa, who lived across the street from the United Church minister. They were great friends.

Many years later, writing about her mother in *Herizons,* Muriel recognized the limits of her mother's influence: "In spite of her intelligence, quick wit, and commitment she never sat on any of the policy boards in the church; nor did any other women." Muriel, a generation later, had different expectations.

Muriel's two unmarried aunts, one her mother's sister and one her father's, also were important role models as she grew up. Eva Westover trained as a nurse in New York state around 1900 and spent most of her life as a public health nurse. Muriel often visited her on Cape Cod. Her father's sister, Abbie Ball, stayed home with her parents until she was past forty. She earned money teaching school and sewing. When both of her parents died she went to Boston where she studied drama and public speaking at the Emerson School of Oratory. She then taught at the Ontario Ladies College, a Methodist girls' school in Whitby, Ontario. Muriel came under her Aunt Abbie's influence when she went to the Ladies College following high school.

Muriel's family home was a great gathering place for the extended family who provided Muriel with early exposure to politics. She recalled many a hot and heavy political discussion among her relatives.

> The adults in my mother's family loved to talk politics. They would argue at the top of their voices and got very mad at each other. The politics they had, they held firmly and believed firmly. My parents always said that they were of two different parties. We thought my father was a Liberal and the fact that my mother wouldn't tell which party she supported made us conclude that she was a Conservative. There was always a lot of political discussion which she entered into heatedly like all the others. When they were both in their late fifties, they learned to play bridge and the bridge table became the centre of much lively political talk. When there was talk about Canada being taken over by the United States, Mother would joke that if it would make the climate warmer she would be all for it.

Note

1.   Nicholas Austin. *The Quaker and the Township of Bolton.* Knolton, Quebec: Brome County Historical Society, 1971.

Muriel's ancestors at Memorial Stone to Nicholas Austin; Muriel visiting there 100 years later.

Chapter 2

"Poisoning the Student Mind"
University Years

uriel's older sister, Evelyn, took a two-year domestic science course at the Ontario Ladies College in Whitby where their Aunt Abbie was teaching. Three years later, when Muriel finished high school (then Grade 11) at age fifteen, her parents thought she might try teaching in a country school. However, her Aunt Abbie would not hear of it. After careful consideration of her own low salary, Abbie offered to pay Muriel's fees for her senior matriculation year at the Ontario Ladies College. Piano lessons would be included as a credit course.

Her aunt provided one of Muriel's earliest memories of someone who objected to the inequality between men and women. Though it was taken for granted that there had to be a man, an ordained minister, at the head of this girls' school, the vice-principal, Miss Maxwell, really ran the school. Muriel recalled Aunt Abbie being quite frank about how they did not need a man at the head of their school.

She remembered too how her music theory teacher was the first to make her aware of the historic union of Protestant churches that year. One day her teacher came to the school terribly upset about the prospect of church union. The United Church of Canada was formed in 1925 through the union of the Methodist church, the Congregational church and part of the Presbyterian church. She was a Presbyterian and was so upset she was practically in tears. She could not teach but had to talk to Muriel, her teenage student, about it. Her point of view was quite different from that of the college, which was Methodist. In Magog, union was not an issue because there was no Presbyterian church and no Congregational church. The Methodist church simply became

Muriel Ball, 16 years old.

the United Church.

The college provided a good transition year between school and university. It functioned somewhat as a finishing school and allowed Muriel to make friends and feel a bit less unsophisticated when she entered McGill University. Muriel, still very shy at Whitby, never got involved in drama even though her aunt was the drama coach. Living in residence, she was terribly homesick. By fifteen Muriel had grown tall and felt very big next to her tiny, dainty roommate. The school offered languages, history and math, good instruction in piano and voice, but little science, which was a bit of a handicap at McGill. Once a month guest speakers came to address the student assembly. These were generally United Church people. One she particularly remembered was Jim Endicott, a very tall, handsome young man who impressed all the students with his good looks. His talk about China, where he was a missionary, awakened Muriel's interest in China. Over the years he kept reappearing in the Duckworths' lives and stayed with them on one occasion, fifty years later.

The McGill Years, 1925-29

The Reverend Wesley Boyd, minister of the Magog United Church, had a lot to do with Muriel's going to university. He must have seen her potential and encouraged her parents to find the means to send her to McGill. Unwittingly, Anna Ball secured a bursary for her daughter as well. As Muriel told it:

> I was very keen to go and they were happy to send me except for the cost. There was never the slightest discussion in my family that it was not worthwhile my going, because I was a woman. My mother had it figured out that they could probably manage if we could find a room for $4.00 a week. So my mother went in with me and registered me at Royal Victoria College. When she said we were looking for a downtown room for me, her sixteen-year-old daughter, for $4.00 a week, the staff person who registered me said "one moment please" and went to see Miss Hurlbatt, head of Royal Victoria College, who was known as the warden. So Mother and I went to talk to this warden and she immediately offered me a bursary so that I could live in the women's residence, for the same price.
>
> Even with this help my parents could give me no allowance. I hadn't a cent to spend. My Aunt Abbie provided me with $2.00 a week spending money. On top of that, before I was finished we borrowed from her. I think I owed her about $400.00 when I graduated. While the bursary was a great help with the living accommodation I was ashamed of it. I didn't want anybody to know

that I was on a bursary because it wasn't the same as a scholarship. It didn't occur to me that they wouldn't have given me a bursary if they hadn't thought I would be a pretty good student and I had done well in high school. To me a bursary just meant that you were poor. It took me a long time to realize that there were other students there who were from the Eastern Townships and other rural areas and from Montreal who were also there on bursaries.

The other thing that I was very stupid about was that I didn't want my friends to know that my mother worked because there was no indication that any of the other students' mothers worked for money. I wasted a lot of energy not wanting anybody to find out. I had the feeling that I would not be accepted if they knew.

Despite her feelings of insecurity Muriel made friends with students from two families that she had first met through her mother's tea room and these helped her bridge the gap between her rural background and life in Montreal. One of these was the family of Dr. Richard Roberts who vacationed along Lake Memphremagog the summer before Muriel entered university. The Roberts had three daughters at McGill. Their youngest, Gwen, was a member of Muriel's class and became her best friend. Muriel became a lifelong friend to all the women in this family. They all married students of theology, colleagues of Muriel's husband.

At McGill female students were referred to as "McGill women." Muriel reflected that not being called "girls" certainly added to their dignity and was an early step in later identifying herself as a feminist.

The Student Christian Movement

Muriel's self-consciousness as a rural girl coming from a farm family was not easily overcome. She felt that most of the other women students, having gone to private schools, were better prepared for university. Her old shyness reasserted itself and she might have remained that way were it not for joining the Student Christian Movement (SCM). This Canadian university organization was founded in 1921 as a "fellowship of students who seek through study, prayer and practice to know and follow Jesus Christ." It was held suspect through the 1920s and 1930s by the traditional churches because the SCM tended to challenge their received wisdom.

On the McGill campus, the SCM was in Strathcona Hall which had been built as the student YMCA. Strathcona Hall became the centre of Muriel's university life; she ran in and out of it as often as she was in and out of the Arts building. Muriel thrived on the informal atmosphere of the SCM. She felt she learned a great deal from the SCM staff, who were called "secretaries," and she shared Christianity as a core value with other students there.

This song was composed by scmers in the 30s who were attacked
for inviting a socialist to speak at a conference.

I was particularly influenced by the SCM secretaries, Harry Avison,
Jean Hutchinson and Chuck Stewart. I never got over being intimi-
dated by teachers at McGill. There wasn't a single professor that I
felt comfortable with, and that's probably why the SCM meant so
much because there I felt freedom. Looking back over the years I've
felt always that the experience of the SCM was the most important
thing that happened to me, probably the most important aspect of
my college life, more important than any of the courses that I took.

Some of the top students came there to sort out their own

thinking in small group discussions. There was a lot of political thinking going on and sorting out of political philosophy and I was certainly on the edge of that. But it wasn't aimed at political action except on the campus. I got involved for instance, in the fight to prevent sororities on the campus. We worked very hard on that and the sororities were voted down by the McGill Women Students Society, though in later years they crept back in.

The SCM conducted study groups according to a method developed by Dr. Sharman, who held summer courses for study of the Gospels at a camp at Lake Minnesing in Algonquin Park. There, people met in small groups where each and every person had to look at the evidence of the records of the life of Jesus and determine for themselves what was or was not historial.

This was an agony for a person like me brought up where everyone knew the answers. To go into a group and set aside everything you knew about Jesus was a very trying discipline to go through. I had always before treated the Gospel as though its authors had set down day by day events in the life of Jesus as they happened. To face the implication that nothing was written down until after Jesus died was itself a shock. But this question of free and open discussion, that everything needed to be challenged, to be questioned, to be talked about, that was completely opposite to the authoritarian approach in the church—that this is the answer, and this is what you must believe—which I had.

Although I don't think of my parents as dogmatic, there's no question that they thought: "of course this is what you believe; this is the natural thing that you believe." And it was a fantastic experience to be in a small group of people who were asked to shed what they had been brought up to believe, and just look at the material and start from scratch, and make up your own mind about it—is this what the Gospel is really saying?

This kind of disciplined study had great social and personal implications for me. The emphasis was not as much on applying the Gospel to the times as on applying it to your personal self, finding the way, finding "the pearl of great price," finding what is the essential, important thing in life. What does it mean, "straight is the way and narrow is the gate that leadeth unto life?" These were very personal. Looking for implications for ourselves as individuals— The Rich Young Man, the Widow's Mite, The Good Samaritan— who was neighbour to the man? That one made a great impression on me. It is hard to convey sitting around with six to eight other students with long periods of silence. There was a great deal of

emphasis on individual searching, on straightening out what you
really believed, without pressure.

Brought up as she was to be conforming, it must have been a great
challenge to Muriel to dare to differ from the status quo. In a lecture
delivered to the Quaker Canadian Yearly Meeting in 1986 Muriel recounted
how these discussions marked a profound turning point in her life:

> In my copy of Sharman's *Records of the Life of Jesus* I wrote a few
> notes in the margin. You remember the story of Jesus being
> criticized by the Pharisees for working on the Sabbath. They were
> so angry with him for this affront to their rigid religious practice and
> to their authority that they "took counsel against him how they
> might destroy him." Here I wrote, "question attacked is law and
> authority. Jesus is substituting new understanding of relation with
> God. Man must act in direct relation with God." This was the
> beginning of my adult search for truth and my sense that all things
> must be open to me. It was unsettling; it was painful. It was exciting.
> Silence in the group was still not comfortable for me, though I know
> now that it was an integral part of this experience.

The practice of determining her own personal beliefs made Muriel a
very independent thinker. This was all the more surprising because Muriel
never liked to step on toes. She was not given to arguing with others or to
trying to win them over to her views. She preferred to question them as she
quietly formulated her own opinions. What began as a result of her own
insecurity and shyness became an entrenched habit. She always seemed
more interested in finding out what others thought and felt than in promoting
her own views. Besides fostering Muriel's own sense of personal responsibility, the SCM marked the beginnings of her struggle against anti-Semitism
and anti-racism.

> Prejudice was very much a topic of discussion at the SCM at
> Strathcona Hall. Jewish students often came for discussions and felt
> at home there. One of the big campus issues was that Jews were
> under a quota and there was a lot of anti-Semitism. Everyone knew
> there was a quota on the admission of Jews. Jewish students found
> their best support in the SCM apart from their own organizations.
> One day one of my classmates, who lived in the women's residence,
> wrote a nasty article about Jews in an editorial in the *McGill Daily*.
> I was very upset, and I remember sitting and crying about it. There
> was a great reaction to this student's article and fortunately she was
> dropped from the staff of the newspaper.

When I was eighteen I attended the week-long National Annual Conference of the SCM at Elgin House on Lake Muskoka. I saved up the money to pay for it. It was the first time I had stayed in a summer hotel. That week made a great impression on me. There was a young Rabbi Eisendrath who declared with great force, "Jesus Christ was a Jew!" I did not feel as if any of us had paid attention to this before.

It was in the SCM that Muriel encountered an early feminist role model in the person of Jean Hutchinson.

The person whose group I was in was Jean Hutchinson. Jean was a feminist without ever knowing it. She was such an independent woman that people were sorry for her husband. She was a very important person to me and I was a member of her group during the four years I was at McGill. Jean Hutchinson was a founder of the SCM. Her father was a general secretary of the YMCA in Halifax and he was an independent thinker. Jean told me that she used to sit up till all hours talking with her father. This was very different from my relationship with my father who was always determined to be thought right.

The SCM also sowed the seeds which eventually led to Muriel's becoming a Quaker.

Several of the speakers who were brought to McGill by the SCM were Quakers. John Macmurray, an Anglican clergyman, I think became a Quaker when he was over seventy. He wrote a book about his spiritual pilgrimage. He gave a series of lectures at McGill which I'm sure had some influence on my thinking. Another was C.F. Andrews, close friend and companion of Gandhi, whom I would much later realize was "Charlie Andrews" in the film on Gandhi's life.

Other notable visitors to the SCM included Tagore, the Indian poet; Henry Hodgkins, one of the founders of Pendle Hill, the Quaker Study Centre; Kagawa, the great Japanese-Christian pacifist; Reverend Harry F. Ward, the socialist teaching Christian ethics at Union Theological Seminary (UTS); Helen Nichol, later a fellow student at UTS; and the national SCM secretaries Gertrude Rutherford and Murray Brooks.

Muriel had a lot of fun at the SCM. Their leader, Jean Hutchinson, had a great sense of humour. Muriel was reminded of her whenever she sang a hilarious song "Poisoning the Student Mind"(composed by SCMers of the

thirties who were attacked for inviting a socialist to speak at a conference).
The chorus went:

> The SCM has found its true vocation, poisoning the student mind
> Its leaders by astute manipulation are poisoning the student mind
> And pious souls are sure that we will go to toast our toes in furnaces
> below
> If we give heed to leaders that we know are poisoning the student
> mind.
> Bad men, bold women, villains double-dyed, 'neath their smiling
>   countenances hide spiritual arsenic and moral cyanide
> For poisoning the student, poisoning the student, poisoning the
> student mind.

Though she remained nervous about speaking in public, Muriel did
learn in her graduating year at McGill that it was possible to conceal her
nervousness. In her final year Muriel took the education courses required for
a high school teaching diploma, in addition to a full schedule of studies for
a B.A. All education students did supervised practice teaching. One such
teaching period required each student to teach a class with all their fellow
students sitting around the walls of the classroom full of girls and boys. The
day came for Muriel to do her practice teaching lesson in geography.

> You knew your classmates were watching you. The professor was
> also watching you. Another man was there, a visiting professor
> from Scotland. I was so scared that when I was home for the
> weekend I hoped the train would go off the track so I wouldn't have
> to go back to do it. But I did it!
>   The dean was six foot four with a broad Scottish accent and he
> was quite intimidating. When I finished the class and the children
> had been dismissed, he then asked my classmates, "what was the
> best thing about Miss Ball's presentation?" Somebody said, "She
> wasn't nervous." He said, "Yes, that's right. She wasn't nervous."

Muriel made a determined effort to acquire public speaking skills. She
made herself enter a public speaking contest at Royal Victoria College (RVC)
sponsored by the McGill Women's Society. When her turn came her voice
trembled and she felt very nervous. To get over her reluctance to speak
publicly, Muriel also volunteered to take minutes at student meetings. The
note taking was not stressful but when she read the minutes aloud her heart
would beat loudly and she would have to struggle to conceal her nervousness. In school she had never had the opportunity to debate or to practice
public speaking. She had felt that every time she opened her mouth she was

subject to criticism. As a child she feared being asked a question in case she got the answer wrong. Even at home her father was inclined to make fun of her whenever she made a mistake.

Romance, Graduation and Marriage

In addition to the many lifelong friends Muriel made through the SCM, it was here that she met her future husband. Jack Duckworth was a theology student whom Muriel found very attractive, partly because at twenty-eight he was much more mature than the other male students she knew. Muriel admired Jack for his athletic vigour, his progressive ideas and his excellent speaking ability.

The first occasion when Jack asked her for a date, when she was in her sophomore year, she had to refuse because her uncle was taking her out to celebrate her birthday. When Jack learned that she was only turning eighteen he almost decided not to see her again. He also discovered that she was not even a basketball player on the McGill women's team, as he had supposed. He had confused her with a cousin, Edith Ball, also at McGill, who was an outstanding member of the basketball team. Muriel was not even an athlete. Muriel herself was not ready to settle for one boyfriend and enjoyed the company of a number of young men so Jack soon dropped out of the race.

By eighteen Muriel had become a tall, attractive young woman with clear blue eyes, a high forehead and soft, curly brown hair. She loved going to the tea dances at the Ritz Carlton Hotel and once she went to both the matinee and the evening performance of the same play on the same day at His Majesty's Theatre with two different escorts.

Muriel and a half dozen other women students lived in "the Annex," a house on University Street for the overflow from Royal Victoria College. Some of the young women at the Annex were friends with some of the men at the United Theological College just up the street. Often at 10 o'clock at night when they had finished studying they all gathered at a favourite restaurant for coffee. One evening Muriel got a phone call from one of these young men saying that Jack was ill and wanted her to come to his bedside. Jack had sustained a neck injury from a fall while diving over a horse in the Y gym. He was in considerable pain. Gwen Roberts, her best friend (who later became Gwen Norman), remembered what a tizzy Muriel was in. Should she go? Or was it a practical joke? She thought she had not treated him too well earlier and decided that she would go. Jack was thrilled to see her and from then on their romance blossomed. They became engaged in her third year at university. During her final year at McGill Jack was continuing his theological studies at Union Theological Seminary (UTS) in New York. After obtaining his Masters and the first year of theology at McGill, he decided to do the final two years of theology at UTS.

I met Jack around the SCM. He was very active in campus activities. He had come to McGill as a mature student. He had been working as a volunteer in the Vancouver YMCA and at their summer camp. He was so good at working with boys that he was encouraged to become a YMCA secretary. But first he was required to have some college education and some courses in religious education. His choices were McGill or Chicago and since he had been born in Montreal and lived there until he was around twelve he decided to return east.

Even during the university term, to finance his way he carried two jobs. He taught gym classes at the Westmount Y and on weekends he was a student minister first at Grand'Mère then at Beloeil Ste. Hilaire, where he gained experience preaching. He discovered he was a very good preacher. He spoke with a lot of conviction and he liked discussing ideas with people in his congregation. This made him decide to take the full theological course and not just the part that was required to become a YMCA secretary.

Jack was living at the Presbyterian college when union [of the churches] took place. He was always on the side of new thinking and he did not identify with those who were resisting union. So he was happy to pack his suitcase and hike across the campus to the Methodist college.

Following his M.A. Jack went to Union Theological Seminary in the fall of 1928 after we became engaged. I graduated from McGill in May of 1929. We were married in June, and I went eagerly to New York with Jack in September for his final year at Union.

Muriel and Jack were married very informally in the American Presbyterian church (actually United) on Dorchester Street. One of Jack's friends, Errol Amaron, was the assistant minister and officiated. Muriel had prevailed upon her mother not to host the wedding in Magog because she did not want her mother to go to the trouble she had taken for Evelyn's wedding, where she and Evelyn had done all the cooking and sewing. Muriel wanted a simple open affair. She and Jack just invited their friends by word of mouth and the church was packed. Afterwards the minister invited them to come into the church parlour to receive their friends' good wishes. There was no reception and no one made speeches. Later Muriel's family and a few friends had dinner at the Queen's Hotel before seeing the bride and groom off at the Windsor station where they took the transCanada train to Vancouver. Like the Royal couple, they waved from the balcony at the back of the train. Muriel's wedding dress, a short two-piece lace Alice blue gown with a dropped waist, was to become a favourite family costume. She unearthed it many years later and wore it to the weddings of two of her granddaughters when she was over seventy-five.

Jack took Muriel to Vancouver to meet his family. They arrived at a time of great excitement in that household too, since his sister, Mildred, was also to be married within two weeks. The families made much of the coincidence that Jack had two sisters named "Evelyn" and "Mildred," the very names of Muriel's sisters. Jack's sisters were obviously surprised that he had married someone as tall as himself and Muriel felt rather conspicuous next to her tiny sisters-in-law. And she had very few clothes and felt rather self-conscious about that. Muriel found that Jack's family was quite different from her own. They seemed to be very forthcoming, while she came from a family that was more reticent about expressing their emotions. She did not think that they shared Jack's interests, although his mother obviously doted on him. Muriel loved exploring Vancouver with Jack and particularly enjoyed being introduced to his favourite haunts.

A Year At Union Theological Seminary, 1929-30

Muriel registered at Union Theological Seminary in New York City as a full-time student and worked as a part-time field student while Jack completed his second year there. If Muriel had found the SCM stimulating she and Jack revelled in the richness of life at Union. They attended UTS during a period of much social ferment. The stock market crash of October 1929, just after they arrived in New York, inaugurated the Great Depression. During these financially precarious times the academic and practical experience Muriel and Jack gained was invaluable. They had a series of remarkable professors: the president of UTS, Henry Sloane Coffin; Harry Emerson Fosdick, who was also the minister of Riverside church across the street; Dr. Moffat, noted translator of the bible; Sophia Fahs, sister-in-law of Dr. Sharman of SCM fame; Mary Ely Lyman; Reinhold Niebuhr; and Harry F. Ward, a fiery defender of civil liberties. Charles Webber, a socialist ordained minister, supervised Muriel's field work and became her friend.

It was at UTS that Muriel first began to explore what she had in common with those of different ideologies, later one of her chief characteristics as a peacemaker.

> There are times in life when things make a tremendous impression and this was such a period. Being in New York that year and being a student at Union Theological Seminary was radicalizing with the kind of ideas that were floating around, the actions that people were involved in, the work that I was doing in Hell's Kitchen with teenaged girls, first generation Americans, and the other students who became our friends. At Union they were very open to all streams of thought. For the first time I really got exposed to the role

of psychiatry and psychoanalysis.

Also at that time there were the beginnings of a dialogue between Christianity and Communism. This to me was really very exciting because they had Marxists coming to talk about this very serious search, what is it that we have in common, Christians and Marxists, and finding what we have in common, and working together as far as we could move together in the same direction. I remember debate and talk in the classroom and in the common room about the relation between Christianity and Communism and looking for the common thread, knowing that Communism was meant to be at the service of the "common man" and Christianity was meant to be the religion of the common people. I suspect that might have been the beginning of my feeling that you go along with people as long as you feel comfortable that you are going in the same direction and that's a decision that you have to be constantly making.

At Union they related theological teaching to public trends and to the field of psychiatry. Harry Emerson Fosdick taught homiletics [the composition and preaching of sermons]. He made a terrific impression and Jack was one of his most appreciative and also one of his best students. Among the courses I took was one on Christian ethics and modern literature, taught in the first half of the year by Harry Ward, and the second half by Reinhold Niebuhr. Harry Ward was a socialist and a strong supporter of the civil rights movement. He was one of the people who went to Russia because he felt people should know what the social experiment was all about. Reinhold Niebuhr was an outstanding scholar who had good relations with his students, as did Ward.

At Union, the open relationship between the faculty and the students meant a great deal. They treated us like people and it made a great difference. There was Dr. Moffat, for instance, the Dr. Moffat who wrote the Moffat translation of the bible, one of the first attempts to put the bible in contemporary language so people could really understand. He had open house every week, he and his wife, in their own apartment. You could always drop in and talk to them. There was Dr. Eugene Lyman, a professor of New Testament who had Jack as a student and his wife Mary Ely Lyman who was one of my teachers. I also took a course in religious education from Sophia Fahs. She was the sister of Dr. Sharman, who had introduced his method of studying the Gospels into the Canadian SCM. She too had this open point of view about people learning for themselves and not to be given the hierarchical approach to what religion was about.

Many of these teachers and contemporaries would continue to have important meaning throughout Muriel's and Jack's life. At a later time she and Jack helped set up a public meeting in Montreal for Harry Ward. He was hissed at by some of the audience both for having recently visited the USSR and because he spoke positively about some of the social changes he found there.

Muriel recalled enthusiastically her friendship with Miles Horton and Rosa Parks' connection with him.

> Rosa Parks had attended mixed racial conferences at Highlander Folk School in Tennessee where Miles was the director for many years. Horton, one of my classmates, spent his life as a leader of integrated adult education camps and conferences in the South. He made a big impact, so much so that the campsites were burned by the Klu Klux Klan in the South and people were discouraged, of course, from going there. I think one of the exciting links in the stream of history is that years later, Rosa Parks, the woman who refused to move in the bus, had just taken one of Miles Horton's seminars, which gave her the courage to act because she knew she had those people out there behind her. When she came back after she had been working all day and she was tired, she just sat down at the front of the bus and refused to move. It has always been exciting for me to know that Miles Horton and the Highlander Folk School were involved. That alone wouldn't have given her the courage. She already had ideas and strength of her own, or she wouldn't have been at Highlander and become an important member of that community.

As young theological students they subscribed to the views of Social Gospellers who put much less emphasis on supernatural dogma and life hereafter. God was viewed primarily as a loving, forgiving father whose children were to love and care for one another on earth. Social Gospellers saw the workplace and the community's customs and institutions as what shaped personal morality. Because of this they were in the forefront in organizing social services and adult education. They considered the economic system, with its emphasis on profit-making at the expense of the workers' welfare, as the greatest evil of the times and the depression confirmed their views.

> Certainly pacifism was very much to the fore. The Social Gospel and pacifism were linked in my mind. I remember Norman Thomas being one of the speakers and hearing about Eugene Debs, who had died in 1926, a labour hero who had gone to prison for opposition

to the First World War and who ran for president of the US while he was in jail. I recall a well-known Catholic priest talking about the confessional. To go to a Protestant theological college and have them feature a priest as a speaker was quite an eye-opening experience. There was a series of public lectures that was very popular. All the students flocked to them.

The influence of some of these Social Gospellers would long be felt. Sixty years later a poster hung on Muriel's kitchen wall quoting Eugene Debs:

> While there is a lower class, I am in it
> While there is a criminal element, I am of it
> And while there is a soul in prison I am not free.

Of all the learning opportunities at UTS none had greater immediate impact on Muriel than the field work she did in New York. Here, for the first time, she saw life through the eyes of poor young women who were first generation Americans. Her field work was at a community church where she met these working teenagers in a Sunday School class and in a recreation group in the middle of the week. Muriel won them over the very first time she coached basketball. She demonstrated a free throw and it actually went into the basket. But she would soon realize how ill-equipped she was to deal with some of the harsher problems in their lives.

> Working with teenage girls on the Lower West Side, "Hell's Kitchen" was in itself a huge experience for me. Apart from the wonderful students . . . in my class, and the kinds of professors who were also our friends, those sixteen- and seventeen-year-old girls were as important in my growing up as anything. I was in their homes and I saw what it was like. They were living in those days, many of them, right beside the 7th Avenue elevated trains, which were just booming and clattering next to their bedroom windows. And they lived in flats—I'm sure it wouldn't be allowed now— where there would be a window at the front and a window at the back and a string of rooms between them, without any windows. Despite these really very bad conditions they were cheerful. They had left school and had gone to work. We met as a group twice a week, and so we got to know each other very well.
> Just a couple of things that I remember very well. One of the girls was raped. And these girls, although they were sixteen and seventeen and I was twenty, felt I was too innocent to know. They didn't tell me for quite a long time. And I don't think I would have

known what to do anyway to respond. I knew something was going on. But it was hard for them to tell me, because they thought I was an innocent young thing who wouldn't have been exposed to such experiences, and looking back now, I'm sure I wasn't any help.

And I remember how they talked a lot about their relationships with their own mothers, because most of them were first generation Americans. Many of them were of German background, and there was the usual difficulty to get their mothers to accept that life was different for them. And we did role-playing away back then. I didn't run into role-playing again until about, I guess, 1965. And that was 1930, thirty-five years earlier! It seemed a very natural, spontaneous thing to do. We invited the mothers one night. Each girl took the part of a mother and each mother took the part of a girl and then everybody got into the discussion.

Muriel was not at all nervous working with these young women. She felt that their lives were already dominated by school, church and home and that what they most needed was a chance to be themselves. She wanted to make them feel accepted and not tell them what they ought to do or feel.

The stock market crashed within two months of Muriel's arrival in New York. Muriel and Jack were already living on a shoestring and to that extent were not affected. While the impact of the Great Depression was not immediately felt at UTS, both students and teachers were certainly aware of the economic crisis, which put everything into a state of question. The following year UTS was greatly involved with the unemployed.

In October of 1929, just after we had come to New York the stock market crashed and everybody was theorizing and speculating about what had actually happened. The consequences of the stock market crash got worse and worse after we went back to Montreal, and Union Seminary was more and more affected by it after we left. Nobody knew in the beginning how long it was going to go on or how bad it was going to get. Nobody that I was exposed to was in a position to predict how bad.

We were very hard up. Jack had a part-time job in a church which was his supervised field work. He travelled to East Orange, New Jersey. It took him an hour and a half to get there and he went twice a week. He was an assistant minister and I think he earned $125 a month. I earned $85.00 a month from my part-time job of supervised field work in Christ Church Community Centre in Hell's Kitchen. I had in addition a little job helping to serve tea one day a week in the common room. I got $2.00 a week for doing that and it paid for the laundry. We just managed and we got back to

Montreal with something under $50.00 at the end of the year—
absolutely nothing else in the world except our wedding presents.
At Union we had always known that if I should get pregnant we
would have to leave. But we did have the security of a job to go back
to because Jack knew he was going to work for the YMCA in
Montreal and he could have taken up his job any time so it wasn't
such a bad worry.

The year at Union Theological Seminary not only opened new worlds
for Muriel but it reinforced what she had learned at the SCM, to seek out the
truth for herself. She listened carefully to the opinions and theories of those
around her, seldom making up her own mind definitively. She saw merit in
more than one argument and while she tended to discount her own lack of
sureness as insecurity, this habit of listening for what she could agree with
in others became characteristic of her. She became adept at questioning

others for their opinions rather
than putting forth her own.
Although Muriel hesitated to
hold forth about her views
she could be passionate in
identifying with and advocating the interests of other
people. Her enthusiasm for
learning through small group
discussion made her very effective in youth and adult education.

Muriel and Jack left UTS
with the strong convictions
of the Social Gospel. Their
central purpose in life was to
work for the Kingdom of God
in this world. The "brother-
hood of man" meant that cooperation and not competi-
tion should be the basis for
economic life. They proceeded
to implement in their lives
the teachings of the Social
Gospellers. For them, Christianity required a passionate
commitment to working for
social justice.

Muriel, wearing her original wedding dress to her
granddaughter Marya's wedding, playing with
another granddaughter, Anna Duckworth, 1986.

Chapter 3

A Wife and Mother Striving to Build "
... A Life of Her Own"

By the time Muriel and Jack returned to Montreal in 1930, the city, as with all North America, was quickly sinking into economic collapse. One-third of its population was on relief during the depression years and many skilled people could only find work selling apples, raking leaves and shovelling snow. Jack came into immediate contact with the harsh realities of unemployment when, as a YMCA secretary, he saw men in bread lines and tried to find them jobs. The Y itself was able to retain all its staff by dint of wage cuts and not replacing retirees. Jack worked at first in an uninsulated shack on the Y's Notre Dame de Grace property, with only a wood stove for heat in the winter. Later on a local business rented them a store-front office on Monkland Ave.

Muriel was able to get a half-time job for the next two years earning $500.00 a year at the McGill SCM organizing speakers and discussion groups. They found a four room walk-up apartment on Côte St. Luc Road for $50.00 a month. Most of Muriel's spare time was spent either in church work or going to meetings with Jack. They were involved in a number of organizations being formed at that time, exploring alternatives to capitalism. Muriel joined study groups of graduates of the SCM and they were both involved in founding the Fellowship for a Christian Social Order (FCSO).

Writing about Jack Duckworth during this period, Roby Kidd, a colleague of Jack's, said:

> In Montreal a dynamic group of ministers and YMCA secretaries were exceedingly active through the FCSO and gained much publicity through their efforts to arouse the churches and community to action to redress the threatening conditions of labour distress, bad housing, the armament race, etc.[1]

Jack and Muriel also joined the League for Social Reconstruction (LSR), forerunner of the Cooperative Commonwealth Federation (CCF), which in turn was the precursor to the New Democratic Party (NDP). The goal of the LSR was to establish a new social order in Canada that would promote the enforcement of decent basic wages, low-rent housing, unemployment insurance, socialized medical care, adequate old age pensions, family allowances and free education for all up to age sixteen.

Muriel found the LSR very exciting, but she had less and less time to be involved after the birth of her first child, Martin, in 1933.

> We were on the edge of the forming of the CCF, but it came at a time when I was having my children, and without much help. Therefore I felt on the edge of it; but it was exciting and we were both somewhat involved in all these movements. I remember going to the conferences out of which eventually came the CCF.
>
> The Canadian Association for Adult Education was also formed at about the same time, and we were very much involved in founding the NDG (Notre Dame de Grace Community Council.

They also belonged to the Fellowship of Reconciliation (FOR), a religious pacifist group that was non-denominational and international. FOR was founded in England following the First World War. Among its founders was the Reverend Richard Roberts, father of Gwen (Roberts) Norman, a lifetime friend of Muriel's. In New York, Jack and Muriel had been introduced to the FOR which, by the early twenties, had spread to the United States. FOR was actively committed to non-violence and sponsored debates at large public meetings. Although it never gained the same importance in Canada, Jack and Muriel formed part of a newly organized FOR group in Montreal in the early thirties that met at their home. Muriel was the only woman member among the YMCA secretaries, several ministers and others who gathered each month at the Duckworths' for discussion about the works of Sherwood Eddy, Eugene Debs, Norman Thomas and John R. Mott. Margaret Kidd, a close friend of Muriel's, found a reference to Jack's involvement in her husband's, Roby Kidd's, notes:

> Jack was the news correspondent for Quebec in the Fellowship Of Reconciliation magazine, *The World of Tomorrow.* About 1940 over 20,000 ministers of U.S.A. and Canada declared their pacifism in a questionnaire in this magazine. Most of them reneged when the U.S. declared war on Germany.

Muriel and Jack's biggest volunteer commitment was to their own church, Wesley United, because they felt that the church was where social change should be expected to come about. Jack had every intention of being ordained a United Church minister when he returned to Montreal. The practice was for a minister to be "called," that is, invited by a congregation to a church before being ordained. Jack tried to argue that serving people through the YMCA was equal to having a call to a church. This was unacceptable to the church officials and they refused to ordain him. Although he was disappointed, he had already chosen the YMCA as his life work and he became general secretary of the Notre Dame de Grace (NDG) YMCA in the west end of Montreal. He organized this suburban Y as a family Y, a new idea at the time. They ran recreation and adult education programs for youth and adults, using local schools. By 1938 construction began on the NDG YMCA which was opened in 1940. Fifty years later Muriel attended its anniversary and she recalled that the Y was known as "the house that Jack built."

After spending time at the Union Theological Seminary, Muriel and Jack found the conservative atmosphere at Wesley United Church rather stifling but set their hopes on the next generation. Despite Jack's differences with church officials over his ordination he still felt very much part of the United Church. Muriel and he both decided that whatever disagreements they might have with the adult congregation they could at least work with the children. Jack became the superintendent of the Sunday School and Muriel worked with the leaders and girls of the Canadian Girls In Training (CGIT). She was responsible for the program for seventy girls and their seven leaders and Sunday School teachers. Yet, in working with the youth they could not entirely escape some of the more conservative elements of the church.

> Jack went on having periodic scraps with adults in the church. There were some people who felt that he was leading the children astray. One day at a church meeting one man asked Jack straight out, "Are you a communist? Or are you a loyal member of the British Empire?" It was so absurd that we just laughed about it. This man was known to be such a right-wing character! But that was the sort of thing that Jack had to cope with all his life. He was always very straightforward, he couldn't dissemble about what he thought was important and it was always getting him into trouble. But the minister of the church, Reverend B.B. Brown, never seemed to have any doubts about him.

Muriel had fewer differences with the leaders of the CGIT program and enjoyed working with them right up until the birth of her third child, John, in 1938. In fact her last meeting with the program leaders occurred around her hospital bed following his birth. Soon she became a member of the Girls' Work Board of all Quebec churches with CGIT programs. She always favoured the CGIT over the Girl Guides because each group had so much more autonomy in deciding its own program and the organization seemed to her to be less authoritarian and more democratic. The CGIT made an effort to promote "world mindedness" with disarmament and peace-centred themes, and they introduced a "CGIT Peace Week" in 1936.

During the summers of 1931 and 1932 Muriel was a volunteer leader at

Cedar Lodge, the CGIT summer camp at Lake Memphremagog across the lake from her aunt's cottage, which she later inherited. During the second summer she was no doubt the subject of much camper interest, being pregnant at twenty-three with her first child. Besides teaching bible study she had a group of sixteen-year-old campers learning about "The World Today." She found conversations with them very stimulating because they were so eager to learn about everything that was happening in the rapidly changing world scene. Muriel knew that encouraging them, giving them an opportunity to understand and having a positive relationship with them were the keys to their learning.

Friends she made at the summer camps would be lasting ones. More than fifty years later Muriel would still count among her close friends Ida Stabler and Lois Chipman, both of whom she first knew as CGIT campers.

Family Life

Because of the depression Muriel and Jack felt nervous about the birth of their first child, Martin, in 1933.

> I recall lying on a couch waiting for the baby to be born and hearing on the radio that Roosevelt was closing the banks. The YMCA held onto its staff but everybody took a 15 percent cut. When Martin was born Jack earned an annual salary of $1,800.00, but the monthly grocery bill was only $30.00 and the rent $57.50.

The family had moved to a larger four-room apartment across from a park on Côte St. Antoine Road where Muriel took the baby on outings. She loved caring for Martin but found that having a baby meant that she was cut off from her former contacts. She missed her friends at the SCM and, were it not for her sister Mildred who worked downtown and kept in frequent touch with her, she would have felt even more isolated. Jack worked long hours and often evenings as well. Muriel and other wives of YMCA secretaries realized that they were all in the same boat and about ten of them decided to form a book club. They met weekly in one another's homes to discuss novels and biographies and before long these friends became her main support group.

Eleanor, born in 1935, was named after Eleanor Roosevelt whom Muriel greatly admired. By the time John was born in 1938 they had moved to an eight-room house on Benny Avenue in the western part of Notre Dame de Grace. When war was declared, their landowner panicked and put the house up for sale. With help from Muriel's father, they were able to buy another house just a couple of blocks away at 4059 Westhill, across the street from Benny Farm, which provided an expanse of several acres of fields. Muriel felt the children had the best of both worlds growing up in the city yet surrounded by the country. In the spring the boys and their friends would build rafts to sail the water-filled gullies on the nearby vacant lots. Eleanor, dressed in her pink skating costume with flying cape, would leap over the gullies with great abandon as she and John played Superman and Mary Marvel. The family pets included a dignified Irish setter named Flynn, a white cat named Prince and a budgie named Jerry.

In a CBC radio public affairs broadcast made in 1947, Muriel was asked to describe how she managed to retain a "life of her own" during the early years of her marriage.

> When the children were tiny and all in bed very early, my life was mostly after dark, and made up of interests I had had before they were born. Like many other young mothers, I was determined to keep a corner of my life for myself, if for no other reason than to have something else to talk about than babies and household problems. Besides, I firmly believed I would be a better mother for keeping in touch with the world outside our four walls even though it took effort and time.
>
> A good many times, in spite of my determination, the walls threatened to confine me. There would be illness and there was never enough help with the work and of course little children need their mothers, but my husband and my friends and the volunteer group work I was doing were always pulling me back into circulation. . . . It has been possible to have a "life of my own" because I wanted to and because my husband also believes I should have one and has always helped to make such a life possible for me.

Muriel and Jack did not always agree but they usually argued in private. In those days women were not supposed to differ from their husbands in public. However Muriel did recall an incident when she felt it was important to take a different position from his before a group of Hi Y teens. She felt it was a very good thing for those students to have seen a couple that they knew got along well together being able to disagree in public.

Jack was always good around the house, a fact that astonished Muriel because Jack's mother did not believe in men doing "women's work." Jack's mother was quite disapproving when Jack changed the babies' diapers, washed dishes or prepared breakfast. But Jack had seen his mother being a slave to her whole family and he just did not think that was right. Also he had acquired some useful skills during the summers when he worked as a dishwasher on the dining cars of the trans-Canada CPR trains. He put Martin to sleep by rocking his crib and making the sounds and motion of a moving train. And as the children grew up Jack always led the dishwashing brigade. Cleaning up after dinner was a family affair. Jack washed, the kids dried and

Muriel put things away.

Muriel obviously struggled to maintain a balance in her busy life. She loved raising children but she also wanted a life of her own. Sometimes she worried that the two could not be combined, but one evening as she was putting Martin to bed she realized he saw some benefit in her activities. Urging her to get to her meeting on time he told her, "hurry up Mummy so you won't be late to learn to be a better mummy."

Another favourite memory was of five-year-old Eleanor rushing through the house and down to the basement to invent creations with some old chemistry lab equipment that a friend had given her. Eleanor always referred to these as her "inventments."

Muriel would never forget when Eleanor had polio in Grade 1 that it was neither the doctors nor the nurses, but rather a hospital ward maid who took the trouble to phone her the first time Eleanor began to walk again. Eleanor herself recalled a drawing she did when she was eight years old showing all the things she wanted to be when she grew up—a weight lifter (inspired by physiotherapy following her bout with polio), a doctor, a scientist, a ballet dancer and a "housewife with lots of committees." Obviously Muriel had left her mark. Eleanor also remembered growing up listening to "Citizens' Forum" on the CBC and to the discussion groups which were held in the Duckworths' living room.

For the most part, the children just took their mother for granted, and when interviewed about their early years tended to recall incidents about Jack. As their father left to walk to work in the morning he would often turn and do a little tap dance on the sidewalk and tip his hat *à la* Maurice Chevalier to the watching children. He always came home early for birthday parties to organize the games. And often on hot summer days he would hustle home carrying ice cream cones which he would shade with his hat.

On Sunday afternoons in the wintertime, the ritual was to have tea in the living room served in front of the fire. The family would listen to a CBC radio program broadcasting the weekly sermon of the famous preacher, Dr. Fosdick, the minister at Riverside Church in New York. For Jack especially this was a high point because he felt that no matter what they were getting at church, they could always be sure of this little bit of good preaching from his old teacher at Union Theological, a man he loved and admired greatly.

In the warmer weather the family sometimes went for excursions by streetcar to favourite city parks—Mount Royal, Murray Hill and Westmount. This, according to Eleanor, was the one activity that made not going to church acceptable.

Summer holidays meant going to Magog by train and usually they stayed by the lake in "Aunt May's" cottage. When they visited Muriel's parents in Magog, Eleanor remembered her grandmother always busy baking, with flour on her clothes. The children's favourite places to play were the nearby dock, the sawmill, the railway station and the farm machinery store that was kitty-corner to their grandmother's house. Some mothers might have worried about the children's safety around such potentially dangerous areas but Eleanor never felt the slightest constraint as she and her brothers explored these fascinating places.

Martin especially remembered Christmas in Magog and going by train. He was aware that his father was deeply attached to this part of the world and on summer holidays he gave Martin a kind of "royal treatment," fishing, rowing and storytelling. In later years Martin would try to replicate these types of holidays for his own son, Nick.

Though very busy with her own young family Muriel reached out to friends and to her immediate community. Margaret Kidd recalled Muriel's kindness during her early days in Montreal. She related:

> I first came to know Muriel in the early days of my marriage and my first experiences in Montreal from September 1941 to June 1943, when my husband worked for her husband at the family YMCA in Notre Dame de Grace. She was such a source of strength and support for me—I was a stranger in Montreal—knew no one apart from my husband. . . . She was busy with her young family and involved in the Y, the church and the Home and School, yet her home was always open.
>
> When I was sick in pregnancy at Christmas 1942 she brought me to her home and cared for me even

Muriel with Eleanor and John
in Phillips Square, Montreal, 1946.

Martin, 11, Eleanor, 8 and John, 5, 1944.

though her house was busy with all the Christmas goings-on. I was in bed in her house for at least a week, saving both me and the baby! And her comment to me, when I expressed my gratitude, was "One often can't repay a giver, but you can always pass it on to others." To me this is the way Muriel has always operated, giving and showing others how.

One of Muriel's early volunteer activities came about from noticing the need for organized play for three-year-old John when she joined a house-wives' swim and gym class two mornings a week at the Y. They had hired a babysitter at the Y but had not thought about providing any equipment or materials for her; they expected her to entertain the children with stories. Muriel soon noticed that John just sat in the corner with nothing to do and was not at all happy. Luckily, a young woman joined the mothers' group who knew about Montessori education, and she was horrified at the children's inactivity. So, before long they had a little meeting in Muriel's living room and things began to change. The mothers organized a cooperative play school at the Y. Muriel had learned something about day care from her friend Margaret Kidd who worked in one of the much-needed day care centres that flourished during the war years when women were encouraged to work outside the home.

While helping to start their own cooperative nursery school, Muriel met several other women who were undertaking similar efforts in other parts of the city. This in turn led to her efforts to organize a nursery school association in Montreal. Although there were established standards at that time for day care, there were none for nursery schools, and Muriel's earlier experience at the Y made her aware that they were needed. With the help of Agnes Matthews, principal of St. George's School in Montreal, and her staff in charge of preschool children, Muriel participated in working on provincial legislation that would set standards for nursery schools in Quebec.

Working for a Peaceful Community

During the war years when Muriel and Jack deliberately chose to keep children and youth as the focus of their attention, they were founding members of three Home and School Associations in Notre Dame de Grace at Rosedale, Kensington and Willingdon schools. Even before their eldest, Martin, started school they had helped to organize the first Home and School in their community.

There was no kindergarten in the neighbourhood school attended by Martin and Eleanor. The children had to walk a long distance to attend one in another school. The summer before John was due to start school, Muriel and three other women in the Home and School started going door to door to get support for their petition to the school board for a kindergarten in their school. The board agreed and granted the kindergarten. Muriel and her friends in the Home and School were astounded at such an easy victory. Later they learned that the principal had always been in favour of a kindergarten, but thought the children in this neighbourhood were well cared for and that there were other schools in greater need of kindergartens.

Next Muriel got busy on a committee to found a school library. They not only raised the money for a library but they had the audacity to present the principal with a list of books which they thought should be in the library. That, the principal explained, was not their privilege! They moved on to further challenges and also succeeded in having Kensington school be one of the first to offer evening courses for adults.

Early in the war, Muriel formed part of a training group of eight or ten women who met weekly to prepare themselves to lead parent education discussions. The course was given by Muriel Hughes of the Mental Hygiene Institute and the group met in her home. They explored ways to encourage parents to deal with such problems as how to discipline their children, whether they should spank them, the right of parents to get angry and what to do about their own guilt feelings. A woman who was in Muriel's class asked to see her privately. She quietly confided in Muriel that she was a battered wife and wondered whether she should be preparing herself to do parent education because she felt that her problem disqualified her. That was the first time Muriel realized that there were women whose husbands beat them.

Muriel credited the artist Fritz Brandtner, who later became a friend of the family, for bringing a very exciting dimension into her life, that of children's art. She first heard him speak at a Home and School meeting where he brought children's paintings for them to look at. She was infected by his attitude towards children's art, probably the more so because she was already interested in the kind of education that was going on at the Little Red School House in New York. Soon after, she encouraged Roby Kidd, Notre Dame de Grace YMCA staff member, to organize Saturday morning art classes for neighbourhood children with Fritz Brandtner as teacher.

Being elected in 1946 to the provincial council of the Home and School Association brought Muriel into closer contact with the politics of education in Quebec. These were politically dangerous times in Quebec when the Duplessis government introduced fascist measures such as the Padlock law which meant that bookstores as well as private homes were raided in search of communist literature. As a member of the provincial council of the Home and School Association, Muriel received the nomination list for the slate of officers. Somebody in the Duplessis government found it unacceptable. Muriel was invited to an off-the-record meeting in a private home to discuss the matter. There she learned that the government suspected one of the women on the slate of being a communist and wanted her name removed.

Muriel knew her well having worked with her the previous year on a study on the education of Jewish children in Outremont. Jews did not have separate rights and were educated in the Protestant schools. The study revealed anti-Semitism in the school system. For instance, Baron Byng, a high school in the area where most of the children were Jewish, had no Jewish teachers.

In the course of doing the study Muriel had developed great respect for her colleague and she objected to the government's political interference. She was further angered when the Home and School did a cover-up; they sent out a letter removing this woman's name from the slate on the pretext that there were too many nominees from the Montreal area. In righteous indignation, Muriel objected to the new slate of officers at the annual meeting of the Home and School Association. Muriel was with a group of dissenters who had met prior to the annual meeting and who now proposed another slate of officers, including Muriel's name as president of the council. She had never expected that she would be elected president but when the dissenters' alternate nomination slate was totally defeated, including her friend's name, Muriel rose to her feet. She, who could only open her mouth in a public meeting when she felt passionate about something, exclaimed dramatically, "Father forgive them for they know not what they do!"

Muriel also objected vigorously when the government insisted that the Home and School change its name to the Protestant Home and School Association when they went to become incorporated. She believed that as long as they retained their present name, the Home and School Association, there was the possibility of a province-wide association of all parents, English and French, Catholic and Protestant and Jewish, which would be in a far stronger position to influence the government on education policies. But her view was not acceptable to the Duplessis government which did all it could to keep Catholics out of the Home and School movement.

If Muriel had been shy and inarticulate in her earlier years, she was quickly becoming a passionate opponent of racial and religious prejudice. She still felt nervous when she rose to speak, and sometimes her voice quivered as she was overcome with emotion and felt on the verge of tears. But she persisted.

Muriel's heavy volunteer work load also meant that she taught herself to be well organized. The piece she gave on the CBC broadcast in 1947 related how she coped with her busy life.

> But the big question always is, of course, how do you do these things with three children and no help? When I talk about planning and organizing, you see my home is also my workshop where I prepare for committee work, etc., and I had to learn some working techniques. (I wish I knew more.) Once a week I make a big list—

things to do, people to see, letters to write, etc. I put them down on paper and then my mind isn't all cluttered up trying to remember them. I also note meetings and appointments in a date book, and I have the simplest kind of filing system—a few manila folders where materials for different committees and also family activities can be kept separately.

Having my own desk (which we bought instead of a dressing table when we were first married) helps a great deal to simplify my work. I try to make the telephone a useful servant and not the master of my time. If I'm rushing through some housework which no reasonable degree of flexibility will allow me to postpone any longer, the telephone goes unanswered, unless, of course I'm expecting an important call.

I often do necessary reading and preparation for meetings in the mornings when I'm fresh and alone in the house except for the telephone. In the afternoons after school, I plan to be at home. The children are in and out and busy, but I like to be there then and I can often do housework during those hours. Most of my endless mending of socks is done in committee meetings—I can't bear to waste my time on it when I'm alone.

As for the actual work of the house—for years now we have shared the routine everyday tasks. Each child has his [or her] schedule which he [or she] has helped to work out, and Daddy has his jobs too. Nobody really works hard to cover these chores and there isn't a great deal of grumbling. . . .

I have found that in order to do community work seriously, even though voluntarily, there are times when [housework] accumulates and seems to get out of hand. Telephone calls make housework nearly impossible, a deadline must be met on a report, and so on. At those times, washing, ironing, mending and cleaning take second place and have to be fitted in whenever possible. At those times a regular schedule cannot work any more than it can when there is a crisis, such as illness, within the family. So I learned not to worry if, for instance, the ironing doesn't all get done during the week, or the washing has to be left until Wednesday afternoon. Some people might call it gross neglect of household duties. I call it flexibility.

Recently I asked my eleven-year-old daughter if she thought my outside activities had any good results in the family. Her quick reply was "Humph, we certainly learned to look after ourselves!" and then, more thoughtfully, "I guess it is a good thing we know all that about the education of Jewish children in Quebec that you have been learning this year."

Muriel was always eager to incorporate new ideas into managing the household. One that she read about in *Parents Magazine* and instituted at the cottage was the card system. On the backs of cards cut from Nabisco Shredded Wheat boxes she wrote a household job: set table, wash dishes, sweep the floor, make a fire in the fireplace, make breakfast, sweep veranda, pick a bouquet, get milk and feed the pig (at the farm up the road), make a dessert, prepare the vegetables, feed the dog, empty the pee pots (in the early days). And then the weekly jobs, with the day specified: wash the kitchen floor, wash the veranda, wash the row boat, sink the tin cans, rinse laundry in the lake (acceptable procedures in those days!). Every evening the cards were shuffled and each one drew an agreed number of cards. If they got a weekly job on the wrong day they were delighted. Even guests were incorporated into this nightly routine.

Jack almost always encouraged Muriel's full involvement in volunteer work outside home, and he would complain only on those occasions when he found buttons missing on his shirts or holes in his socks. He was fastidious about his clothes and wished Muriel could keep up in the mending department too. On the whole, no one gave Muriel more emotional support than Jack. Whenever she was hesitant he would jokingly quote Emile Coué, a pop psychologist, and tell her to repeat: "Every day in every way I am getting better and better!" When Muriel was faced with a real difficulty or a new challenge she would rather not have to meet, Jack used to say: "You can do it! If anybody can do it, you can!" In retrospect Muriel recognized the incentive his support provided: "I think that made quite a change in my life—that confidence!"

If Jack was Muriel's source of strength, Muriel in turn was Jack's. Their mutual support clearly made each of them more effective. Eleanor remembers her parents as playful and industrious with nothing depressive about either of them. She felt they lived full lives. There was always something needing to be done and so they did it. Martin came to see his father as "a missionary, a preacher, a mover of men." Muriel and Jack themselves had been raised in strong religious families where much was expected of them. At McGill and at Union Theological Seminary Muriel and Jack were educated in the best tradition of the Social Gospel. Taking responsibility and leadership in the community came quite naturally to them.

Note

1.   Margaret Kidd, letter to Marion Kerans, Toronto, 1983. In the author's possession.

Chapter 4

Pacifists in a "Good" War

Besides striving to be a good wife and mother and to keep a "life of her own," Muriel waged another interior struggle. Although she—as was the norm for women of her generation—was brought up to be and sought to be pleasant, she continued to question received truths, no matter what the cost. Her quest for truth was painful in two important areas, her views on communism and her pacifism during the war.

Communism

After Martin's birth in March 1933, at the bottom of the depression, Muriel looked to Mildred as her lifeline to what was going on in the world. Among Mildred's friends were radical thinkers, and Muriel came to know some of them. During the depression times were so bad and the future looked so bleak that serious-minded people were engaged in a widespread search for alternatives to capitalism. Many intellectuals were eager to examine the Soviet system and some more progressive church members who advocated the Social Gospel were also sympathetic to communism, as were political leaders among social democrats. Communist-based political movements cropped up both in the west and in Ontario. Certain communists enjoyed much prominence. Muriel recalled the packed house at His Majesty's in downtown Montreal when Paul Robeson sang and the great crowd that came to hear the Red Dean of Canterbury.

Muriel recalled discussions at UTS and she continued to be intrigued by the thought of a connection between the ideals of Christianity and of communism—everyone producing according to their ability and receiving according to their need. Jack, on the other hand, was adamantly opposed to communism on theological grounds. Although Jack often identified with the working class, according to his son, Martin, Jack believed in making a better world by making better people out of capitalists. Muriel saw Jack as opposed to violent revolution and a Godless society. Meanwhile, Muriel remained curious and interested in the progressive social programs she heard were going on in the Soviet Union. There was a certain tension between Jack and Muriel over how radical they should become.

Martin recalled the Christmas Jack tried to give Muriel a fur coat.

> He cashed in a paid-up insurance policy to buy an expensive coat to show his love for her. She refused to accept it because she could not see herself wearing a fur coat as though she were a women of means.

Muriel's tendency to resist propaganda was another reason why she remained open to new political systems. The bogey of communism was constantly being raised by the establishment in order to silence criticism of existing conditions or demands for reform. Muriel developed a particularly keen aversion to propaganda in her efforts to try to know the truth. A childhood experience had left its mark.

> During the First World War we were given such a horrible picture of the Germans. I was visiting my aunt in Boston just after the US entered the war in 1917 when I was eight years old. I remember the horror stories about the Germans chopping off the hands of babies and throwing the babies against stone walls and afterwards I knew that that wasn't true. I remember a terrible nightmare I had about a German coming into my bedroom and chopping me up. I was absolutely terrified by this dream. And I remember the horrible pictures of Bolsheviks that would give you nightmares. They always had wild hair standing out in all directions, great big bushy beards and evil eyes—and knowing later that that was propaganda.

In 1939 Mildred invited Muriel to attend a meeting in her home. Young people were gathering there to hear Stanley Ryerson, later the secretary of the Communist Party of Canada. Ryerson had just come back from the World Youth Congress, an international communist youth gathering in Europe, and was to speak at a youth conference in Montreal. Muriel hesitated about going and indicated that she did not think she should do something that Jack would not like. Mildred in a disgusted tone remarked, "I never heard you say that before!" On the one hand Muriel felt she wanted to know more about what these young people were saying because she did have some confidence in them. But on the other hand she did not want to be identified in public with communists. She waffled over going because she feared that to do that sort of thing was a threat to Jack. The YMCA would have taken a dim view of her association with communists and Jack himself genuinely did not approve of communism.

Already there had been one incident that had gotten Jack into trouble. During the textile workers' strike in 1937, Muriel and Jack attended a large meeting in support of the strike. A newspaper reporter from the *Montreal Star* who knew Jack chose to report in the paper that he was there. Just being in the audience was an affront to the president of the Montreal board of the YMCA, who was also the president of Dominion Textile. The general secretary of the Montreal YMCA informed Jack that his presence had put the Y in an awkward position. Jack did not back down and insisted on the propriety of upholding the right of the workers to organize and to strike.

Despite her anxieties over not involving Jack, Muriel went to the meeting.

> I remember feeling kind of vulnerable because I went to it. It represented

my real ambivalence about it. I want to know these people and I have some confidence in what they are saying, yet I don't want to be identified with them publicly. I don't really feel like I belong.

It was not only a question of divided loyalties for Muriel but of internal conflict over the old question of seeking out the truth. She wanted very much to please people—Jack, Mildred, her friends, her parents—yet she struggled to clarify her own convictions.

As her children grew and asked all kinds of questions—about God, war, Santa Claus, communism, love, evil—Muriel encouraged their questions, enjoyed the openness of their minds, and tried to help them understand that there were questions they might or might not find answers to as they grew up.

Eleanor recalled once hearing a sermon on the evils of communism. "What's that?" Eleanor asked her mother. Muriel looked torn and refrained from giving Eleanor an answer in support of the minister's diatribe. She replied cryptically, "No one should have more than they need!" Discussions about communism were not a regular occurrence in the Duckworth household. When Martin as a teenager discovered in their home a communist pamphlet on the theme of "workers of the world unite!" he thought communism was some secret thing. He wondered why it was that his parents had not told him anything about this wonderful topic and immediately developed a suppressed fascination for it.

Over the years Muriel always respected her communist friends' intellectual approach towards their beliefs. Her sister Mildred suffered enormously when a number of her close friends were accused at the Gouzenko trials in 1946. At the time, Mildred worked in the Czech embassy in Ottawa and she used to spend her lunch hours sitting in the courtroom following the trial. Mildred's friends were exonerated but Muriel too felt they had been unfairly attacked. As a result Muriel felt closer to them and they remained her friends.

> My feelings about communism are related to my life experience, not so much to what I read. Nothing that I have read seems to matter so much as the experience I had with people.

Muriel never let people's ideologies stand in the way of accepting them as individuals. Her warm personal interest conveyed the feeling that our common humanity is what bonds us. Muriel's devotion to her communist friends and her reluctance to fracture family relations came first. Her openness and acceptance caused narrow-minded people to brand her as a communist on a number of occasions throughout her life. At times she would be distressed and even frightened, as when during her Voice of Women tenure accusatory telephone calls came in the middle of the night. For the most part she simply shrugged off such accusations.

Pacifism

Muriel and Jack had strongly resisted the very idea of war before it broke out, while at the same time opposition was collapsing all around them. After the declaration of war, Jack remained a staunch pacifist. Even though Muriel felt less sure of her own position, she continued to support Jack's. While she had not been brought up to be a pacifist, during her undergraduate years Muriel had sympathized with the inherent pacifism in the Student Christian Movement. She leaned towards a pacifist interpretation in her reading of the *Records of the Life of Jesus*. Muriel recalled that the First World War was supposed to have been the war to end all wars, and now many of her friends and most of her family insisted that Hitler had to be stopped and the only way to do so was to go to war. Because Muriel was so suspicious of propaganda she tended to discount horror stories about the war.

She felt pained by the conflict between Jack's position and that of her family and her various friends. She knew her brother Norman was likely to enlist if war was declared.

> I felt caught between my parents' strong position of support for the war and their fear for Norman's life, and Jack's very strong opposition to the war and my uncertainty, and because of all my friends at all levels. I had friends on the left who had opposed the war when Germany and the USSR had signed that mutual non-aggression pact. . . .
>
> There was another group of people, politically sophisticated, who were close to government. I remember this woman saying almost with enthusiasm—and how it shocked me— "There is going to be a war!" I was still going around thinking that there had to be another way. Surely there doesn't have to be a war! I think I was probably pleased with Neville Chamberlain when he came home with his umbrella saying "peace in our time," not knowing too much about the situation, the political price they paid then for peace.[1]
>
> The way I have come to look at it, looking backwards over history, Europe had many opportunities to deal with what was going on in Germany short of war, and they did not [act on them]. And the reason they did not was that they were more concerned with stopping communism than they were with stopping fascism.
>
> At the time of the signing of the Treaty of Versailles, June 28, 1919, there was a very good cartoon in the *Daily Herald*, London, done by the cartoonist, Mike Dyson. It was a picture of the men coming down the steps of the palace of Versailles, having just signed the treaty, Lloyd George for England, Clemenceau of France, Orlando for Italy, Wilson for the United States, and all looking very pleased with themselves for what they had just done. Clemenceau was speaking and the caption underneath the picture was, "Curious! I seem to hear a child weeping!"

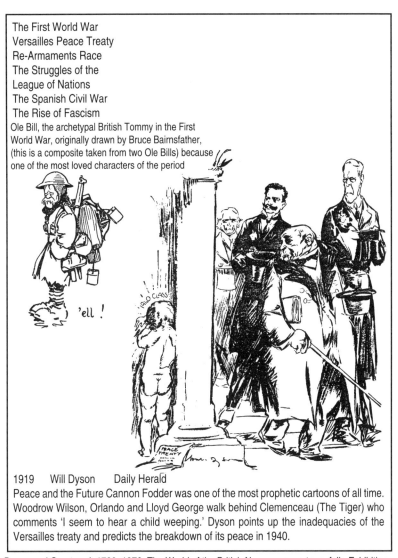

The First World War
Versailles Peace Treaty
Re-Armaments Race
The Struggles of the
League of Nations
The Spanish Civil War
The Rise of Fascism
Ole Bill, the archetypal British Tommy in the First
World War, originally drawn by Bruce Bairnsfather,
(this is a composite taken from two Ole Bills) because
one of the most loved characters of the period

'ell !

1919   Will Dyson   Daily Herald
Peace and the Future Cannon Fodder was one of the most prophetic cartoons of all time.
Woodrow Wilson, Orlando and Lloyd George walk behind Clemenceau (The Tiger) who
comments 'I seem to hear a child weeping.' Dyson points up the inadequacies of the
Versailles treaty and predicts the breakdown of its peace in 1940.

Drawn and Quartered, 1720–1970, The World of the British Newspaper cartoon, folio Exhibition,
National Portrait Newspaper Publisher's Association Gallery. Published by Times Newspapers Ltd.

Around the corner of the building is this little baby crying, naked except for a banner across his chest which said 'Class of 1940.' Isn't that incredible? Dyson was a famous cartoonist who could see in the terms of the Treaty of Versailles the seeds of another war. It was a very punitive treaty, an impossibly punitive peace which brought desperation to the German people and the rise of fascism in Germany. [Muriel wept as she remembered this prophetic cartoon.]

She had begun by thinking that, purely and simply, you do not cause the death of a great number of people in order to deal with Nazi fascism. Her theological beliefs led her to see all people of the world as God's children and that God's children must not go around killing each other. Beyond that she had no answers, but her quest for answers would be lifelong.

> How do you talk about dealing with the evil that was Nazism and fascism in any other terms than war? I think that is probably one of the big searches of my life, trying to find an answer to that. I am still convinced that there is an answer, that we have to find it.

Church Leaders Back Away

The declaration of war caused fractures between social democrats. J.S. Woodsworth adamantly insisted that Canada should remain neutral but the CCF party split from their leader. Even the MP Agnes Macphail, formerly a confirmed pacifist, concluded that contemplating a world without opposition to Hitler seemed more terrible than even war.

Jack found himself one of very few leaders in the church who remained true to pacifism. The little FOR group begun by the Duckworths disbanded, although two United Church minister friends, Lavelle Smith in Westmount and Bill Halliday in Montreal West, did retain their pacifist position in public.

When Jack and Muriel returned to UTS in the spring of 1940 for a tenth anniversary class reunion, they discovered that, while many of the students there were still pacifists, Reinhold Niebuhr was not. This was very hard on Jack who had always greatly admired Niebuhr. And even though Niebuhr was not at all unfriendly to the students who had held to their pacifist position, he made it quite clear that, in his view, they were wrong. It was not easy for Jack and Muriel to face the division which that brought about. And it forced Muriel to rethink her own theological view of pacifism. Was she a pacifist because of Jack? Or was she herself convinced that this war was wrong?

Reinhold Niebuhr castigated the pacifist position as self-righteous in an article he wrote in the winter edition of *Radical Religion*. Dr. Richard Roberts,[2] founder and first secretary of the FOR in Britain, and father of Muriel's long-time friend, Gwen Norman, replied to Niebuhr, and the correspondence was printed in *Christianity and Society*, a magazine of which Niebuhr was one of the editors. Dr. Roberts was a fine theologian and a brilliant preacher who came from a Welsh mining background and was in close touch with organized labour. In the 1920s he went to the United States and from there to Canada where he became a United Church minister, and later moderator of the United Church of Canada. He regarded what was going on in Germany as evil but his position was that nevertheless the Christian church cannot condone killing as the answer.

In his reply to Niebuhr, Roberts referred to the sense of alienation from one's own people, the coolness of friends, the suspicion of disloyalty and the lacerating conflict of loyalties which the pacifist must undergo. This helped Muriel to understand better why she herself had had such a difficult time maintaining a pacifist position during the war. Roberts had agonized over these same questions, but he had not wavered from his position that a Christian minister cannot support war. Remembering her own inner conflict, she greatly sympathized with him and she was proud that Jack remained steadfast in support of Roberts.

Dr. Roberts was a visiting professor at Pine Hill Divinity School in Halifax when war broke out. In 1938 he signed a declaration along with a group of seventy-five United Church ministers which was printed in the *United Church Observer*.[3] It stated:

> Neither the state nor any other power has the right to compel a person to engage in what his conscience declares to be a sinful act. . . . Some may sincerely hold that obedience to that divine command leads them to abstain from participation in any war, some that it forbids them to participate in unjust wars, some that in the present unredeemed state of the world that state has a duty under God to use force when law and order are threatened or to vindicate an essential Christian principle, i.e. to defend victims of wanton aggression or secure freedom for the oppressed. The Church recognizes the conscientious right and action of each of these groups.

In a letter sent from Montreal to one of his daughters, dated October 5, 1939, Dr. Roberts had reported:

> And it is not the ministers only, but the laity. Jack Duckworth told us on Sunday night that he sat with a company of laymen, Y.M.C.A. directors, who started discussing the matter and they all agreed that fomenting the war spirit was not the business of the church. . . . It is very cheering to me. . . . I had to resign from my congregation in 1914 for saying the things that apparently all the United Church ministers are saying in these days. It is not that they have become pacifists, but that they have come to see that the Gospel and war are at extreme antipodes from one another.

But Dr. Roberts would soon learn that during the Second World War the official church was no longer receptive to his message. Jack continued to support him and, although Muriel had not worked out her own theological reasons for opposing this war, she felt it was wrong and continued to support Jack.

Muriel claimed people used to say that Jack was the most militant pacifist they had ever met. His board of directors recognized how much they needed him in the demanding job he was doing at the YMCA, but they also saw him as somebody who had this strange notion about not being in favour of the war.

Sometimes he would get involved in a quarrel with one or other of the board members about his convictions. He would try to discuss them but never made much headway in bringing the board members around to his point of view. Muriel felt that Jack did not ever realize how unrealistic it was to expect the board members to see things differently. He would go on exhausting himself trying to persuade them of another viewpoint. Sometimes when Muriel and Jack would talk over these incidents, they felt "it's us against the world!" In correspondence with Roby Kidd some years later Jack wrote about this period of his life:

> [I had] many confrontations with my YMCA associates, my college friends and professor [and] unhappy experiences with church officials and directors as I tried to interpret my understanding of Jesus' teachings to the modern scenes around us. Whether I was challenging the war system, unemployment, or the exploitation of resources or people, I was made to feel that I was a disturbing influence . . . yet the social gospel embattled industrial combines and proclaimed the dignity of mankind. It challenged militarism and war. It began the foundations in our society of social theories on which have been built family welfare and social welfare programs as well as medicare and retirement allowances.[4]

Family and War

Muriel recalled how tense she and Jack felt because they held viewpoints about the war which differed from those of her parents. Early in the war all of them worried about her brother Norman, who would have enlisted right away had he not been recovering from double pneumonia. Their fears for Norman's safety were well founded. He joined the Air Force and went to England in 1941 where he was attached to a British crew. In 1942 Norman was killed over the Netherlands returning from an air raid on Kassel, Germany. He was buried in a Canadian cemetery in Bergen, the Netherlands. Norman was a very precious member of the family. He was outgoing and friendly and Muriel's children worshipped him. He loved horses and the outdoors. As John grew up he was always proud when family members would say how much he reminded them of Norman.

Even though Muriel's parents did not accept Jack and Muriel's views on pacifism, Norman's death brought the family closer together. Muriel and Jack immediately went home to Magog, and Jack offered considerable support to Muriel's parents in their grief. He helped to plan a very beautiful memorial service. The minister of the church, Philip Matthams, was himself a pacifist. He had been recommended as pastor to the Magog congregation by Muriel and Jack before the war.

One way that Muriel expressed her disapproval of the war was to refuse to do "war work." At that time it was common for married women who remained at home to engage in volunteer work to support the war effort. The civilian population put much energy into organizing victory bond campaigns, victory gardens, Red Cross circles and emergency defence, but Muriel chose to keep working with children instead. She did make a feeble attempt for a few weeks to join a Red Cross sewing group but her heart was not in it and she felt quite sure the women there did not want her around. Once when she ventured the opinion that it was important to keep on working with children even though there was a war on, she was emphatically told by one woman that what she was doing was not important, that what was important was the war effort.

At the outbreak of war Martin was six and a half, Eleanor was almost four and John nearly a year old. Martin always asked insistent questions about the war and about the young men who were joining up and going away from the Notre Dame de Grace YMCA. He was badly affected whenever news came that one of them had been killed. Muriel felt troubled too as she looked at Martin's paintings, filled with strafing planes and red skies, vividly portraying air battles. Although she tried to keep the children's minds off the war she was amazed at how eagerly they would identify by sound the war planes that flew overhead.

An acquaintance with some German-speaking prisoners of war helped Muriel to keep a human face on the "enemy." The Y was called upon to work with some interned young Germans of military age who had been caught in England at the outbreak of war and shipped to an internment camp near Sherbrooke, Quebec. Some of them, mainly young professionals, volunteered to work in Montreal in a tool and dye manufacturing plant in the suburb of Lachine where specialized labour was needed. The Y got involved through their

Norman Ball, 1942.

prisoner of war services, and once a week some of these young workers came to the Y for socializing. The Duckworth children made friends with two of these young men, who came to their home for Sunday tea, and they in turn became very fond of the children. One Sunday afternoon they all went together to a Van Gogh exhibit at the Montreal Museum. Muriel remembered how one young man carried little Eleanor around on his shoulders so that she could see the pictures too. The family lost contact with these young friends after they left Montreal, but many years later one of them was to surface again in Toronto as the eye doctor of two of Muriel's best friends and Muriel and Eleanor had a great reunion with him.

Throughout the war Jack wrote monthly letters to all the young service men who had come to the Y as boys. They always came to see him whenever they were home on leave and gave him news for these letters. He would mimeograph copies for each service man. Many of them replied and he would relay their news in his next monthly letter. He felt it was important in this way to keep a sense of community among these "boys" whom he loved.

Muriel's family continued to be plagued with tragedy during the next three years. Muriel herself had two miscarriages, the first a few months after Norman's death. She always remembered how Mildred's husband, George, came to comfort her and sat on her bed cheering her up. Only a short while later, in the spring of 1945, George himself contracted meningitis and died at the age of thirty. Then in January 1947, Muriel's mother, Anna Ball, died after a brief illness, leaving her family in further shock. Anna, so attentive when it came to looking after others, had not paid much attention to her own health and neglected to go to the family doctor on her own account. It cost money and she could "doctor" herself. Muriel always felt that her mother had died prematurely and might have lived had she had medical attention sooner.

Notes

1. Muriel is referring to a meeting in Munich in September 1938, between Hitler, Mussolini, Sir Neville Chamberlain (prime minister of Britain) and Edouard Daladier (premier of France). Hitler had threatened to invade Czechoslovakia; England and France were committed by treaty to go to war against Germany in that case. At the Munich meeting, they backed away from that commitment in their attempt to achieve "peace in our time." Historians generally agree that they not only sacrificed Czechoslovakia, but gave Hitler a precious extra year for a war he was able to unleash at a time of his own choosing.
2. Gwen Norman, Unpublished biography of Dr. Richard Roberts, p. 185. The manuscript was graciously lent to the author by Ms. Norman.
3. "Declaration upon War Made by the General Council." *United Church Observer*, 1938. Cited in Gwen Norman, Unpublished biography of Dr. Richard Roberts.
4. Letter from Margaret Kidd, October 1983, to author.

Chapter 5

Becoming an Adult Educator: Halifax 1947-67

*M*uriel felt very disappointed for Jack when he missed the one job he really wanted, general secretary to the YMCA of Vancouver. An opening for this position came in 1943 and he wanted to return to his home town. Although he was fully qualified Jack was not invited to apply and he felt that the reason was because he was a known pacifist. Muriel would have been happy to move to Vancouver.

The next opportunity for a challenge came in 1947. Halifax was looking for a general secretary who could raise sufficient money to build a new YMCA. The old Y on Barrington Street was in very bad shape. Even the marble doorsills were worn down from the traffic of men over a period including two world wars. The board of the Halifax YMCA was glad to hire Jack as he was known to be an able fundraiser. And after the experience he gained in building the Notre Dame de Grace Y Jack was pleased with the opportunity. During the next two years he succeeded with his board and a great many volunteers in raising over a million dollars to build the YMCA on South Park Street, the largest capital sum ever raised by a social agency in Halifax to that date.

On September 20, 1947, the Duckworths moved into their new home, at the

John, Muriel, Martin, Jack, Eleanor, Halifax, 1947.

corner of Oxford and London streets. Though she knew virtually nobody when she arrived, Muriel gradually found her way into the community largely through the children and by attending Home and School meetings. Jack used a parting gift of $500.00 given to him by the Notre Dame de Grace Y to fix up their basement and this became a "hang out" for John's gang and for dances for Martin's "Ten Minutes More Club." Martin fell in love at age fourteen and Eleanor made a strenuous effort to be accepted by the girls in her class. John quickly made friends.

Muriel and Jack assumed that Halifax had an undenominational school system because it had just one school board, only to discover that there were still separate schools for Protestants and Catholics. They soon became aware of the divisions between Catholics and Protestants and how pronounced political partisanship was. The Protestant and Catholic high schools were situated practically across the street from each other and Martin and Eleanor were quite conscious of the rivalries between students. Although Muriel worried about the quality of her own children's education, she later learned through her job in the Department of Education that the children in her neighbourhood were not nearly as badly off as children in the Black communities.

Family Sorrows

The early years in Halifax continued to be marked by family tragedy. A few months after Muriel's arrival in Halifax she was shattered to hear that her sister, Mildred, had a mental breakdown and was hospitalized in Montreal. Mildred had responded with great stoicism to her husband's death for the sake of her two little daughters but, finally, the accumulated sorrow over the loss of her husband, her mother and her brother all within three years proved too stressful. And even before these sad losses, the Gouzenko affair had taken its toll on her. Mildred had been working in Ottawa as the liaison officer for the Czechoslovakian embassy, and she lived through the harrowing trials of some personal friends.

When Muriel and her family moved away at such a critical period in Mildred's life, she felt all the more bereft. Muriel and Mildred had always been very close and Muriel's children adored their aunt. Muriel remembered her sister as a popular, pretty child who had grown up to be a vivacious, independent-minded woman. She had not anticipated that the outcome of Mildred's anguish could be mental illness and had difficulty believing this could have happened to her sister. Muriel felt guilty that she had not been sufficiently sensitive to Mildred's sorrow.

After several months in hospital in Montreal, Mildred recovered enough so that Muriel and Jack invited her and her children to come and stay with them in Halifax. Jack had been able to find a large six bedroom house on Cambridge Street for a reasonable price. Here Mildred could have her own quarters on the third floor and she accepted. That winter Mildred tried to rebuild her life and took further studies at Dalhousie, but her illness returned and she was hospitalized in

Dartmouth. Her children remained with Muriel for the next year and afterwards went to live with Evelyn, Mildred and Muriel's older sister, and her family on their farm near Belleville, Ontario.

Mildred was in and out of hospital for nine years and Muriel faced with her the ups and downs of her depression. Eleanor recalled how her mother, with no show of effort, took the bus and ferry to visit her aunt every week. Muriel would always remember Mildred as a highly intelligent woman filled with the love of life. She saw her sister's illness as a great tragedy. Having a member of her own family mentally ill made Muriel much more sensitive to the pain felt by mentally ill persons and their families. She thought that medical and community understanding of mental illness was very limited.

Paid Employment

Muriel felt she was at a turning point. The children were well along in school and she had already been working full-time as a volunteer. Dr. Harry Hall, head of student counselling at that time, and later principal of Sir George Williams College, Montreal, encouraged her to pursue employment. She decided to follow his advice but once Muriel arrived in Halifax she did not rush into it. After some of the tensions in the Home and School Association in Montreal she wanted to draw breath and get to know the scene in Halifax. She spent the first few months settling the family, going to meetings of the Home and School and to various organizations and keeping herself very much in the background.

Muriel, 1956.

During that first year, Muriel came into contact with Tom Parker, the progressive principal of Bloomfield School. They met through an adult education program which Parker had introduced in the school. This was based on the YMCA's "So Ed" program. Muriel was pleased when, after learning of her background, Tom invited her to co-teach a course for parents of preschool children, one evening a week for six weeks. She enjoyed doing this and prepared a reference list of toys, records and books appropriate for preschoolers for distribution to the parents who took the course.

While working at Bloomfield School, Muriel met Guy Henson, director of the newly established Adult Education Division of the provincial Department of

Education, and Donald Wetmore, advisor in Drama. Henson drove her home the night of the season's closing and on the spot invited her to come and work for them as an adviser on parent education. He offered her $300.00 a year for a half-time job but Muriel held out for $500.00 so that she would have enough money to pay her streetcar fare and for help at home.

Olive White came two days a week to help out with the housework and baking and she became a lifelong friend of the whole family. Muriel always felt she could never have coped without Olive's assistance. Many years later, when Muriel received the Person's Award at Government House, she invited Olive to come to Ottawa as her special guest.

From 1948 to 1962 Muriel worked part-time as parent education adviser for the Nova Scotia Department of Education. The staff of the Adult Education Division, besides Guy Henson, included Betty Murray, John Hugh McKenzie, Don Wetmore, Charlie Topshee, Tom Jones and Reverend W.P. Oliver, who was also part-time. In Muriel's opinion, these educators had an approach to education which could well have been adopted by the whole Department of Education. Guy Henson was a progressive and creative administrator.

The Adult Education Division attracted public attention in the fifties due to its folk schools, arts festivals and the Nova Scotia School of the Arts. The Adult Education Division set about encouraging young artists and musicians and providing a showcase for their talent. As early as 1947 they set up a series of travelling exhibits. In the early sixties they held an art exhibit in the lobby of Province House. Muriel bought her first original painting at one of these exhibits, a lively picture by Robert Annand, a young artist then living in Truro. She bought this picture for $60.00 out of her first pay cheque as a full time worker and she felt it was quite a bold decision, first to choose a painting and then to pay so much money for it. She still prizes it.

Muriel's functions as a volunteer and as paid staff often overlapped, and a good deal of her volunteer work was done from the office of the Adult Education Division. Muriel encouraged parents to see themselves through the Home and School as partners with teachers, administrators and the Department of Education. She felt that the Home and School Association gave parents some influence, but at times she felt frustrated that they did not have enough power or demand more. What she most enjoyed was gathering people into small groups and getting them to talk about what they thought needed to be done, to decide on their own group process and to make their own decisions. She found that few parents had any previous experience in making decisions about their children outside of their own homes.

As part of her job she travelled throughout the province organizing mental health discussion groups with parents about their children's behaviour. Either Dr. Frances Marshall, Dr. Robert Weil or Dr. Frank Dunsworth accompanied Muriel to these meetings as resource persons. After she got the discussion rolling, the psychiatrist or psychologist would respond in a low-key way to the typical childhood problems the parents raised.

Muriel also met with a group of ten Halifax women every second week in the Adult Education Division office to discuss parent education. For these sessions she prepared cases for discussion. In the intervening week each woman met with parents in her own school. Muriel recognized that this was parent education from the perspective of mothers only.

> We called it "parent education" but it was always exclusively mothers who got involved. The men had nothing to do with it. We became a support group for each other. We laughed a lot.

As a staff member, Muriel participated in province-wide programs designed to teach people how to run meetings according to Roberts' Rules of Order. But Muriel was always sceptical about the appropriateness of formal procedures in small groups. She found them artificial and preferred dealing with questions informally and trying to reach common views. Muriel thought that women in particular had other ways of reaching decisions than through passing motions. She always favoured going around the group in a circle to have each person say how they felt about an issue. Muriel liked techniques that made it easier for people to express themselves and found that often simply asking the person one was sitting near, "what do you think about that?" was all it took to get people started.

The Adult Education Division staff also organized ten-day long folk schools for adults, including folk schools for native people in Nova Scotia.[1] The goal of the folk schools was to give adults confidence in themselves to undertake whatever they thought needed to be done in their own communities and to work together. Muriel thought these events were an ideal form of education as people came together in an informal manner, and were not a captive audience but were there because they wanted to learn. She had great faith in the techniques the division developed for adult learning. It was clear they increased people's self-confidence.

As Muriel met with parents around the province she frequently travelled with the famed Nova Scotia educator Dr. L.A. DeWolfe. She strongly supported his philosophy of education. He believed that a teacher's job was to develop a love of knowledge in their pupils; it was not so much to inform as to create a desire for information. When he wanted to change the way teachers taught, he managed to overcome their resistance by using the Home and School forum to disseminate sound ideas about education. Every issue of the Home and School magazine contained a page of his writing.[2] Muriel felt he was the leader who should have been the principal of the Teachers College. But he was ahead of his time and his ideas were "too far out" for the establishment.

Muriel thought that the philosophy of adult education should apply to the education of youth. She would insist, "it isn't a question of pouring ideas into kids but of getting things out of kids' heads." And she was fond of quoting John Holt, author of *How Children Fail:* "The only answer that really sticks in a child's mind is the answer to a question that he asked or might ask of himself."[3] She would often remind parents that "play is a child's work and it has got to be taken seriously."

In 1962, at the age of fifty-three, she accepted an appointment to her first full-time job, secretary to the Adult Education Division. From 1962 to 1967 she also continued doing parent education and researched and helped set up literacy programs.

At times Muriel did a delicate balancing act between her volunteer and paid work roles. Once she publicly questioned the statistics in a Department of Education report after Gordon Cowan, a member of the Halifax school board, phoned to tell her he thought the report was inaccurate. He then gave the report to the press who checked it with Muriel. Newspaper headlines the next day ran "Duckworth says . . . ." The deputy minister of education came to Muriel's office to ask her whose side she was on, but she pointed out that apart from being a part-time employee (at that time) she was also the president of the Nova Scotia Education Association and as such she felt she had the right to comment publicly.

Combatting Racism in Nova Scotia

Although Muriel credited her colleagues with creating a very stimulating work environment, she thought that she gained the most valuable experience from her exposure to Black communities in Nova Scotia. During her travels she was invited to speak in several Black communities. There she saw the poverty, the poor roads and lack of public services. She visited some of the schools for Black children on the edge of Dartmouth and in East Preston. In New Roads, the children were going to school three shifts a day. In another Black community in Halifax County, a white woman was teaching Black children in her own kitchen. Nobody had questioned why there was no school for these children. Instead, the press made a hero of the woman who taught them. Muriel tried to alert influential people to these appalling conditions only to find that often they knew what was going on but chose to remain silent. Once when Muriel raised the subject, the hostess who was entertaining her cut the discussion short, remarking curtly, "it doesn't do any good to talk about it."

Racism was pervasive throughout Nova Scotia even where one would not expect to find it. Jack once suggested to his YMCA board that they invite the well-known leader of the US human rights movement, Martin Luther King, to speak in Halifax. But his board members would not have King because some of them thought that he was probably a communist. Attitudes like that shocked and angered Muriel.

Muriel was always inspired by the story of Juanita (de Shields) Chambers, a brilliant Black student who had graduated from McGill in 1934. She was the first woman member of the McGill intercollegiate debating team. When she took teacher training she was told by the dean of education that she was wasting her time studying education since she would never be hired. He was right. Selling Christmas cards from door to door was one of the ways she earned money during the depression. In the 1940s the Nursery School Committee of the Notre Dame de Grace YMCA invited Juanita to take charge of this part-time program. At the time she was supporting her two young children and her nearly-blind husband. Jack encouraged her to continue graduate work so that she would have the status to match her ability. Juanita did obtain a Ph.D., studying psychology in French, at the University of Montreal. In the 1960s, Muriel caught up with her again when she was at the University of Alberta. By then Juanita was chairperson of the department of educational psychology. Muriel was certain that if employment, housing and educational opportunities for Blacks were improved in Nova Scotia there would be many more success stories such as Juanita's.

To help combat social injustice towards Blacks Muriel joined the Nova Scotia Association for the Advancement of Coloured People (NSAACP), an organization formed after the war and open to both Blacks and whites, although few whites joined. Reverend W.P. Oliver helped to found it and was the first president. Blacks who had been in the Canadian Services came home thinking that they had fought for equality and now they would have it. They found instead that the war had made no difference, so they formed the NSAACP to help themselves. Muriel remembered that their meetings were exciting and well-attended.

In the mid-sixties Muriel joined another group, composed largely of Quakers, in support of the Students Union for Peace Action (SUPA). This was a combined peace and civil rights organization which came out of the Combined Universities Against Nuclear Disarmament. SUPA organized a number of projects across Canada where young people would engage in community development. One such project brought a young activist, Rocky Jones, to Halifax in the summer of 1965. He wanted to work in the inner city but the organization had only raised a small sum which did not allow them to pay him enough to support his young family. The Quakers, hearing of this, initiated a group called The Friends of the Nova Scotia Project. Among them were Muriel and Jack Duckworth, Doug and Sidney Shadbolt, Gus Wedderburn, Dorothy and Steve Norvell, Don Trivett, Anne and Ian Maxwell and David and Peggy Hope-Simpson, all of whom had a background in the peace movement and the civil rights movement. This support group took on the responsibility of raising funds to pay for the project, including Rocky's salary.

What Rocky found astounding was that he was given the mandate to organize youth in the inner city with no strings attached, no political or moral direction, and no attempt to control him. The support group gave him no specific directions. They believed in what he was doing and gave him the freedom to do it. Rocky remembered that on many occasions he would go to them to talk about problems in the community, or about dealing with certain officials or even about personal problems. He felt free to take anything to these meetings. In turn he received support and complete open and unqualified acceptance. For Rocky this support group provided an incredible experience.

The project continued for nearly three years and formed Kwacha House (from the Zambian word for freedom), a centre for Black and white kids from the inner city. Kwacha House attracted many young people although it had to move on several occasions. Up to 150 kids would attend meetings. They held dances, sewing classes, kayaking and all kinds of activities. Through Kwacha House, the political momentum of the Black community in the Halifax area began to build.

As the community drew together they moved towards the concept of Black power and began to call community meetings where only Black people could attend. At a public meeting a speaker from Montreal talked about the need for Blacks to make themselves strong. Soon afterwards, in 1969, the Black United Front was formed. Muriel was elated. As she anticipated, much of the Black strength from the NSAACP went into the newly formed Black organization. She watched with interest and some cynicism as the Nova Scotia government immediately gave the Black United Front generous sums of money because they were fearful of what was going to happen with all the Black people getting a sense of their own power.

For Rocky, Muriel represented a woman who was able to move from the upper class environment of the south end of Halifax through the whole community and not be out of place, not be pretentious and not be opinionated. Black people who had no jobs or even access to places of entertainment in the south end generally resented the "Blue Bloods" from that part of town that came to hand out whatever it was they were handing out—a little scholarship or the Gideon bible. Rocky never found Muriel to be patronizing. He recalled:

> I don't remember ever a situation when I couldn't phone Muriel Duckworth and feel free to call upon her and, secondly, having the feeling that she would give me wise counsel, not necessarily what I wanted but very wise and fruitful counsel. She was and is a hell of a woman!

Notes

1. Public Archives of Nova Scotia (PANS) MG 1 Vol. 2917, No. 35.
2. PANS MG 1 Vol. 2914.
3. John Holt, *How Children Fail*. New York: Pittman, 1964.

Chapter 6

An Expanding Horizon: The Maturation of a Pacifist

Two trips which Muriel took in her forties and fifties opened up the world outside Canada to her. During the rest of her life she would retain a vivid sense of the world as her backyard. She had an ability to grasp how international events affected people and readily identified with their struggles and their pain. In later years she would use every chance she got to urge young people to travel.

An Unexpected Trip to Paris

Muriel took an unexpected trip to Paris in 1955. Jack's board of directors raised money to send him to the celebration of the one hundredth anniversary of the World YMCA. However, there was no money for Muriel to go. Jack was not happy about it because he wanted to take Muriel with him, but he knew they could not afford it. Then a couple of weeks before Christmas, Muriel was bringing in the mail from the letterbox when she saw a large brown envelope with her name printed on it. She opened it and found a sheet of red tissue paper with bills laid out spelling the word "Paris" and a tiny note, typewritten on foolscap paper saying, "we think that you should go too. A Happy Christmas to you both!" The money totalled $600.00 which would cover the boat trip to Europe. Try as she would to find out who had played Santa Claus, she never did discover her benefactors.

For Muriel, at forty-six, this was the trip of a lifetime—six weeks abroad and her first trip to Europe. They sailed from Montreal to Liverpool in July on a luxury Cunard liner. Jack, always an early riser, would go up on deck to enjoy the fresh air and eventually Muriel would join him for his second breakfast. She revelled in the chance to sleep in, eat delicious meals with no end of selection from the menus and no dishes to wash—every homemaker's dream! She and Jack felt expansive towards everybody on board ship and not just towards the forty fellow delegates who were part of the Canadian delegation to the Centennial Conference.

Soon after their arrival, they took a train to Manchester and flew from there to the Netherlands to visit Muriel's brother's grave in the Allied cemetery on the outskirts of the little town of Bergen. There they were hosted by a couple, the Sluyters, who had undertaken the care of Norman's grave. Muriel and Jack had written beforehand and asked them what they might bring them. The Sluyters had replied "nothing" for themselves, but

Ms. Sluyter, who had been a refugee in the Netherlands from the First World
War, replied that her relatives in Hungary could use anything they might
care to bring. Mr. Sluyter told them what it had been like under the German
occupation. Like many other Dutch people, they had provided sanctuary for
Jews. He talked about the resistance of the Dutch people and their acts of
civil disobedience during the Nazi occupation. He himself used to climb
telephone poles, on the pretence that he was a telephone repair person, and
send messages over the wire to the underground. His main underground job
had been to prepare false identification papers. Towards the end of the war,
Mr. Sluyter was arrested for sheltering a young Jewish girl in their home.
He was incarcerated in a concentration camp in Germany. In his library,
behind other books, he had hidden a large volume in fine print that recorded
the resistance movement in the Netherlands during the war. He was still so
uneasy that even ten years later he kept this book hidden and only brought
it out to show persons like the Duckworths whom he trusted.

After a while Ms. Sluyter, who could not speak English, indicated that
they had had enough war talk and kept saying "Kinder? Kinder?" Muriel,
realizing that Ms. Sluyter was asking whether they had children, brought out
pictures of Martin, Eleanor and John. It was probably the first time Muriel
discovered that she could communicate with women from other countries
without even speaking the same language. In years to follow she would
become very good at this.

The Duckworths were introduced to other villagers as the relatives of
one of the Canadian pilots shot down over the Netherlands and buried in
their local beautifully kept cemetery. They were invariably greeted with
such warmth that it was almost as if they themselves had fought by the Dutch
people's side. After two days of hospitality, Muriel and Jack took the train
to Amsterdam, and from there to Cologne.

Muriel was startled to find that on crossing the border into Germany she
still harboured feelings of fear and anger towards Germans. This was
precipitated by the sight of the customs officers who came on board to
conduct their inspection. The officials' uniforms and caps reminded Muriel
of Nazi officers. She had to pull herself together and remind herself:

> These pleasant, friendly young men are not much older than your
> own sons. They had nothing to do with shooting down your brother
> nor anybody else, nor with putting people in concentration camps.

But the unpleasant feelings persisted. Once more she was shaken when
she and Jack arrived in the Cologne railway station late at night and heard
over the loud speakers what sounded like harsh commands that they could
not understand. Her emotional reaction took her by surprise. But the next
day her feelings for Germans began to soften when she and Jack went to visit

Muriel and Jack on way to Liverpool, en route to Paris World YMCA Centennial, 1955.

the bombed-out cathedral near the railway station. They watched how workers carefully marked every stone to indicate where each would fit in rebuilding the cathedral, and Muriel realized that it would take years to accomplish the task. The following day, they saw further bomb damage when they took a steamer on a romantic trip up the Rhine river to Mainz. All the bridges had been destroyed and not one had yet been rebuilt ten years after the end of the war. Arriving at Mainz, they took a taxi whose driver miraculously found them a room and who told Muriel and Jack that 85 percent of the city had been destroyed by bombs.

From Germany they went on to spend ten happier days in Switzerland, visiting Lucerne and Geneva, staying with friends at Lake Thun and walking with them in the majestic Swiss Alps. From there they visited Rome, then on to Paris for the two-week YMCA conference where over eight thousand delegates from seventy-nine countries gathered. Here too there were constant reminders of the war. The conference itself was held in an arena, a large gymnasium into which Jews had been herded together at the time of the Nazi occupation. From this site the Nazis decided to which camp the Jews were to be dispersed. And just across the street from Jack and Muriel's hotel near the Sorbonne was a little commemorative plaque on the wall of a lycée, honouring the memory of a boy of nineteen who was killed on that spot on the day of the liberation of Paris in August 1944. In the midst of having a wonderful time sight-seeing Muriel would come upon similar plaques outside the entrance to the subway at the Place de la Concorde or beside the fountain at the foot of Boulevard St. Michel.

Muriel and Jack were delighted to meet an old friend who had studied medicine at McGill, Dr. John Karefa Smart of Sierra Leone, then with the World Health Organization and one of the conference speakers. One night they sat with him at an outdoor cafe discussing how the youth of the world could best serve the cause of peace.

While Jack was at the conference, Muriel enjoyed exploring Paris on her own. One day she realized she was spending half of her time underground getting from one place to the next by subway and decided henceforth to use the buses so that she would see more of Paris. Together they celebrated Jack's birthday, August fifteenth, by going up the Eiffel Tower only to find it was jammed with great lineups of people who were celebrating Napoleon's birthday that same day.

Muriel's enthusiasm for travel did not include interest in other tourists who boasted of the hard bargains they drove with merchants, or in those who expressed annoyance because every attendant in the Paris subways could not speak English. She noted that North Americans could afford to swarm all over Europe while scarcely any of the people they met in Europe could think of being able to pay them a return visit. But at the conference itself, Muriel and Jack were impressed with the attitude of the United States delegation. They found the Americans had a conciliatory approach to divisive issues. The Americans' desire to carry their share of responsibility was apparent, without in any way dominating the proceedings. Muriel felt the conference itself was a healing event. Later, writing about the very moving closing ceremony, she commented:

Experiences such as this, based on common aspirations and values really do help to displace the bitterness of the past. At this closing assembly, I stood beside a German youth, talked with him, and laughed with him, and really felt comfortable about it.[1]

A First International Conference

Muriel was a delegate to her first international conference when she attended a World Mental Health conference in 1955 in Toronto. She was sent by the Nova Scotia Federation of Home and School and the Adult Education Division. The conference was to have been held in the United States but because communists from the Soviet Union and East European countries were barred from entering the US during the Cold War, the event was moved to Toronto.

Muriel was quite thrilled to hear Eleanor Roosevelt speak to a packed Convocation Hall. It was the first time she saw a speaker receive a standing ovation. Ms. Roosevelt spoke about shell shocked soldiers from the war. She told a story about her shyness when first going to visit a hospital for the mentally ill. She asked her husband what she should do and President Roosevelt told her to ask to see the kitchen and to go and lift up the lids to see what the patients were being fed!

A memorable session, and one which was not on the original program, was a brilliant addition giving witch doctors a chance to speak and answer questions from a huge meeting of fascinated people who overflowed a large room.

A Cruise to the Black Sea

In 1962, when Jack retired, he and Muriel decided to take a holiday. Their family persuaded them that they could afford a cruise to the Black Sea on an old luxury liner, Cunard's *The Caronia* (known as the "Green Goddess"), especially when they were offered marvellous accommodation for the lowest price following another passenger cancellation. They left in early October and returned just before Christmas.

Many of the people on board were seasoned travellers and complained about this old-fashioned ship designed before the Second World War, but Jack and Muriel thought the "Green Goddess" was the height of luxury. Initially they had supposed that all the passengers were wealthy people who went on yearly cruises, but gradually they made friends with others like themselves: retired school teachers, a young couple from New York, an artist and a teacher who had worked for a long time to afford such a trip. They went ashore several times with these new friends. It was understood that picnic lunches were available so Muriel and Jack always had the steward provide them with a delicious box lunch from the dining room to take ashore, even though they sensed he looked down his nose at them for ordering one. Most of the passengers headed for the nearest modern hotel. They were not about to take box lunches, but Muriel and Jack were only too glad of this service. It gave them a chance to sit on benches and to talk with the people they met.

When they reached the beautiful city of Odessa on the Black Sea, their young artist friend, who was of Russian Jewish background, went along the backstreets to find a certain address of relatives he had never met. When he came back he told them about some of the poverty tourists normally did not see.

The Cuban crisis occurred while they were sailing in the Black Sea. While the US seemed willing to risk a nuclear war, Kruschev was not and backed off. He called off his ships and they went home thus averting a nuclear attack by the US. Because of the tension between the Americans and the Soviets, the cruise ship was not allowed to go very close to shore so passengers had to go ashore in life boats. They saw a big friendship banner overhanging the docks in Odessa with a picture of Kruschev and of Castro. Loudspeakers were blaring news of the Cuban crisis. A second big banner welcomed the mariners as belonging to the worldwide alliance of workers, but the tourists were ignored, as if to imply the mariners were their kin and tourists did not matter. Muriel and Jack themselves felt that they did not wish to be identified with the rich American passengers either, but they had no way to communicate this to the people they saw. They were disturbed by the hysterical tone of the American news about the Cuban crisis on the ship's radio. They preferred reading the news from England in the ship's daily paper that contained a more reasonable presentation of the crisis. It was only after they got home that they learned that the USSR had threatened to close off the Black Sea because the United States was refusing to allow the Soviets to go to Cuba. Relations between the United States and the Soviet Union were to occupy much of Muriel's attention for many years to come.

Full-time Employment

Jack's retirement was a turning point for Muriel. Just before he retired from the YMCA in 1962 she began to work full-time for the Department of Education as secretary to the Adult Education Division. Their roles began to change. As Jack had more free time he spent many hours helping Muriel with her volunteer work, although he did continue to work half-time, fundraising for the Heart Foundation and later for the Canadian National Institute for the Blind. Eleanor recalled the enthusiasm with which her mother always spoke about her job. Like many postmenopausal women Muriel had a lot of wind in her sails and her vista on the world was ever expanding. She even moved about with a new independence as she learned to drive a car at fifty-two. Eleanor said that Muriel drove with great flair and confidence once she got the knack of it, but at the start she was nervous and had to take her driver's test three times in her much prized Mini Minor.

Interweaving Adult Education and Peace Education

More and more of Muriel's spare time went to a newly formed national women's peace organization, the Voice of Women (VOW). Muriel was a founding member in 1960 and was active both at the local and national levels. She integrated peace issues into community and adult education. She saw education partly as a process of preparing children for world citizenship. The education of women and the role of women in the community also increasingly occupied her attention.

Representing VOW, Muriel and Ghislaine Laurendeau from Montreal, attended the Canadian Conference on Education, held in March 1962, at the Queen Elizabeth Hotel in Montreal. It was a mammoth event involving two thousand delegates touching on all aspects of education. Muriel sat on one of the committees preparing for the conference. She had also been sent by the Adult Education Division and the Home and School. Delegates representing organizations as varied as the Canadian Labour Congress, the Bar Association and the Imperial Order of the Daughters of the Empire, met for four days. Muriel attended a forum on New Developments in Society that dealt with such questions as how to educate for changes in value systems, communications, transportation and industry.

Later she reported back to the organizations that had sent her that of the seven discussion groups she attended at the forum, only two emerged with resolutions containing any reference whatever to the international scene or to "education for change." Muriel observed in her report that perhaps the greatest influence on the atmosphere of the conference was the presence of large numbers of enthusiastic and dedicated French-speaking Canadians who made it clear from the first evening that they saw Canada as a bicultural country and that there must be recognition and understanding of this fact.

Originally the conference was to have been held in Toronto but a hotel employees strike made for a change in location. As no translation equipment was available many English people who were not bilingual were quite startled to hear French being spoken all around them. Standing beside Muriel at the back of a large hall Roby Kidd commented to her on the Anglophones' attitude: "They will just have to get used to it."

It was as a result of this conference that Muriel proposed a National Education Committee within the Voice of Women to make the peace movement more active in the education world and to encourage study groups on education within the VOW. She suggested that they work cooperatively with the Adult Education Association and the Canadian Teachers' Federation. She was rewarded for her enthusiastic ideas by being elected national chairperson of the VOW Education Committee.

In the autumn of 1962 Muriel attended a conference in Toronto entitled "The Real World of Women" organized by the CBC.[2] After it she began to speak about the need for women to do career planning and to advocate changes to make it possible for women with children to work outside the home. In a speech given to the Nova Scotia Nursing Association, Muriel pointed out that the life expectancy of women currently was almost double that of their grandmothers.[3] In 1964 women constituted 28.8 percent of all those employed, and married women made up 51.2 percent of all women in the labour force in Canada. Muriel insisted that because rapid social change was affecting women, society needed to reorganize to cope with this change. She wanted to encourage married nurses to stay with their jobs.

Educators whose ideas Muriel incorporated and advocated included the sociologist Elise Boulding from the University of Michigan and S.R. Laycock from the University of Saskatchewan. Laycock wanted educators to foster and develop creativity and critical thinking in children. Boulding thought that educators must help the next generation to grow up feeling that it is responsible for the world community. She advocated research for redesigning the entire school curriculum (particularly world history and geography to teach the known world as a global unit) to prepare young people for coping with tomorrow's world. Boulding insisted that new concepts of world citizenship meant that children would not love their own country any the less because they felt an additional loyalty to the planet as a whole.

Muriel took these ideas and tried to apply them. As the chairperson of the National Education Committee, she assisted local VOW groups throughout the country to set up projects and programs on education for living in a world community. This included researching what was being taught in Canadian schools in social studies, history, geography and the arts that was conducive to tolerance and based on the concept of the world community. She encouraged VOW study groups to emphasize projects which would contribute to Canadian unity, such as bilingualism and interprovincial student exchanges. She suggested they encourage schools to "adopt" schools in other countries and to initiate correspondence between Canadian children and those of other lands.

In the spring of 1965, through the Nova Scotia Voice of Women, Muriel organized the Halifax Committee for the United Nations International Cooperation Year. This committee, comprised of a variety of community organizations, brought to Halifax a remarkable exhibit of one hundred children's paintings from thirty-five countries. The art collection was compiled by a Voice of Women member, Betty Nickerson of Winnipeg, who was invited to open the exhibit at the Nova Scotia School of Architecture.

In her report, as vice-president for the Atlantic Region of the Voice of Women, at the annual general meeting in 1965, Muriel talked of the excellent response to a public meeting they organized in Halifax on Military Toys and Television Violence. Speakers included a child psychiatrist and CBC's regional director of school broadcasts and youth programs. For many years Muriel also supported the anti-war-toy campaigns that Voice of Women sponsored.[4]

Opposing Nuclear Testing

Muriel met many people from other countries through Jack's long-term work with the YMCA's International Affairs Committee. She came to understand in very concrete ways Canada's connection with world problems and took to heart her own individual responsibility as a citizen. In 1954, when Muriel heard the story about the Japanese fishers who were contaminated aboard their boat, "Lucky Dragon," by radioactive fallout from the US hydrogen bomb test at Bikini, she immediately grasped the monumental danger of nuclear testing. Muriel believed the warnings of Linus Pauling and Albert Schweitzer; these two who were among the very few scientists at the time who stated that testing nuclear weapons posed a danger to the very survival of everyone on the planet.

Muriel insisted that an international treaty to prevent nuclear testing was the overriding issue of the era. Over and over again she brought her concern before every group to which she belonged. Muriel would raise the subject with the staff of the Adult Education Division as an issue they should be publicizing. And she brought it before the Home and School Association in her parent education activities. In later years educational authorities came to see it differently, but at the time they did not particularly appreciate her views that the survival of everybody's children was threatened by atmospheric testing of nuclear weapons. They would imply that nuclear testing was neither a relevant nor an appropriate issue for education. Undaunted, Muriel continued to pursue the subject. She sometimes felt that people were fed up with her. At a National Home and School convention held in Halifax in the early sixties, she even tried single handedly to get a resolution through the meeting condemning nuclear testing in the atmosphere. She got absolutely no support from the committee formulating the resolutions, and her concerns never even came to the floor of the convention.

In November 1960, Muriel was the only woman on a panel of nine who appeared on the first national CBC telecast out of Halifax. The topic was, "should Canada stop trying to be a world power?" Muriel felt she would never get a word in, and the half-hour show was nearly over when she burst out, "you've got to get away from war as the solution to the world's problems!" Afterwards she received several letters congratulating her for taking a peace position. As one woman wrote, "that's one reason I want to tell you how sure I am that your sharp protest struck them—how they all fell to gabbling to cover up their discomfiture."[5]

In the late fifties, when the Committee for Nuclear Disarmament was founded in Canada, Muriel and Jack became members, and Jack was the co-chair of the Halifax group. They looked in vain to their United Church congregation for support for their activities. Instead, they found kindred spirits among a small emerging group of Halifax Quakers.

A Peace Witness

While speaking at the 1986 Canadian Yearly Meeting of the Society of
Friends, Muriel traced a series of small events in her life that acquainted her
with the Quaker tradition and that eventually led to her "becoming a Friend."
As a Christmas gift in 1939, her sister Mildred had given her a book entitled
We Didn't Ask Utopia—A Quaker Family in Soviet Russia. It was the story
of a couple who lived for ten months in a new town on the Volga six hundred
miles from Moscow. They worked as a team, a doctor and a nurse, on
research and treatment of malaria and the husband died of typhus before the
year was out. Muriel recalled the emotional impact of that story and how
impressed she was with the couple's devotion to the people they served,
although neither tried to proselytize the other people.

Another time, while reviewing educational materials that she had
ordered for the Adult Education Division, Muriel came upon a pamphlet put
out by Quakers about working in groups. It emphasized the need to respect
each individual in the group and to avoid making any attempt at manipulation. The methods for searching out and achieving consensus that were
described in this pamphlet were consistent with Muriel's own experiences
of working with people in groups. They rang true to her.

In 1962 Helen and Murray Cunningham moved to Halifax and started
a Quaker group. Helen knew Muriel through the national Voice of Women
and she invited Muriel and Jack to attend a Friends' Meeting for Worship,
as the Quaker service is called. This invitation came at a point in the
Duckworths' lives when they were having serious difficulties with their own
church.

When they first came to Halifax, Muriel and Jack chose St. Matthew's
United Church because of its historic connections. The first nonconformist
United Church in Halifax was originally built in 1749 down near the
harbour. The present St. Matthew's was also very old. It was a charming
church with little gates to the pews, a very high Presbyterian pulpit, a good
organ and a choir with four paid soloists. While Muriel and Jack found the
music and the church building very pleasing they did not feel at home in the
congregation. The minister visited Muriel just after they had joined. On
hearing that she had worked with teenagers he asked if she would be a
Sunday School teacher. Muriel replied that she would be delighted and
would use his weekly sermon as the basis for discussion with the teenagers.
This was too much for him. He dropped the subject and never asked her
again! It did not take long before Muriel and Jack realized that it was of more
benefit to meditate during his sermons than to listen to them.

Their discomfort with the church came to a head over the church's lack
of involvement in the movement for nuclear disarmament. Jack and Muriel
were working hard to gain public support to stop nuclear bomb testing in the
atmosphere and they got no help from within their own congregation. They

felt it was "the last straw" when the moderator of the United Church, the Reverend James Mutchmore, personally made a point of denying support to the anti-nuclear movement.

Mutchmore had been invited to briefings by the Department of National Defence which was engaged in taking opinion makers to see the NORAD establishment in Colorado. The moderator had come home from one of these trips making speeches about what great bargaining power Canada had with the United States because they needed Canada's North to build up their defences against the USSR. Muriel happened to go on a tour of Newfoundland for the Home and School Federation just after Mutchmore's speaking tour in that province. It was as though she were following his footsteps. She came home incensed at Mutchmore's political message. Jack wrote to Reverend Mutchmore recalling the pacifist position of Richard Roberts, a former United Church moderator. Mutchmore wrote back very sharply defending his own position. Muriel and Jack concluded that the moderator's stand meant that the United Church could not take any effective position with regard to nuclear disarmament or atmospheric testing. Recalling the peace positions of so many other United Church ministers in the past, Muriel and Jack felt this was a denial of their heritage.

They felt so alienated that when the Cunninghams invited them to the Quaker meetings which they were holding in their home, they gladly accepted. They did not drop their membership in the United Church immediately, and for a short time they went sometimes to their old church and sometimes to the Quaker meeting. Gradually the Quaker group became their community and they wrote a letter of resignation to their former church. No one replied and only one couple ever mentioned their absence.

At first, Muriel and Jack were really quite baffled at the experience of a Quaker meeting. They were aware that Quakers were known for their peace witness but otherwise were unfamiliar with Quaker practice. The Meeting for Worship was enveloped in silence, and this made Muriel feel uncomfortable just as periods of silence had back in her early SCM days. However, Muriel and Jack did feel at home with the Friends' community. They started reading Quaker literature and learned about the history of the Quaker pacifist position and about Quaker practice and discipline. Gradually they began going also to the Quaker business meeting, referred to as "the monthly Meeting for Worship for Business." They found the process of a Quaker business meeting to be quite different from any business meeting they had ever attended. Whenever a person spoke, their contribution was surrounded by silence, just as it was in the Meeting for Worship. The person who was speaking was never to be interrupted and was listened to closely. Respondents were to stay silent for a little while before they replied. Each person considered that they were there because this was a part of God's will for them and that they were seeking to conduct business under God. This was quite a change from the kind of meetings where people argued or expressed impatience and interrupted each other. As Muriel described it:

> You were supposed to be honest, to express your honest opinion, but when you are aware of doing that under God's guidance then you think a few times about whether it is your honest opinion— really are you seeking the truth? Or is it you trying to put yourself forward, trying to influence other people to your position, which might not really be justifiable in terms of what is the good for everybody in that meeting and for that meeting extending itself out into the community.

She agreed that it was a slow way to get business done, but it was the secret to "getting a sense of the meeting," the Quaker expression that the time has come to take action or record a decision in the name of the meeting. Quaker actions are only taken as a result of the meetings for business and are never made at the Meeting for Worship.

Although they attended the Quaker meetings regularly Jack never officially joined the Quakers. However, they both became actively involved: Jack was treasurer for more than ten years; Muriel worked on the committees for finance, ministry and counsel and served on the Canadian Yearly Meeting Representative Committee. Jack had no desire to formally join any organizations in his latter years and Muriel was reluctant to join without him. Referring to historic Quakers such as Stanley Jones, John Macmurray and Muriel Lester who wrote prayers and poetry, and to the martyrs in Massachusetts, Muriel was convinced that Quakers were "a company of saints" and that she was only in the process of "becoming a Friend." Eventually she accepted that she was in the company of seekers, not of saints, and she applied for membership in 1975, following Jack's death. Reflecting on the meaning of being a Quaker, she acknowledged:

> It has meant a lot to me in my life, that's only during the last twenty years of my life. It seemed to me to be a kind of simple, basic, direct approach to God and to the Word and to other people, which to me was fairly straightforward, comprehensible and meaningful. I have always found it very hard to define God. I've held onto God; I've given up God; I've tried to redefine God; I've found God undefinable and I know that I will never define God the way George Fox did.[6] I doubt whether many Quakers do feel about God the way George Fox felt, but I can relate to George Fox's feeling that there is "that of God in every person." And that, I think, has been a very important thing to me. I know that in me I am faulty enough, that I find it very hard to see "that of God in every person." There are people that I

give up on, that I set aside and don't really care to bother to take the time to find "that of God" in that person. This isn't admirable but that's how it is. "That of God in every person" is the inner light. If you believe that there is that inner light of God in you, then you must grant that there is that inner light in other people.

This "inner light" that guides a person and "that of God in every person" were tenets of Quaker belief that Muriel could accept. These came to underpin her belief in human rights and pacifism, to which she was already committed. She could not stand arrogant power that destroyed people nor violence in any form.

The simplicity of the Quaker approach, with their silent Meeting for Worship and their view of themselves as searching for the truth appealed to Muriel. She had always felt impatient with dogmatic people who insisted that they had the truth. She had never invested heavily in the Christian belief in supernatural doctrines. Rather, she believed that caring and loving relationships were the centre of spirituality.

For several years Muriel did not publicly identify herself as a Quaker in her work in the peace movement because she did not want people to think that only Quakers were "for peace" or that you had to be a Quaker to "be for peace." Yet the influence of "the Friends" was strong in the Voice of Women. Quakers who also belonged to VOW included Ursula Franklin and Nancy Pocock of Toronto, Helen Cunningham of Montreal, Muriel Bishop of Winnipeg, Mildred Osterhaut of Vancouver and Peggy Hope-Simpson and Dorothy Norvell of Halifax. These Quaker women acted as a powerful generative force to the Voice of Women. Muriel derived strength from each of them and in turn was often a source of inspiration for them.

Notes

1. M. Duckworth, "We Felt Our Way Through Europe" in *Food for Thought: Journal of the Canadian Association for Adult Education,* Winter 1956.
2. PANS MG 1 Vol. 2913, No. 52.
3. Banquet speech given by M. Duckworth to Registered Nurses Association of N.S., 19 May 1965. Women Today and Tomorrow. PANS MG 1 Vol. 2932, No. 4.
4. National Archives of Canada (NAC) MG 28 I 218 Vol. 21, File 8.
5. Letter to M. Duckworth (awaiting archival deposit).
6. George Fox (1624–91) founded the Society of Friends in 1652. He sought to find a new way in which people could gain direct access to God and developed the idea of the inner light within each person.

Muriel on a vow Peace Walk to a church service in Toronto, 1963.

vow in Halifax Natal Day Parade, 1977.

Betty Peterson

Anti-submarine demonstration, 1983.

Chapter 7

Finding Other Voices

A Women's Peace Movement

The Voice of Women, begun in 1960 during a time of international crisis, became an all-consuming interest in Muriel's life. During the six years from 1960 to 1967, when she was already working full-time for the Nova Scotia Department of Education, she managed to be actively involved as a volunteer in VOW both at the local and the national levels. Home responsibilities had lessened as her children were now adults living in other cities. Jack, having retired from the YMCA, was working half-time for the Heart Foundation and Muriel took advantage of his spare time and his typing skills to involve him in VOW secretarial tasks.

Finally, Muriel became so absorbed in the women's peace movement that she decided to resign from her paid employment to become the national president of VOW in 1967. The story of the Voice of Women during the four years of her presidency was also the story of Muriel's life. It was in VOW that Muriel's political education flourished and where she became a political activist. Years before, during the Duplessis regime in Quebec, she had engaged in some politically contentious issues in her work in the Home and School Association where she had always been an advocate for children. She was also involved in anti-racist activity, both in the Voice of Women and

Betty Peterson

Muriel making a speech on Parliament Hill at the Peace Petition presentation, 1982.

87

in the Halifax community in general. Protesting nuclear arms and advocating disarmament revealed to her what women are up against when they try to influence politicians. Like many others who started out in the Voice of Women, she assumed that if the government was properly informed it would do the right thing. With her background in adult education, she felt that a citizen's job was to become knowledgeable about important issues and persuade the government, through well-researched briefs and letters, to act in the best interest of the country. While Muriel never abandoned these techniques, her political activism was to take on a passionately public form. Because she had spent so much of her life working as a volunteer with women, Muriel felt very much at home in a women's organization. But she was not at all used to criticizing government policy in public. In the Voice of Women Muriel met other women whose attitudes and experience led her to become increasingly radicalized.

The feminist movement spread throughout Canada within ten years of the founding of the Voice of Women, which did not initially think of itself as a feminist organization. However, a considerable number of its members came to understand how women are excluded from political decision-making while first dealing with disarmament issues. Muriel was one of several such women who went on to become feminist leaders in Canada, and she readily acknowledged that her springboard to feminism was through the women's peace movement.

The original declaration of VOW proposed "to make possible a women's movement, through which they can assert resistance to war and the threat of war, and in which they can engage in purposeful action towards the easing of world tensions and the turning of men's minds from war."[1]

The Voice of Women came into being in the spring of 1960, when an international crisis brought the world to the brink of nuclear war. Gary Powers, an American pilot of a high altitude U2 spy plane, was shot down over the Soviet Union. At that very moment Kruschev was in Paris, participating in the Summit Conference of the four big powers. In a fury, Kruschev immediately broke off negotiations, proclaiming publicly, "we won't stand for this!" Newspapers headlined the threat of war.

Lotta Dempsey, a columnist for *The Toronto Star*, wrote in her column on Saturday, May 21, 1960, that "humankind were closer than man has been since creation to writing the last postscript to the history of civilization." "Where are the women?" she pleaded, "The men aren't able to cope. Where are the women?" Women readers, many of whom had lost loved ones in the Second World War, responded by the thousands. A group in Toronto, led by Helen Tucker and Josephine Davis, began to organize a women's peace movement and to make contact with women across the country who felt the same sense of urgency. Their first public meeting was called on June 10 in Toronto's Massey Hall, with Britain's Nobel Peace Prize winner Philip

Noel-Baker as principal speaker. A month later an organization was born called the Voice of Women/la Voix des femmes. Members often refer to themselves as "the Voices." In less than a year, over three thousand women had joined VOW from across Canada. With registrations pouring in at the rate of a hundred a week, the membership climbed to six thousand. Later, when the international crisis had subsided, many women dropped out leaving a core membership of two to three thousand.

A national office opened in Toronto. Annual general meetings and meetings of the VOW council and executive were regularly conducted in various Canadian cities. Voices soon learned to issue press releases on their positions. And following annual general meetings, delegations often went to parliament to press for the implementation of their resolutions. At both the local and national levels active members went on radio and TV, and wrote news stories about VOW campaigns and their views on disarmament and international peace questions. Muriel had had a little radio experience as president of the Nova Scotia Home and School Association and of the Nova Scotia Education Association, but she found early interviews on behalf of VOW a much more threatening experience. Voices tried to cope with their nervousness by consulting among themselves and supporting one another. Muriel would always remember how Ann Gertler, an experienced member from Montreal, actually sat across from her and prompted her with written placards during an early radio interview.

During the sixties and early seventies, VOW made representations to government and issued briefs on the dangers of radioactive fallout, foreign aid, Canada's role in NATO and NORAD, the illegality of war, science policy in Canada, multinational corporations, Canada's participation in the Vietnam war through its Defence Production Sharing Agreement with the United States, Canada's activities in research on chemical and biological warfare, biculturalism and bilingualism in Canada, the status of women in Canada and the invocation of the War Measures Act. In their communications with prime ministers and ministers of external affairs, VOW addressed a host of issues concerning Canada's foreign policy and Canada's participation at the United Nations and at international disarmament meetings.

Various campaigns were initiated by the national council and by provincial and local branches. Hundreds of women across Canada participated in a University of Toronto Faculty of Dentistry research project monitoring nuclear fallout. They collected thousands of children's baby teeth for testing of the strontium 90 content. The children who contributed wore buttons saying "I gave my tooth to science" instead of getting 10 cents from the tooth fairy. VOW campaigned and raised funds for the Canadian Peace Research Institute. Its members gave leadership to the United Nations' International Cooperation Year (1965) programs across the country through sitting on local citizen committees. They set up information centres and essay and painting competitions, "twinned" cities and arranged exchange visits. Great numbers took part in annual anti-war-toy campaigns. During the Vietnam war, the Voice of Women involved hundreds and hundreds of women in knitting baby clothes for the children of Vietnam. Members boycotted products of firms which manufactured weapons parts for the United States, and staged regular public appeals to end the war in Vietnam. Special days such as Hiroshima Day, Mother's Day, Armistice Day, Human Rights' and United Nations' Day were marked by public meetings, vigils, services and film showings.

VOW put particular emphasis on having its member delegates meet with women around the world who were concerned about peace and disarmament, especially with women from those countries deemed by the government to be "the enemy." To this end, they sent representatives to European countries and to Moscow. In September 1962, they initiated an international women's conference, the first meeting in Canada which included women from the Soviet Union and other socialist countries. Muriel chaired the VOW annual general meeting following this conference. From it, VOW sent a delegation to the United Nations that met with Prime Minister Nehru, who led the India delegation, and proposed an international year of peace. Although the UN was not ready to declare an International Year of Peace, the negotiations did bear some fruit. Nehru proposed to the general assembly an International Cooperation Year (ICY). This was adopted and came about in 1965 and Muriel was on the Canadian ICY Committee.

Nova Scotia Voice Of Women

Muriel, like many other VOW members, first got involved at the local level. Muriel heard of the Voice of Women through Peggy Hope-Simpson. Peggy's husband, David, belonged to the Canadian Committee on Radiation Hazards. Jo Davis, a founding member of VOW, had written to David to ask him to publicize the new women's organization. David did not think Peggy could take it on. She had her hands full with four young children, including a new baby. He urged her to think of someone who could. As Peggy thought about who might be of help Muriel's name sprang to mind because she was well known. Although Peggy had never actually met Muriel, she decided to phone her. Muriel responded with enthusiasm and subsequently Peggy and Muriel invited others to a first meeting of the Voice of Women in Halifax.

It was November 23, 1960, when twenty-three women gathered in Muriel's living room on Cambridge Street. These women had wide community contacts whom they resolved to reach as they talked with growing apprehension about the prospect of war. Some were so alarmed that they were in tears. Joan Marshall, one of five women commentators on CBC, chaired the meeting. As the women thought about what they could do, Margaret Hathaway proposed a public protest against the dumping of

vow in Halifax Natal Day Parade, 1977.

nuclear wastes by an American company, 150 miles off the coast of Yarmouth. They all agreed with this suggestion and they decided to call a public meeting two weeks later to protest this dumping.

Excited preparations consumed the next few days as the new women's peace group prepared for their public meeting, the first protest of its kind in Canada. Harold Hathaway, director of public affairs CBC, Halifax, arranged for CBC television coverage and the women organized press interviews to follow the meeting, called for December 7 at Sir Charles Tupper school. They invited four prominent Halifax citizens to speak about the danger of long-term radiation hazards to the international fisheries. The organizers made arrangements to collect signatures to a petition drawn up by the Canadian Committee for the Control of Radiation Hazards to ban the dumping of nuclear waste products. The publicity generated by the meeting did contribute to the federal government putting an end to the dumping, even though Muriel initially felt the reporters treated the women with an air of scepticism. She felt the media's attitude was, "what did these women know anyway?" But they had carefully prepared themselves with plenty of facts and the public meeting gave credibility to their protest.

Afterwards, Muriel and Peggy continued to spend much time on the phone and at speaking engagements urging women to join VOW or to raise disarmament issues in any organization to which they belonged. Their enthusiasm was catching and within six months VOW had fifty Nova Scotia members.

Early in its history, the local Halifax group divided into two main working committees, a political study group and a committee on human rights. All VOW members then came together for regular general meetings. The first group educated itself on the risk of nuclear war and the effects of nuclear testing in the atmosphere, reading such books as *Speak Truth to Power*, by the American Friends Service Committee, and Robert Jungk's *Brighter than a Thousand Suns*.[2] Much of the writing about peace and disarmament at that time was done by men. In later years Muriel tended to look with a certain scepticism at writings about peace that did not include women's views.

The second committee examined race relations between the Black and white people of Nova Scotia. Muriel belonged to the political study committee but was also recruited by the human rights committee to help in a research project on the employment of Black people in the Halifax area, the first research of its kind in Nova Scotia. VOW members telephoned local employers to ask about their employment policy with respect to Blacks.

When Muriel called Simpson's personnel department she was told, "oh yes we employ Black people," to which she replied, "I'm glad to hear that, but it just happens that I have never seen a Black person on the floor selling anything." The woman taking her call replied, "oh well, of course you wouldn't want to buy a hat from a Black woman!" Other local firms such as Olands thought their token employment of Blacks covered the situation. Voice of Women then called public meetings to reveal their findings and issued press releases about them. Fran MacLean, chairing that committee, was interviewed on national CBC TV. Her report stated,

> Upon interviewing personnel managers in private industries, we found that of approximately 3,000 workers only nine were Negroes and everyone of these was engaged in maintenance work. Several employers told us candidly that out of deference to anticipated public reaction and employee opinion, they did not have Negroes.[3]

At first, Voices found it very tough dealing with the media. Muriel thought members were rather shocked that reporters did not feel obliged to interview them politely. After a while Voices came to expect that they would often be challenged by a less than friendly press for their views and for their peace activities. Muriel claimed that women and peace were never given "equal time" with men and war on the media. To gain confidence, the women would help each other prepare for interviews and generally had more than one spokesperson present. Gradually they became adept at communicating with the media.

The women found it even more difficult to undertake public demonstrations. As middle-class women, they were not used to staging public events on the streets to call attention to their political beliefs. Demonstrations and outdoor rallies were unheard of in Halifax at that time. Other than labour demonstrations, people gathered only for such affairs as the Natal Day parade, the veterans parade to the war memorial on Armistice Day and Labour Day parades. Muriel recalled how Nova Scotia's Voice of Women had scarcely been in existence a year when one of the members proposed that they observe Armistice Day by holding a silent public vigil for peace. This suggestion was first met with great reluctance but it generated heated discussion. Finally one member startled them all by saying that if they did not do it, she was going to resign, whereupon another woman threatened to leave if they did undertake a public demonstration. At length they agreed to hold a silent vigil.

On a cold and windy Sunday, November 12, 1961, they gathered at the Sailors' Memorial which, at that time, was located on Citadel Hill. Muriel remembered how, quaking in their boots, they timidly walked back and forth in front of the memorial during an hour of silent meditation, carrying a poster that said "Vigil for Peace." Several of the women's husbands had joined them and helped hold the poster. Quizzical onlookers and Mounties on motorcycles watched them. Eventually, on the strength of their poster, they were joined by a few persons returning from church. They wanted to focus attention on the urgent need for serious peace negotiations, but only later realized that because this was a silent vigil they should have had leaflets to hand out to passersby to explain what they were doing.

By Hiroshima Day the following August 6, Muriel, along with other Voices, had grown bolder and had decided to join in a public action that was highly controversial. Jack, who was the chair of the Halifax Committee on Nuclear Disarmament, had announced that its members intended to lay a wreath at the foot of the cenotaph to mark the seventeenth anniversary of the dropping of the A-bomb on Hiroshima and to commemorate those who died. Goaded by an editorial in the *Halifax Mail Star* asking Legion members if they were going to let this happen to them, members of the Royal Canadian Legion formed a party of twenty Legion members to "defend" the cenotaph. With quiet dignity, Jack carried the huge wreath of dahlias and carnations over to the president of the Legion branch, stopped and shook hands with him and asked politely where he should lay the flowers. The Legionnaire, completely disarmed, indicated that Jack should lay the wreath at the flag staff. The press snapped pictures and a reporter from the local newspaper, the *Chronicle-Herald,* interviewed Muriel. He wrote:

> She [Muriel Duckworth] thought the cenotaph was the right place to lay a wreath as it not only honoured men and women who died in battle but also all those who died as a result of war. "I had a brother killed in the Second World War. I don't think the placing of the wreath at the cenotaph would have dishonoured him. But it does not really matter where the wreath was laid, as long as it was

done and those who were killed by nuclear weapons are remembered."[4]

At a national meeting in 1969 the Voices decided to support American women who were protesting the development of anti-ballistic missiles (ABMs). They sent tiny paper umbrellas to members of parliament bearing the legend, "an umbrella to protect you from the bomb, cheaper and just as effective as an ABM." In order to reach the wider public, members distributed similar ABM paper parasols on the streets of Canadian cities. Muriel, as the national president of VOW, showed no reluctance about issuing a press release pointing out that there was already the equivalent of fifteen tons of TNT to blow up every man, woman and child on the face of the earth, and that the ABMs might be "a political or economic asset to military-minded governments but as protection for the people they are a farce."[5] However, she did not so easily overcome her shyness when it came to talking to people on the streets about the issue. The Halifax group passed out the tiny paper umbrellas and their messages to people along downtown streets. Muriel was assigned Spring Garden Road. As she distributed hers, she kept hoping she would not meet anyone she knew. But before long she recognized a woman and crossed the street rather than meet her face to face. In later years such encounters did not faze her.

The public may have viewed them as extremists, but the Voices strongly believed that they had to do something to make people pay attention to these issues even if it was uncomfortable to do so. Gradually, with the support of her group, Muriel, like others, found it easier take part in public demonstrations. Often the women would go back to some member's house afterwards and talk and laugh about their experiences. But it never became any easier for Muriel to address a demonstration. Once when she was handed a bullhorn to address an outdoor labour rally in downtown Halifax she felt she wanted to run away and hide. And she recalled what consternation she felt the time she addressed a large crowd in Winnipeg from the back of a truck. Yet each time people asked her to speak, she rose to the occasion.

In later years Muriel even began to enjoy being part of street action. Once, to help out Voices who were doing street theatre, she dressed up as an old derelict man to hand out leaflets to people coming off the Dartmouth ferry. Another time she supported a demonstration staged by "MUMS," a local organization of single parents. As an elder, Muriel became a well-known figure at such public protests.

> I got over feeling self-conscious doing it because I realized I was only one of many. It came to the stage that it meant something to the people who were doing a demonstration if I turned up. When something like that is going on in the interest of what I believe in,

that is where I want to be—not at a coffee party—but out there with those people because it does something for me. It keeps up my inner sense that these are the things I care about.

When she addressed a young Katimavik group Muriel explained herself by quoting Luther, "Here I stand. I can do no other."[6]

Even in the early years, protests in the name of peace caused painful political divisions among the Voices. The originators of VOW intended it to be an organization that would include women of differing beliefs and backgrounds who would work together for peace. They wanted to cut across the barriers of racial, political and religious prejudices that lead to war. According to its constitution, VOW was non-partisan. But, as soon as the organization moved beyond generalities to the specific problems of nuclear politics and the arms trade, some of the members confused "partisan" with "political" and became upset when the executive or council of VOW criticized government policy. Some insisted that political stands should be avoided because they would cause divisions in the membership. They thought that members ought to act as neutral peacemakers, otherwise the movement would be weakened. But more radical members insisted on the need to confront the government or its policies.

The first test came in 1963, within a year of the Cuban crisis, when Prime Minister Pearson reversed his anti-nuclear stance and allowed nuclear warheads into Canada. The Voice of Women executive rose up in public opposition and led demonstrations in several cities. But not all VOW members felt it was right to oppose the Liberal government. Feelings were bitter and a number of women resigned, including several women on the VOW human rights committee in Halifax. These women thought, "maybe Canada needs nuclear warheads, how are we to know?" Muriel argued that Canada could not oppose nuclear weapons for other countries if it did not have the same policy for itself. She was firm in expressing her conviction that women joined Voice of Women for the express purpose of eliminating nuclear war. She felt that coming face to face with the political realities could not be avoided. Nonetheless she found it hard to see women dropping out.

The National Voice Of Women

Muriel played an active part at the national level of the Voice of Women from the time of its first annual general meeting. She was vacationing with members of her family at her cottage in Quebec when she received a request from Sylvia Kaplan of the Nova Scotia VOW to represent them at the meeting in Toronto. Because she was looking after her grandchildren it was inconvenient for her to go; she agreed somewhat reluctantly. Afterwards she was glad that she had gone because she was so inspired by such strong women as Betty Mardiros of Edmonton and Hilary Brown of Hornby Island, BC, both of whom were deeply committed to preventing future wars. From then on she seldom missed a VOW annual general meeting and became well-known as an active representative from Nova Scotia.

Muriel was quickly drawn onto various national committees becoming the first chairperson of the Education Committee, formed in 1962, to compile and distribute information on international affairs. She also sat on the national committee to study the inclusion of China at the United Nations. Women who remember Muriel from meetings saw her as a real asset to the organization. She was a good listener and known for her careful attention to democratic process in meetings. Muriel was well informed and often had vital information readily at hand, having long developed the habit of noting things down that would be useful in discussing disarmament issues. She could always be counted on to keep impeccable minutes.

Dr. Helen Cunningham, recognizing Muriel's ability, suggested that she chair the annual general meeting which followed the first International Conference in Montreal in 1962. This meeting was attended by over two hundred women from many countries. Muriel agreed, feeling unequal to the job, but she knew that the other members of the planning committee had all been involved in the two-day conference prior to the annual general meeting and that they were exhausted. Despite feeling that she was pushed into it, Muriel did her best to conceal how nervous she felt.

Whenever she chaired meetings, Muriel combined those rare qualities of attention to detail, patience and good humour. She had a talent for building consensus which conveyed to people her genuine belief in their ability to reach a common understanding and to decide on the best course of action. Her natural, spontaneous manner put people at ease and she was immensely skilled at reducing personal tensions in discussions, all the while clarifying the issues under consideration. Ursula Franklin, recalling those early years of the VOW, said that Muriel's presence meant that standards were ensured. What amazed Ursula most of all was that Muriel never lost her temper no matter how contentious the meetings were. Muriel would talk to all parties of a dispute and attempt to come up with a proposal acceptable to all. Under extreme stress she was occasionally known to break into tears, which had an instant sobering effect on everyone around her.

Muriel was elected as regional vice-president for the period of 1963 to 1967, and became president in 1967. Helen Tucker, Thérèse Casgrain and Kay Macpherson preceded Muriel as presidents of VOW in the sixties. Near the conclusion of Kay Macpherson's term, the question of who was ready, willing and able to become the next president loomed large. Many competent women had returned to the work force or were actively involved in emerging organizations in the women's movement. During a council meeting one winter afternoon in December 1966, at Ann Gertler's home in Montreal, Ann pointed to Muriel and said, "you should be the next president!

Betty Peterson

Muriel at anti-submarine demonstration, 1983.

You are the obvious choice."

At first Muriel objected. She could not see herself as national president. In addition to her own full-time job, she could not envisage how a national organization with its office in Toronto could have a president living in Halifax. The executive and council and the women who ran the national office persuaded her of their support. Because this organization was so important to her, she decided that she would quit her job with the Department of Education and give her full attention to the women's peace movement. Referring to her presidency from 1967 to 1971 Muriel said,

> It was probably the hardest thing I've ever done and the one from which I learned the most—from just having to do it and feeling overwhelmed by it from the beginning.

She always gave credit to Kay Macpherson for her tremendous help during Muriel's term in office.

Muriel felt that she was frequently pushed into accepting leadership, not because she was ready nor because she was the most suitable person, but because she was available. Such modesty does not take into account the experience she had gained while working in the field of adult education and as a member of the Home and School. At fifty-eight she was well up to the challenge. In turn, VOW inspired and motivated her because it addressed the most meaningful goal of her life—that women working together in groups take responsibility for bringing about peace and non-violence in the world.

A Visit To Moscow

With Muriel's presidency in the offing, Kay Macpherson phoned her one day early in January 1967, to say that the executive thought that as the president-elect, she should be their representative at the celebration of International Women's Day, March 8, in Moscow. An invitation had come from the Soviet Women's Committee, in honour of the fiftieth anniversary of the Revolution in 1917, to send a VOW representative to an International Conference of Women for Peace. VOW had encouraged exchange visits with Soviet women on three former occasions because VOW advocated face-to-face contact between the women of countries deemed to be enemies. They also invited Soviet women to come to the international conference they were planning for their centennial project in June 1967 in Montreal. The Voices firmly believed that the women of the world were not enemies.

There was much discussion over the wisdom of accepting this invitation to Moscow because all expenses were covered by the Soviet Women's Committee, and VOW was all too conscious of frequently being accused of being communists. They did not want to put themselves into a compromising position, and yet they felt it was important to meet with women from communist countries. Because they never received government grants, they were dependent on their modest membership fees and any money they could raise to run the organization. They decided that it was worth the risk, and afterwards they would jokingly refer to the "Moscow gold" that enabled Muriel to get to this conference.

Few people from Canada visited the Soviet Union during those years and Muriel found the idea of going there quite overwhelming. She talked it over with Jack and with her boss, and everyone agreed it was an opportunity not to be missed. She had already resigned her job to take effect in June and so had no trouble getting a leave of absence.

On the plane to Moscow, Muriel met six American women and the only other Canadian delegate, Doris Mailman from Winnipeg, who represented the Congress of Canadian Women. In Moscow they joined 225 women from eighty-five countries. Women were asked what they wanted to see during this two week visit to the Soviet Union. Muriel, as she requested, was taken to see nursery schools, kindergartens, and elementary and high schools, always accompanied by an interpreter. She found it relatively easy to talk with students, teachers and doctors and to question them about their work.

The visitors were taken to see the war memorial and Red Square, the Kremlin, the Moscow metro, a marriage palace and a children's culture palace. For recreation, they were treated to the Bolshoi ballet and the Moscow circus. In Leningrad they spent several hours at the Hermitage Art Gallery and in the very beautiful square surrounding it. They were overwhelmed by the sight of the cemetery where so many thousands lay buried following the tragic siege of Leningrad.

The highlight of the trip was the celebration of International Women's Day, a national holiday in the Soviet Union observed by everybody—men, women and children. Their hosts began the day with a gala breakfast at the hotel and brought presents to all the guests. Muriel received a beautiful orange shawl. Everywhere there was a wonderfully happy atmosphere. Even the huge billboards that ordinarily had party slogans exhorting the people to work harder, carried messages of congratulations to women. It was even more festive than Mother's Day in Canada. The foreign guests joined six thousand people who assembled in the Palace of Congresses at a concert to honour women. Muriel was moved by the passionate proclamation made by the delegate from the National Liberation Front of Vietnam, Madame Nguyen Ngoc Dung, who declared: "We, like all women, are dreaming of bringing up our children in independent peace."

The following night, every foreign woman at the conference was invited to a private home for dinner. Doris, Muriel and their interpreter were guests of a couple, both of whom were engineers. As Heroes of the Revolution, this family had been among the first to get new housing in Moscow, but by North American standards it was very modest. Dark narrow hallways and stairs led to their small three room apartment. Despite the cramped quarters, heavy old furniture gave the place a homey feeling. An enormous bookcase was packed with books and the table was set with lovely old china. The six of them sat around the dining room table laden with food. Muriel immediately warmed to this cheerful couple and their nineteen-year-old daughter who was studying French. In the midst of lively discussion Muriel decided to give the interpreter a break by speaking French and having the daughter translate for her parents. They brought out maps and an encyclopedia to search out just where in Canada Muriel and Doris lived. Part way through the meal they all hopped up and went into the living room to watch an interview of Muriel on TV which was scheduled to be shown at that time. The evening was so informal and her hosts so friendly that Muriel felt entirely at home.

The conference itself, about women and peace, was in some ways disappointing. It was set up very formally with no opportunity for discussion. The Chinese were absent as relations between the USSR and China had recently deteriorated. And there were no representatives from Israel. Two countries were in disfavour at the conference, the United States because of the war in Vietnam, and Israel because of the tension with the Palestinians. After two to three days of listening to speech after speech with no response or interaction, Muriel made her own brief presentation. She felt that Canada

was very much a bit player and not at all important in this forum. But she
carried away a vivid memory of an informal meeting in a hotel room on the
eve of International Women's Day which she reported in a later CBC
broadcast on Maritime Magazine.

> In this small gathering there were women from the United States,
> England, Australia, New Zealand and Canada and the four women
> from Vietnam with their interpreter. Remember that in Vietnam,
> the hundreds of thousands of troops from U.S., Australia and New
> Zealand are foreign invaders in the eyes of these women. And they
> can't understand why England and Canada don't dissociate them-
> selves completely from the war. Yet when the American women
> invited the Vietnamese to talk with us, they gladly accepted the
> invitation. . . .
>
> They told us how they feel—that they will make any sacrifice
> fighting for their own country against a foreign invader. They gave
> the history of the war as they see it. They answered our questions.
> Of course the main question was the one put by a young woman
> from Washington, D.C., who was there representing Women's
> Strike for Peace, "What are your conditions for peace?"
>
> The answer was, they said, just as it has been stated by
> President Ho Chi Minh and his foreign Secretary repeatedly and
> recently; as soon as the United States stops bombing North Vietnam
> unconditionally, peace talks will begin. We want, they said, inde-
> pendence, democracy, peace and neutrality.
>
> When I read our newspapers now and I think about these quiet,
> determined women, I am almost overwhelmed with the tragedy of
> it. You feel they will never give up. They are sure they can win, even
> if it takes years, and yet the U.S. has the power to wipe them out.
> It sounds like genocide unless the bombing is stopped and peace
> talks begin.[7]

Following the conference all delegates were invited to other parts of the
USSR. The women from North America were taken to Tallin, in Estonia,
across from Finland. This part of the Soviet Union looked quite Scandinavian
to Muriel. She liked the architecture and the atmosphere. The women would
chat informally with Estonians, sitting around little tables with baskets of
fruit, cups of tea and piles of candy. At one of these events Muriel found
herself sitting beside the minister of culture who was talking about their film
industry. Knowing something about the cost of film-making from her son
Martin's work at the National Film Board, Muriel wondered aloud how a
film industry was possible in such a little country. She asked him, "how can
you manage to have a film industry? You know it's pretty hard in Canada

for us to have a film industry." He laughed and replied, "well, we are part of a country that wants us to have a film industry. You live next to a country that doesn't want you to have a film industry."

She also encountered a delightful interpreter who had studied Mark Twain and who had been to England to do research about him. One day while they were riding on the bus together she told Muriel laughingly that her husband was jealous of Mark Twain, because he thought his wife spent more time with Mark Twain than she did with him!

In the Soviet Union, Muriel was struck by the people she met who insisted that only communism could attain such objectives as full equality for women, free and equal education from nursery school through university and adequate housing for all. She was surprised to find that the unions seemed to play a far more important role in the non-working lives of their members than they do in Canada. They were told that the unions that year were spending 12.5 billion dollars on such services as children's and family camps, health spas, cultural services for pensioners and newspapers. When she visited the sumptuous Youth Culture Palaces for the Red Pioneers (a youth organization similar to the Boy Scouts or Girl Guides) she could well believe that their public spending was enormous.

Landing in Montreal she was interviewed by reporters from the *Gazette*, *Le Devoir* and CBC Radio. Shortly after arriving back to work in Halifax, the deputy minister of education, Dr. Moffat, came into her office saying that he had just had a phone call from a man in Montreal (Muriel suspected from a Liberal government official) asking what was this woman up to? They felt she had expressed views to the press which were sympathetic to the Soviet Union. Dr. Moffat treated the matter lightly, Muriel thought, because she had already resigned her job, to take effect in June. She realized that she was spared a confrontation and wondered if her views would have caused her to be fired. On the other hand, she had also expressed criticism of the Soviet school system. Although she was impressed with the warmth in the school classrooms, she did not care for their rigid system of education. But a professor who was head of the education department at Dalhousie University went to the USSR the following year and came back full of praise for the way the classrooms were organized. He quite liked the formal structure and he did not get into any trouble for his views! Muriel knew that the Voice of Women had a reputation for being soft on communists, and the women were always accused of being either pink or stupid—either a red or a dupe. The Voices' insistence that it was important to make connections with the women who were supposed to be their enemies made them targets for such accusations.

The Montreal Conference, June 1967

Muriel chaired the planning committee for the International Conference on Women and Peace, sponsored by the Voice of Women as a Canada centennial project. They invited three hundred women to this second international conference, held June 6-10, 1967, at the University of Montreal. The Voices raised $17,000 to cover the conference expenses. International guests came from Japan, South America, India, Africa, Europe and North America.

Early in the planning process (April 12, 1966) Muriel wrote a lengthy letter, reporting to Kay Macpherson on the first two meetings of her committee in Halifax. Her comments indicated increasing feminist sentiments in this group:

> [There is a] strong feeling that we must not lose sight of the fact that our primary concern is the promotion of the cause of peace and that whatever the emphasis of the conference it must be seen to be clearly related to this purpose.
>
> This brings us to the theme and here we feel that we should relate our theme to the theme and sub-themes of EXPO 67. . . . But as the theme Man and his World and its development at EXPO cuts across national boundaries so must conflict resolution and the provision of adequate supplies of pure air, food and water. . . . From the positive side the words Man the Conserver or Man the Preserver express what we mean but of course the exact words are unsuitable to use. On the negative side, and not altogether seriously, some titles suggested were: Man the Mad Scientist, Man the Monster, Man the Elderly Delinquent, Man and his Illusions, Man the Destroyer, Man the Predatory Animal, Man and Anti-Man.[8]

The committee eventually put its emphasis on stopping the Vietnam war, education for peace and international arms sales. A questionnaire they distributed in advance to each participant is a good illustration of the kind of grass roots research which Muriel believed in promoting. They asked:

> What have women in your country done towards stopping the war in Vietnam?
> What do you consider the most effective instruments or institutions for building peace?
> How is the United Nations regarded in your country? In your community?
> For a peaceful world, what are the proper limits of national sovereignty?
> Bring a text book, preferably from a higher grade in your schools, dealing with the Second World War.

What do you feel about students [from the South] being trained in developed countries?
Does this method of training contribute to the development of their own countries?
What sources do YOU use for factual information on current events?
What additional news sources would you like to see in your country?
Bring your local newspaper for any day in the week of May 15th.
Does your country buy and sell armaments?
What percentage of your country's national income is spent on "defence"?
What are people in your country doing to promote peace?[9]

Because the Voices' first international conference in 1962 had resulted in the United Nations declaring 1965 "International Cooperation Year," the conference planners wanted to build on this achievement in order to further support the UN and strengthen women's influence there. With this in mind they sought a United Nations spokesperson for the opening address, only to discover that the UN would provide only men speakers. Thus it was that a man was the opening speaker at this International Women's Conference. Muriel thought his approach was bureaucratic and not at all inspiring.

VOW had from the beginning tried to be a bilingual organization. Muriel and her planning committee went to great efforts to arrange a completely bilingual conference. Since Montreal had been chosen as the site, they were determined that French speakers must be highly evident, and all sessions were to be bilingual. Since there was no such thing as government grants for translation in those days, one VOW member, who was a professional translator herself, undertook to train bilingual members to do simultaneous interpretation. The organizers experienced a moment of panic when the equipment used by the translators broke down just as a principal speaker, Helen Kazantzakis from Switzerland, but originally from Greece, began her address in French. Thankfully, Madeleine Dubuc of Montreal quickly came to the rescue and translated.

In June 1967 Montreal was in a celebratory mood but the women attending this International Conference on Women and Peace were in a mood of despair. It was a time of serious regional conflict around the world. The Seven Day War in Israel had begun that very week. The civil war in Nigeria had also just begun and the war in Vietnam dragged on. Women at the conference expressed their common despair over the possibility of international peace and asked themselves whether there was anything at all they could do to stop the conflict.

The Americans at the conference were preoccupied with the war in

Vietnam, whereas the European women were interested in nuclear testing, the threat of nuclear war, and the role of NATO and the Warsaw Pact. Women from Third World countries had even more immediate concerns. An African described her attendance at a previous conference where everyone had to stay on the floor to avoid stray bullets being shot through the windows. A Bolivian told of police raiding her home. The delegate from Nigeria, who lived in the part known as Biafra, did not know whether she would get back into her country when she returned because of the civil war there. Another pleaded, "don't send us arms to kill each other." Following the conference, Muriel accompanied a bus load of women to Ottawa to speak with the minister for external affairs about their findings on Vietnam, arms sales and disarmament.

Notes

1. Voice of Women, *Our Declaration: What You Can Do, Some Future Objectives.* Oakville, Ont.: Esperanto Press, 1960. PANS MG 1 Vol. 2912, No. 13.
2. Society of Friends. American Friends Service Committee, *Speak Truth to Power, a Quaker Search for an Alternative to Violence: A Study of International Conflict.* Philadelphia, American Friends Service Committee, 1955. Robert Jungk, *Brighter than a Thousand Suns: A Personal History of the Atomic Scientists.* New York: Harcourt Brace, 1958.
3. "From the Provinces," National VOW Newsletter, November 1962. PANS MG 1 Vol. 2930, No. 23. See also *Maclean's Magazine*, October 1962.
4. PANS MG 1 Vol. 2910, No. 39.
5. Undated press release (April 1969) issued by M. Duckworth. PANS MG 1 Vol. 2910, No. 39.
6. Speech given by M. Duckworth. PANS MG 1 Vol. 2934.
7. PANS MG 1 Vol. 2932.
8. NAC MG 28 I 218 Vol. 13, File 15.
9. Ibid.

Chapter 8

National President of the Voice of Women

*A*s Muriel had anticipated, the logistics of being a Halifax-based president of a national organization with minimum financial resources and a national office in Toronto was no mean feat. Muriel maintained that this was only made possible by the herculean efforts at the national office of the sole paid secretary and a host of volunteers, chief among them the past-president, Kay Macpherson. Early in the history of VOW, Kay and Muriel had developed a strong, mutually supportive relationship. After Muriel replaced Kay as national president, Kay, true to her word, continued to oversee the workings of the national office. The two friends were an excellent team despite their very different styles. Kay, a vibrant colourful enthusiast, propelled people into action, while Muriel was more given to quiet persuasion and to encouraging people to act on their concerns. Each delighted in the other's sense of humour and each paid careful attention to the other's advice. Both women fearlessly stood up to government officials and politicians. Their close friendship was to continue over the years and seldom a week went by when they did not compare notes over the telephone on what to do about the state of the world.

In the early part of Muriel's presidency, Kay was a good coach. Before Muriel started off on her first cross-country trip to meet with VOW members, Kay provided her with two pages of advice in point form: get names and addresses of all present; take notes on suggestions and comments at each meeting; take a local publicity person along for radio, press and TV interviews; include students and daughters of VOWers; take up a collection at public meetings; bring along photos, posters and literature; and take pictures. And after the trip, Kay instructed Muriel to: make a list of everyone Muriel saw; make a report for everyone (a President's Letter); send lists to local groups and ask them to follow up on prospective members and points raised, actions proposed, etc. She concluded:

> Have a lovely time. There is no more wonderful experience, I've found. Cram in everything you can and see as many people as possible. It's well worth every ounce of energy and every dollar spent. Bon voyage—and bless you![1]

Kay was generous in passing on her hard-earned experience from past annual general meetings (AGMs). In a letter to Muriel prior to her first AGM in Winnipeg, Kay suggested tongue in cheek, that they abolish resolution making:

> Your annual meeting planning seems superb to me and I should
> know! . . . After hours and hours of reports and special papers at
> WILPF [Women's International League for Peace and Freedom] my
> chief advice would be NEVER read reports that are reproduced but
> let the reporters introduce themselves, make only if necessary one
> or two points and answer for a very limited time one or two
> questions. . . . Background papers, if any, should be read BEFORE
> any discussion by each member on her own, and do away with
> speeches as much as possible if not altogether.
>   . . . Resolutions? I don't suppose we could combine all our
> policies on Vietnam, Greece, Biafra, Czech (save us PLEASE from
> doing that one) Middle East, etc., etc., in one short statement. NATO,
> OAS, NORAD, etc. No, perhaps it's a hopeless idea. But what good
> are resolutions except either to educate our members or hang a
> delegation on to? Perhaps my resolution should be to abolish
> resolutions.[2]

Nearly twenty years later, while planning the women's international
peace conference in Halifax in 1985, Muriel still remembered this advice as
she urged the planning committee to abandon resolution-making. Certainly,
there were always more issues than VOW could handle.

In one of her lengthy letters to Muriel, Kay started out:

> Today, I listed all our areas of interest just to see what we have to
> keep up in. Bah, how can we? Biafra, Middle East, South Africa,
> Vietnam, NATO, etc., ABM [Anti-Ballistic Missiles], CBW [chemical
> and biological warfare], China, Greece, South America, Violence,
> Women, Indians, Students, Deserters, Blacks. . . .[3]

In Halifax, Muriel worked out of her home on South Street, which had
been christened "the Hive." The dining room functioned as her office, and
from the dining room table she communicated with the national council from
Newfoundland to Victoria, sent out a constant flow of press releases, wrote
speeches and organized petitions and delegations to government. At the
same time, there were countless meetings of the Halifax-Dartmouth VOW as
well as other community groups going on in the kitchen.

VOW ran on a shoestring budget, and Muriel's office practices reflected
this. Her frugal lifetime habits stood her in good stead. Scarcely a piece of
scrap paper was ever thrown away. She would use the backside of flyers,
notices, minutes of meetings or whatever, for drafts of letters, speeches and

endless lists of things to be done. Her letters covered both sides of each page, without benefit of margins, and were written longhand since she did not type.

Memos and letters constantly flew back and forth between Muriel and the national office secretary. Muriel wrote:

> A dozen letters in today's mail all requiring answers. I have got a volunteer who can do routine letters I give her over the phone—at least until she has a baby in a couple of months! Looks as if I have three speeches coming up in Ottawa, Fredericton and St. Andrews, N.B., all on different subjects.[4]

Mediating disputes among the national office and members from across the country was a common occurrence. Another memo to the office manager from Muriel urged:

> Be discreet as usual in using contents of Ms. Jones' [a pseudonym] letter. Don't pass it around—no use getting people's blood pressure up.[5]

Preparations for council meetings and AGMs sometimes got quite complicated with much back and forth communication between the national office, Muriel, and council members across the country. One fiasco occurred when Muriel gave the office administrator a "hurry-up" instruction to photocopy a hand-written document, not realizing that the print would not even be legible.

Muriel's official method of communicating with the office administrator and her executive was to use five-by-eight inch memo pads containing five pastel-coloured carbon copies. She would keep the last copy for herself and mail the others around. Presumably one knew from the colour which copy one received. Kay Macpherson would howl with indignation whenever she received the fourth copy, claiming Muriel's handwriting was illegible. Muriel would counter that she had no trouble reading the last copy which she herself retained. Expensive telephone calls to executive members in other parts of the country were few and far between, and usually made after midnight to get the cheapest rates. During most of her term as president, Muriel had no local typist at her disposal. Jack had typing skills and, as he was home part-time, he would get up very early every morning and frequently type her letters to government and her news releases. Finally, near the end of her term, a Halifax citizens' coalition known as MOVE, of which she was later president, hired a number of people on a federal grant, and Muriel was able to have the services of Margot Sorrel for some of her peace work.

This general lack of resources scarcely affected Muriel's productivity. Her organizing skills and strong sense of self-discipline, developed during nearly forty years of work as a volunteer and in the low-budget education department, meant that she could carry an immense work load with minimal support staff. But there were days when she felt swamped. A six page "note" to the national secretary began:

> Wow, I owe you several letters and about 30 million people at least one each it seems to me. I've written more than 20 today—so I feel a little better—but there is still a huge pile.[6]

Despite all the pressures and deadlines of the work, Margot Sorrel mostly remembered the interesting and lively discussions she had with Muriel and Jack whenever they stopped for lunch.

Soon after Muriel's election as president, she began a monthly President's Letter to members of the VOW council and for distribution to their local executives and membership. These, in addition to the national VOW newsletters, were her way of keeping in touch with everyone. In a conversational tone Muriel constantly promoted actions across the land, did fundraising, and spread her own personal philosophy.

> 1969 is the 100th anniversary of the birth of Gandhi. I am inviting Voice of Women members to join me this year in taking a serious look at his life, his achievements, his failures, and especially at *Satyragraha.* This is the word he invented because "non-violence" and "passive resistance" did not convey a strong enough, a positive enough meaning. *Satyragraha* means literally "truth-force." To Gandhi this meant love-force. Gandhi fasted time and again almost to death, led massive boycotts, and civil disobedience campaigns, to achieve independence for his people, to eliminate untouchability, to stop the partitioning of India, to persuade Hindus and Moslems to live together as brothers. Do you remember the walk of thousands of Indians—241 miles to the sea in 24 days—to make salt from the sea, as an act of civil disobedience to bring an end to the salt laws?
>
> Read some of his own writings and a good biography. I have just re-read *Gandhi* by Louis Fisher. . . . You will probably find that other groups in the community, and university departments would be interested in arranging a series of memorial lectures. You would probably get more yourself from a study group. Is Gandhi relevant to us? I believe he is.[7]

Muriel became adept at fundraising and put VOW's financial needs squarely to the membership, time and again, in her newsletters. Appealing for funds to organize the AGM she wrote about the Vietnam war:

> VOW's basic job is to put an end to the conditions that cause these
> tragic needs. For that we need your money—just to bring people
> together to talk, just to buy the stamps to put on letters, just to pay
> a small office rent and a part-time salary, just to publish information
> not otherwise readily available to the general public and yet essen-
> tial for our understanding of issues.[8]

Every few months Muriel travelled to council meetings in Toronto,
Montreal and Ottawa. After her six-week tour in the autumn of her first year
as president, she wrote:

> Thank you to everyone for my cross country trip—6 weeks, 45
> meetings, 18 radio, 10 TV, 8 newspaper interviews, one speech from
> the back of a truck to 700 people in Winnipeg, many meetings, in
> homes and public places where I met VOW members, their families
> and friends. Your hospitality was magnificent, your imaginative
> efforts for peace inspiring—and I wish I could have met every
> member.[9]

On her return, a letter from Deeno Birmingham of Nanoose Bay
expressed how the Voices from the West felt: "We were all really pleased
to meet you, you inspired a great feeling of friendliness and closeness and
confidence wherever you went."[10]

Muriel had an exceptional ability to organize, to undertake public
education on international issues and to communicate her enthusiasm, in
person and through her correspondence. Her knowledge was extensive.
Often, late into the night, she would seek inspiration and information from
the many periodicals to which she subscribed, including an Australian
monthly, *Pacific*; an English monthly, *Call to Women*; the American *Monthly
Review* and the *Center Diary* from the Center for the Study of Democratic
Institutions; *Liberation* from New York; *Ramparts* from San Francisco; and
her favourite, *I.F. Stone's Weekly*. She firmly believed that if the Canadian
public were only given information revealing both sides of international
disputes they would insist that the Canadian government form its own
independent foreign policy. She felt that it was the task of the Voice of
Women to make the media cover "the other side" of what was happening in
countries which were at war or were deemed to be "the enemy." She
constantly encouraged the regional VOW groups to keep informed through
the alternate press so that they could challenge the mainstream media. At
that time there were no Canadian peace magazines, although there was
research published by the Canadian Peace Research Institute, which was

supported by VOW members.

Muriel was not one to mince words when it came to saying how Canada should make its opposition to American policy felt. In her year-end message to Voices in December 1967 she wrote:

> Canada at the end of 1967, has one major responsibility in foreign policy: to work with other nations for the "alleviation of the causes of war by common action for the economic and social betterment of mankind" (From the statement of purpose, Constitution, Voice of Women Canada). In order to do this, with the singleness of purpose which this urgent task requires and with the full confidence of other less wealthy nations, Canada must act to free herself from her present satellite position in relation to the United States, from the economic uncertainties and limitations of this relationship, from the immoral benefits of exploitation and devastation of other peoples and lands, from the continued waste of money, men and materials on so-called "defence."[11]

Campaigns for peace in Vietnam were continuously undertaken during Muriel's term as president of VOW. Muriel would report in her letters to members the actions VOW groups across Canada were undertaking, including vigils, boycotts of goods made by Canadian and American companies which also manufactured war materials (such as the company manufacturing Saran Wrap which also made napalm), letter-writing campaigns to Prime Minister Pearson and to President Johnson and news releases to alert the public about Canada's role in Vietnam.[12]

When Muriel became president the organization had, for several years, been conducting teach-ins and rallies to protest the war in Vietnam and Canada's involvement in it. A strongly-worded resolution was sent to the federal government from the annual meeting in 1966, urging Canada to recognize that its policies of quiet diplomacy had been ineffectual; that its export of strategic materials (explosives, bullets, aircraft parts, etc.) to the United States for use in Vietnam was destroying Canada's integrity as a member of the International Control Commission; that no solution in Vietnam was possible other than a settlement that would include the withdrawal of US forces and the dismantling of US military bases; and that no lasting peace could be established in Asia without extending full recognition to the People's Republic of China.

The *Ottawa Citizen* reported on Muriel's meeting with National Defence Minister Pierre Cadieux on December 11, 1967. Accompanied by Elsie Saumure, Ann Gertler and Louise Gareau,

> Mrs. Duckworth told the minister that the government should

concentrate its defence expenditure on peace-keeping forces suitable for United Nations deployment. The only defense of Canadians is peace. The organization asked the government to disassociate Canada from further involvement in the Vietnam war by placing an embargo on the sale and shipment of arms to the United States.

Muriel followed Kay Macpherson's earlier leadership in uniting the Voices through public actions, such as rallies and public meetings, against the war in Vietnam.[13] VOW's opposition to the war in turn alerted the Canadian public to Canada's role in Vietnam.

One idea which raised enthusiasm was to bring Vietnamese women to Canada to meet with American women in the peace movement so that they could tell their side of the story. As "enemies" of the United States the Vietnamese women could not cross the border, but American women could come to Canada to meet them. Kay and Muriel advanced this idea when each attended separate conferences in Moscow and Athens. They promoted it again when together they attended an international women's conference in Paris in April 1968. The conference demanded an end to the war in Vietnam.

The Paris Conference

This conference was called by Women Strike for Peace (WSP) of the United States, the Women's Union of the Democratic Republic of Vietnam (North Vietnam) and the South Vietnam Liberation Women's Union (National Liberation Front). As well as Vietnamese women, among the forty women invited were prominent peace activists from the United States, Canada, England, Australia and New Zealand. These countries were invited because their governments (including Canada) were supporting the US in its invasion of Vietnam. The Parisian women made it very clear that they were merely hosting the conference. France was not supporting the US.

Kay and Muriel were billeted in the guest house of a public school with the women from New Zealand and Australia. Every break in the conference gave them a chance to talk with different people: a partisan from the National Liberation Front; Vietnamese MPs; a Vietnamese doctor and teacher; well known peace activist, Eva Coffin; Ann Bennett from the Council of Church Women in the US and wife of the president of Union Theological Seminary; the actress, Viveca Lindfors; Anne Kerr, the British MP who later that same year was maced during the riot at the Chicago Democratic Convention and suffered permanent damage to her eyesight; Vera Rice, the editor of the English *Call to Women*; and Mary Clarke from WSP—a key organizer of this conference.[14]

Even though the conference was meticulously conducted, with all the proceedings being translated into English and Vietnamese, there was nonetheless an informal atmosphere. The women sat around a large table and each session was co-chaired by Ann Bennett and Vietnamese Mme. Binh, later to become the foreign minister of the Provisional Revolutionary Government (PRG) and of the government. Unlike the stiff proceedings of the large Moscow conference the previous year, the format at this small conference allowed for ready discussion and the participants formed close bonds with one another. The WSP influenced the form of this conference. They worked hard to make it as informal as possible in contrast to their experience of a previous conference in Jakarta with the Vietnamese Women, where the proceedings were very formal. Immediately following this conference the Paris Peace Conference was held and the soft spoken, dignified Mme. Binh was named as the head of the PRG's delegation.

Muriel and Kay came back convinced that they were not getting a true picture from the Canadian news media of what was really going on in war-torn Vietnam. The Vietnamese government representatives claimed that 638,000 tons of bombs were dropped in North Vietnam in 1966 and that hospitals, schools and churches were frequent targets. North Vietnam rivers had recently been mined. The aim of the US as seen by the Vietnamese, was to intensify and expand the war in the South and the North despite the US talk of peaceful negotiations. The Vietnamese insisted that bombing and other war acts must stop before the two sides could sit together and discuss measures to bring about peace.

In a press conference called upon her return to Canada on May 9, Muriel cited the efforts of peace groups in the US, Britain, France, West Germany, Australia and Japan. She quoted from the statement made by Senator Wayne Morse in 1965, who stated that US policy in Vietnam was illegal under the United Nations Charter, the Geneva Accords of 1954, SEATO and the American constitution. She repeated what Black American women at the conference had said, that 50 percent of American combat troops in Vietnam were "Negro" whereas they made up only 11 percent of the population of the US. She spoke of Canada's complicity in the war: the fact that the Canadian government had never condemned US policy in Vietnam; that Canada sent arms and strategic material to the US; and that Canada did not provide political asylum for deserters. She chastised the news media for their accounts of Viet Cong atrocities and vague allusions to the "communist threat" while making no mention of the use of napalm, phosphorous, anti-personnel bombs and other barbaric equipment being used against the Vietnamese, often against civilian populations.[15]

What Muriel learned at this conference deepened her commitment to opposition to the war in Vietnam—the central issue during her term as president of Voice of Women. The conference also confirmed that arranging a visit of a delegation of Vietnamese women to Canada was a high priority.

Notes

1. Letter to M. Duckworth from K. Macpherson, 25 July 1967.*
2. Letter to M. Duckworth from K. Macpherson, 1 September 1968.*
3. Letter to M. Duckworth from K. Macpherson, 12 December 1969.*
4. Memo from M. Duckworth to office secretary, 13 November 1967.*
5. Memo from M. Duckworth to office secretary, 20 November 1967.*
6. Memo from M. Duckworth to office secretary, 10 January 1968.*
7. President's Letter, December 1968. PANS MG 1 Vol. 2911, No. 24.
8. President's Letter, 29 August 1968. PANS MG 1 Vol. 2911, No. 24.
9. President's Letter, November 1967. PANS MG 1 Vol. 2930, No. 33.
10. Letter from D. Birmingham to M. Duckworth, 30 October 1967.*
11. National VOW Newsletter, Vol. 5, No. 4 (December 1967). PANS MG 1 Vol. 2912, No. 33.
12. VOW History and Objectives, 1967–72. PANS MG 1 Vol. 2912, No. 13.
13. "Report on Action in the Provinces," National VOW Newsletter, Vol. 6, No. 8 (November 1969). PANS MG 1 Vol. 2930, No. 34.
14. "International Conference of Women to End the War in Vietnam—Paris April 1968," National VOW Newsletter, Vol. 6, No. 2 (June 1968). NAC MG 28–I 218, Vol. 9, No. 9.
15. "VOW President Convinced Public is Ill-informed," National VOW Newsletter, Vol. 6, No. 2 (June 1968). PANS MG 1 Vol. 2930, No. 34.

Note: * indicates document awaiting deposit in the National Archives of Canada.

Chapter 9

The Vietnam Agenda

The Voices Oppose the War in Vietnam

Muriel returned home from the spring 1968 conference in Paris feeling hopeful that world-wide resistance would soon end the war in Vietnam. However, she subsequently learned how difficult it was to shake the apathy of many Canadians, to expose the weakness of the Canadian government and to oppose the power of the American government. For a long time, Canada's politicians turned a deaf ear to the concerns of peace groups and refused to acknowledge Canada's complicity in the Vietnam war. The Voices tried everything—writing briefs; staging public rallies and vigils; organizing petitions and boycotts; letter-writing campaigns; meeting with members of parliament and cabinet ministers; knitting for Vietnamese children; supporting Claire Culhane's public fasts; leading demonstrations against Canadian research into chemical and biological weapons; joining local and national anti-war coalitions; and finally, bringing Vietnamese women to speak in Canada. Their efforts met with few visible results. It was a discouraging business. While some Voices became frustrated and complained that they were getting nowhere, most continued with dogged determination to bring home their message to the Canadian public.

Resisting Chemical and Biological Warfare

While looking into how Canada was tied in with the United States in the war in Vietnam, Voice of Women researchers reviewed the country's defence agreements. They found an agreement between the governments of Canada, the United States, Great Britain and Australia concerning research into chemical and biological warfare and they determined to learn more about research stations in Suffield, Alberta, and Shirley Bay, Ontario. If Canada was researching and producing chemical and biological weapons for use by the Americans in Vietnam, VOW intended to make the matter public. As the AGM was being held in Calgary on September 20–22, 1968, Muriel wrote to the director of the Suffield Experimental Station asking him to meet their delegation. In reply the director invited Muriel and her executive to lunch. When this was discussed at the AGM some of the women who were already planning to demonstrate at Suffield took exception to the executive accepting such an invitation. After considerable debate a compromise was reached. Muriel and the executive would meet with the administrators while the rest of the delegation would conduct a silent vigil outside the gates.

A bus was hired to take the fourteen Voices to Suffield. En route, the women discussed and studied carefully-prepared questions. Muriel felt very nervous. She was only too conscious of some of the Voices' feeling that the executive was not being sufficiently confrontational. Furthermore, she did not feel she knew a great deal about chemical and biological weapons and here she was leading a delegation to challenge government scientists. She was not prepared for the smoothness of the director's welcome and she found it hard to interrogate him rigorously.

According to plan, Muriel was accompanied by past presidents Thérèse Casgrain and Kay Macpherson, and by Mary Reed, the newly elected vice-president from Saskatchewan.[1] Meanwhile the other ten members representing all provinces stood silently at the gate during the entire visit, which lasted nearly four hours. Hilary Brown of Hornby Island, BC handed out copies of a bilingual brochure which stated: "We want peace/Nous voulons la paix." The others carried two placards, one which identified them as Voice of Women, and the other which stated their purpose in coming: "We are concerned/Nous sommes inquietes."

Three officials met with the delegation of four. The scientists attempted to assure the women that their research had only to do with defensive and not offensive materials, that 85 percent of the information on their research was unclassified and readily available through scientific journals, that they engaged in a cooperative arrangement between the four countries for the exchange of research for reasons of economy and they argued that such research was necessary in light of Canada's defence policy. The women questioned the scientists' assumptions that the development of lethal gases provided defense for the public. They asked whether substances were imported, why any secrecy was justified and why Canada exchanged information with the US, a country that failed to ratify the 1925 Geneva Protocol. The dialogue was not particularly fruitful since the scientists considered that they were protecting the public through their work and the women insisted they were not.

Mid-way through the interview Mr. Perry, the director, invited the executive to take a tour around the base. Unfortunately the women were not quick enough on their feet to ask specifically to see the laboratories. They felt that the delegation were being shown only what the officials wanted them to see.

Late that night when the Voices returned to Calgary reporters were on hand to interview them. Muriel was pretty exhausted by this time. When the reporters learned that the delegation had not seen the labs, they contacted Mr. Perry and reported that he said that the women had not asked to see the labs. Muriel tried to straighten out the facts in the fall issue of the Voice of Women newsletter, insisting that the real issue was the intentional and unnecessary secrecy of the Canadian government. She wrote:

Due apparently to a misunderstanding we were not taken to see any laboratory facilities. We did not "refuse" to see labs, as reported in the press. Why would we? Just as we were leaving, Mr. Perry commented that it was too bad we did not have time to see the labs. This was the first time such a possibility was mentioned. We had assumed he showed us what he wished us to see as we drove around. He might have expected us to ask to see other facilities. I have written to Mr. Perry to say that another group of VOW members will be pleased to accept his invitation to visit the labs in the near future. . . . There are many other unanswered questions. Some of the secrecy is intentional and unnecessary, some of it is due to the fact that information is released in highly technical form through scientific journals. This does not really mean informing the public in the sense that it should be informed through the press, popular magazines, radio, TV. Some of it is due simply to lack of dialogue between the public and the scientists. This we have initiated. Soon we go to Ottawa to see the chairman of the Defense Research Board.

Mr. Perry told us that the four scientists in the room with us are the best-informed in the world on the subject of C&B defense, and they assured us they are devoted to the cause of peace. But somehow I am still concerned. *Je suis encore inquiete.* I wish they were working on some of the medical research problems our government feels it cannot afford to support. Having spent the last month in five cities, I could also wish they were working on problems of air pollution for the people already being poisoned. As for defence— our defense is peace.[2]

To further inform the public, VOW commissioned Dr. David Shephard of Halifax to do a paper, *Chemical and Biological Warfare, Some Implications for Society*, which they published in October 1969 with funding from a memorial fund established in memory of a founding member of the Victoria VOW, Jim Lawson.

Resistance to chemical and biological warfare was the focus of the VOW AGM in October 1969, in Ottawa. Muriel urged Voices to come and meet their respective parliamentarians following the meeting.

Voices like ours are needed now more than ever—for peace, against increasing production, sale and use of increasingly horrible means of massive destruction; for civil rights, against manipulation and repression; for children, against corrupting, burning, starving them and poisoning their environment, for a life on this planet for our grandchildren; against the military and industrial mindlessness which is destroying it and the smugness, stupidity, feelings of helplessness and wrong uses of power which allow this destruction to continue. I.F. Stone wrote, when men landed on the moon, "Let the universe beware. Here comes man."[3]

Muriel continued to try to get the truth from Minister of Defence Leo Cadieux about the nature of technical cooperation programs between Canada and the US but failed to turn up any significant information. This, according to the minister, was "classified information."[4]

In June 1969, Muriel and Ursula Franklin presented a brief on behalf of Voice of Women to the Senate's Special Committee on Science Policy urging that all research in the field of chemical and biological warfare be discontinued, and that Canada withdraw from all internationally shared research programs in this field and transfer all facilities and knowledge of personnel to the areas of environmental research and preventive medicine.

At the next anti-chemical and biological warfare (CBW) demonstration organized by Alberta Voices and other peace groups, eight hundred people from across Canada came to Suffield for three days, 29 to 31 May 1970, to protest this experimental station.[5]

From Knitting to Fasting

Muriel maintained that the actions of two Voices, Claire Culhane and Lil Greene, did much to keep Vietnam on the Voices' agenda. Lil Greene, a member of the Ontario VOW, was a superb organizer. Under her guidance Voices recruited at least two thousand Canadian women from church groups, women's institutes, trade union auxiliaries, senior citizens' groups, Brownies, Rangers, Girl Guides, universities and high schools to help knit woolens for Vietnamese children, many of whom lived in caves and holes because their bamboo villages had been destroyed. Thousands of these tiny garments and blankets were sent to the Canadian Committee in Aid of Vietnam in Vancouver, which in turn had them shipped, at no cost, via Soviet ships to Vladivostok and forwarded to the people in the bombed areas. The knitted clothing was distributed to mothers in the North, the Southern liberated areas and the US controlled sections.

Often the bundles awaiting shipment were piled high in the living and dining room of Lil's house. She never neglected the political education of her knitters. Written information about the war in Vietnam was sent along with the dark wool and knitting patterns she and her committees distributed. And women were not only given knitting patterns but were instructed: "The garments *MUST BE KNITTED IN DARK COLOURS.* A baby wrapped in a light-coloured shawl or garment is a deadly attraction for Napalm, 'Lazy Day' or High Explosive bombs in Vietnam, and must be properly camouflaged in dark blending colours." Canadian women, so accustomed to knitting baby clothes in light pastels, were constantly reminded of the anguish of Vietnamese mothers as they knit up brown, navy, dark green or maroon babies' sweaters, vests, booties, shawls and cot blankets. By 1971, under Lil's tireless organizing, more than 46,000 garments and blankets at an estimated value of $72,800 had been delivered to Vietnam.[6]

Even though thousands of women became involved in this project, the press paid scant attention. However, the actions of one Voice of Women member, Claire Culhane, did capture media attention. She figured out a way of going highly public.

Claire returned in 1968 from South Vietnam where she had been an administrator at a Canadian TB civilian hospital. While there, Claire became acutely aware that, although Canada was supposedly offering humanitarian aid, it was also selling arms to the US to conduct the Vietnam war. Claire was deeply committed to ending the war in Vietnam and she wanted to emphasize Canada's part in this war. On her return to Canada, she filed a report with the department of external aid calling for a full parliamentary enquiry into Canada's role in Vietnam. As she belonged to the Voice of Women she sought their support. Soon she persuaded the Montreal Voices to lead public vigils in Phillips Square twice a week and before long she was speaking publicly.

Muriel found Claire to be very knowledgeable. In contrast, Muriel felt rather ignorant, especially when, at their first meeting, Claire took her to task for a news report which quoted Muriel as saying the Vietnam war was initially a civil war. Claire insisted that the blame lay with the US because of their intervention.

According to Claire, the event that galvanized her decision to take action happened after the September 1968 AGM in Calgary. She was with the busload of women that went to Suffield after the AGM to protest chemical and biological weapons research. Just as they were leaving, Charlotte McEwen, a VOW member from Ottawa, handed Claire a copy of a communique announcing that Minister of External Affairs Mitchell Sharp's upcoming speech at the United Nations would support American troops getting out of Vietnam, providing the North Vietnamese withdrew from South Vietnam. This, in effect, was a change in Canada's foreign policy, and supported the American position that the US were in there to protect the South Vietnamese against the North Vietnam communists. Previously, Prime Minister Trudeau had said publicly that Canada's position was "out of Vietnam—we don't mean one-quarter or one-half, we mean out of Vietnam." Claire saw Sharp's position as proof of the direction in which Canada's policy was now going, and it enraged her. The idea came to her to stage a ten-day fast on Parliament Hill, to protest Canada's involvement in Vietnam. For her, leafleting, writing briefs, going to conferences and lobbying were not enough. She was eager to do something dramatic, something that would get a public response.

En route to Suffield, Claire tried to persuade Muriel, Thérèse Casgrain and the others that she was well able to undertake a ten-day fast and sought their support. It was Claire's understanding that the women agreed to endorse her fast providing she would hold off for another week in order to allow time for the press to cover the Suffield trip and the other issues raised at the AGM. Meanwhile, upon her return Claire got busy and formed committees in Ottawa to bring her fresh nurse's uniforms and orange juice daily, to provide a cot, to have someone remain with her when she slept at night in the entrance of the East Wing, and to handle publicity on and off Parliament Hill.

Claire's fast and sit-in on Parliament Hill lasted from September 30 to October 11, during which time she talked with people from all walks of life as well as to parliamentarians. Each day more press across the country covered her fast. As the publicity mounted, more and more people came to Parliament Hill to show their support; even government MPs visited her. As the October 3, 1968, *Ottawa Journal* said in its headline, "Granny Fasts on Hill: she's hungry but not lonely."

The Voices rallied to her support as well. Montreal sent a busload of Voices to stand with Claire on Saturday and ten Voices came by bus from Toronto on Sunday to be with her. Thérèse Casgrain represented Muriel and stood with Claire for the last hours of the fast. During the late afternoon Claire and Thérèse were invited to meet with Prime Minister Pierre Trudeau. When Trudeau congratulated her on her fast she told him what was important was that hundreds and thousands of people across the country were with her in spirit. As they left Claire saw Trudeau's mask slip momentarily. He shook hands with her and said, "You have no idea of the pressures I'm under."

Despite the unprecedented success of Claire's action, it occasioned serious tension within the VOW. Claire had expected Muriel to issue a press release in the early days of her fast, saying Claire's fast was endorsed by the national Voice of Women. But two things stood in the way. Muriel had returned to Halifax on October 2 from her meetings in central Canada, thinking she could get back to Ottawa for the conclusion of Claire's fast. However, once home she found she could neither afford the time nor the cost. Besides, there was some confusion over whether Claire was representing herself or acting with the full support of the Voice of Women. Since Claire was spurred to her action just after the AGM, she had not had the opportunity to air her plans there. Some of the western Voices were mystified that the fast had not been discussed at the AGM and concluded that this was Claire's own individual action. In a rehash of the incident, Alberta vice-president Margaret Fitch, wrote to Muriel from Calgary,

> Some Calgary members were on the bus when Claire's fast was discussed but none of the executive . . . heard of Claire's idea but

thought it would be an individual effort, not a VOW project. They thought some reporter in Ottawa had made a mistake. Otherwise, we felt it would surely have been discussed at the annual meeting.[7]

Claire conceived of her fast right at the point when Muriel was preoccupied with a very difficult action herself—leading the delegation to Suffield. It is unlikely that she gave her full attention to Claire's strategy. Muriel came home to telegrams and phone calls, many of which were from western members of VOW who emphasized that Claire's fast was not a nationally endorsed action. At the time Muriel felt caught in the middle and, realizing that the AGM had ended before Claire proposed her action, she felt she could not issue a press statement endorsing Claire's fast as a national action. When Claire did not receive the national endorsement she angrily telephoned Muriel from the office of a friendly MP, and tried to force Muriel's hand by threatening to resign publicly from VOW. Muriel appreciated that many more Voices across the country did approve of Claire's fast and wanted to be identified with it. Muriel's gestures of asking Thérèse Casgrain to represent her at the conclusion of Claire's fast and sending a telegram to Claire were her attempts to bridge their differences. Muriel's message, read at the final ceremony, said:

> You have focussed attention of all Canadians on the tragedy of the continuing war in Vietnam by your courageous and imaginative act of fasting for ten days. From your own eye-opening experience of six months in Vietnam with a Canadian medical team, and out of your deep compassion for suffering people, you have been moved to carry out this sacrificial act. For the sake of the Vietnamese people and all of us may your efforts to stop the bombing succeed.[8]

Despite Claire's heroic effort, Mitchell Sharp's position at the United Nations did not change. But this did not hinder the Quebec Voices under Claire's bold leadership from instigating a country-wide boycott of American products made by companies which were also chief manufacturers of weapons. One of these was the maker of Saran Wrap. When some of the more cautious Voices objected to such boycotts Muriel came out unequivocally in support of them in a letter to national council members:

> I have had several letters expressing concern that the boycott will not achieve much and that it may lessen the effectiveness of other VOW action. If you re-read Claire's final proposal, you will see that there is no pressure on any group to join this boycott. I do not myself see it as an act of hate. If we are utterly opposed to the use of napalm, it is not a meaningless gesture to refuse to buy Saran Wrap.

Some of your letters also indicate that you think the Canadian public doesn't care enough to support such a boycott. This may be true, but is it a reason for us in VOW not to let the world know why we don't buy Saran, Breck hair products, Melmac dishes, etc.?

One of my friends who works in a medical lab was asked the other day by a doctor, in front of a class, to wrap something in Saran. She said she did not have Saran, and the whole class understood why. Do you think that was meaningless? harmful to VOW? to the cause of peace?

Of course we are all caught up in this war, and others, just because we live on this continent; and we can't fool ourselves that anything we have thought of to do so far matters greatly. War toys don't sell very well any more—the profit has gone out of them— and we did have something to do with that. The aid and comfort we give to draft resisters in Canada and to war resisters in the U.S. are surely of real value both now and for the future.[9]

Muriel also wrote to Nellie Peterson, an Alberta member of VOW:

Claire Culhane's fast and boycott created a real dialogue within VOW. I do think we are on the verge of something new—but I don't know what.[10]

Still, other VOW members grew impatient with maintaining the focus on Vietnam. One member wrote to Muriel:

I think we have become or let ourselves become almost ineffectual as a result of our pre-occupation with Vietnam. Every possible word that can be said as expressing horror and concern about this U.S. problem has been said by us, by concerned Americans, by concerned British and European organizations and by students everywhere. Yet still we go on as if mesmerized. You saw Mr. Sharp; Mrs. Culhane did her magnificent piece of work. The thing has become just about hopeless. It is not within the power of our government to do anything, even if it wanted to. . . . I merely plead now for some action being taken which we can realistically take as Canadians with tie-ups with NATO. And the Commonwealth. Let's fight NATO tooth and nail, by all means, but our actions will be less effective, it seems to me, if we are written off as the "Vietnam bunch."[11]

Although Muriel did vigorously oppose NATO at every opportunity, she continued to protest the Vietnam war spreading throughout Southeast Asia.

Her letters to government grew ever more impassioned. In February 1971, she wrote a public letter to Prime Minister Trudeau.

> Dear Mr. Trudeau,
>
> It is altogether baffling to concerned people everywhere, especially to Canadians, that your government has been able to remain silent on three major issues as the Vietnam war spreads throughout South-East Asia. On behalf of the Voice of Women Canada—and I assure you we speak for thousands of other Canadian citizens when we raise these questions—I ask you to declare yourself now against the Invasion of Laos, for setting a date in 1971 for the complete withdrawal of U.S. troops from Vietnam, against the forced migration of millions of people within South Vietnam.
>
> Tens of thousands of Saigon and American troops have just crossed into Laos, according to some sources, or are assembled at the border ready to cross. . . . You can surely imagine the horrors resulting from bombings by 300 B52's day after day, week after week, month after month.
>
> Will you now speak? Will you now call for an end to the spreading of death and destruction through South-East Asia? Will you call on the U.S. to set a date for the complete withdrawal of American forces from Vietnam?
>
> Mme. Binh has said at the Paris Peace Conference that "if the American Government declares it will withdraw all American troops from South Vietnam before a reasonable and adequate time limit, that is, before June 30, 1971, then the Liberation Armed Forces will refrain from attacking the American forces in process of withdrawal."
>
> Can you not speak and act as a government on humanitarian grounds, seeking justification, if you must, through your obligations as a member of the United Nations? Standing aside from this war, except to allow Canadian manufacturers to continue to profit from it, brutalizes all of us.
>
> South Vietnamese officials have confirmed according to an article in the *New York Times*, January 11, 1971, that between two million and three million people will be moved from the northern provinces of South Vietnam to the extreme south during the next three years. The project is approved by and will be financed by the United States, and is in the final planning stages.
>
> It is surely possible for Canada to raise formal questions about such a "final solution," in the Human Rights Commission at the United Nations or at the International Court or through an international body established to deal specifically with this question.

Indeed how is it possible to remain silent about this openly totalitarian act? How is it possible not to do everything in your power to support the reported 73 percent of American people who want their forces removed from Vietnam.

Will you ask the United States Government to call off the invasion and bombing of Laos? The Voice of Women Canada is not asking you for heroics but for humanly sensitive statesmanship.[12]

Notes

1. NAC MG 1 28 I 218 Vol. 3, File 12.
2. "Suffield Visit," National VOW Newsletter, Vol. 6, No. 3 (October 1968). PANS MG 1 Vol. 2930, No. 34.
3. National VOW Newsletter, Vol. 6, No. 7 (August 1969). PANS MG 1 Vol. 2930, No. 34.
4. Letter from M. Duckworth to L. Cadieux, reprinted in National VOW Newsletter, Vol. 7, No. 2 (March 1970). PANS MG 1 Vol. 2930, No. 34.
5. "Anti-CWB Demonstration at Suffield," National VOW Newsletter, Vol. 7, No. 3 (June 1970). PANS MG 1 Vol. 2930, No. 34.
6. PANS MG 1 Vol. 2911, No. 35. NAC MG 28 I 218, Vol. 28, No. 6.
7. Letter from M. Fitch to M. Duckworth, 23 October 1968.*
8. PANS MG 1 Vol. 2912, No. 10.
9. NAC MG 28 I 218, Vol. 19, No. 2.
10. Letter from M. Duckworth to N. Peterson, 25 November 1968.*
11. Letter from V. Pickett to M. Duckworth, 17 March 1969.*
12. NAC MG 28 I 218, Vol. 20, No. 4.

Note: * indicates document awaiting archival deposit.

Chapter 10

Visits From Vietnamese Women

At the Paris conference of April 1968, as well as during Muriel's earlier trip to the USSR in 1967, the possibility of Vietnamese women coming to Canada had been discussed. The Voice of Women had invited women from Vietnam to its 1967 international conference in Montreal. They were unable to accept, but they said they would like to consider the invitation open for some later date. They also asked Kay Macpherson, then president, to visit Hanoi, which she did the following spring after the Paris conference. Kay repeated VOW's invitation to her hosts.

As mentioned earlier, the VOW executive thought that if Vietnamese women came to Canada, VOW could invite American women in the peace movement to come to Canada to meet them. They hoped that face-to-face meetings with Vietnamese women would strengthen their American sisters' resistance to the war. This plan appealed to the Vietnamese, and preparations were made for them to come in July 1969. Of the three women who came, one was from North Vietnam and the other two were from the National Liberation Front in the South.

Throughout that year, Muriel and Kay and many Voices throughout the country were caught up in a whirlwind of activity leading up to the Vietnamese women's visit. Voices raised $20,000 to pay for the trip and the cross-Canada tour; local committees were set up to arrange events in major cities and at border points; American women, including members of the press, churches, unions, education institutions and peace groups, were invited; support from public figures was sought; security arrangements were made; and a great deal of publicity and interpretation of the purpose of the visit was provided by members of the VOW to the press and to the public. Voices also continued to publicize the monthly letters they received from the Women's Committee of the National Liberation Front (NLF) detailing the effects of the war on specific communities in Vietnam.

Writing to the membership Muriel urged support for the project:

> From the beginning, Voice of Women has constantly striven to keep women in the so-called enemy countries in contact with each other. We have had two international conferences in Canada and they were the origin of this invitation. We believe it is a great privilege for us to be able to perform the service of uniting such people however briefly in a common search for peace. Women are not a voice in the policy making of most nations, including our own.

Meeting with Vietnamese visitors, 1969.

They are not represented in government or in diplomatic circles. Their contacts can only come about through the less formal channels of international meetings and conferences.[1]

In a further fundraising letter to the membership, Muriel asked for a personal contribution of at least $5.00 per member and reminded them that Canada had sold over $2 billion of arms to the US since 1959. She exhorted members:

> I know you will take this responsibility seriously. It is, I think the most meaningful effort imaginable for our movement, to give our fellow citizens and our American neighbours a chance to hear the story of this war and of the Vietnamese people from the lips of women who have lived and suffered and survived through it. We are happy that women from the North and the South are able to come at the same time, symbolizing the fact that Vietnam is one country.[2]

Muriel personally accompanied the women delegates and their two male interpreters to Montreal, Toronto, Vancouver, Nanaimo, Regina and Ottawa, and to centres near border crossings in Quebec, Ontario and British Columbia. The two-week itinerary included attendance at conferences, civic receptions, union meetings, church gatherings, large public meetings, picnics and press conferences.

The first large-scale meeting took place at the Naeve family farm in North Hatley, Quebec, eighteen miles from the American border. Canadian and American peace groups gathered to celebrate the American Independence Day with a day-long program of discussion, films and folk-singing. Three hundred people heard the speeches of the Vietnamese visitors delivered in a huge historic, converted barn, often used for community gatherings.

In Vancouver, a hundred people had to be turned away from the 650-seat Queen Elizabeth playhouse. The Vietnamese delegates also attended a conference of 100 Canadians and 136 Americans in Totem Park at the University of British Columbia.

Everywhere they went the Vietnamese women exerted a magnetic appeal. Although their appearance was sombre, dressed as they were in dark simple Vietnamese clothing, they radiated warmth. As they responded to questions which the audiences asked, they gave vivid and moving descriptions about how it was to live in North and South Vietnam under the rain of bombs and shells. They produced actual pellets of anti-personnel bombs which, they explained, caused deep burns in victims. They described how people were unable to dig shelters in the lowlands to protect themselves from the air raids. Because of this they put their babies in plastic bassinets that floated in tunnels where the water came up to the mothers' armpits, or they would hang up hammocks to put their babies in and try to keep them dry. Oftentimes pregnant women died from shock during delivery. When asked about the prisons they showed pictures which they had brought with them.

They talked openly about the divisions between families where the young supported the NLF and the older people at first continued to give allegiance to the government. Gradually, though, the elders supported the Provincial Revolutionary Government with its goal of self-determination. Because they witnessed this reconciliation within families, the Vietnamese women thought national reconciliation was also possible. They also described the erosion of GI morale. American soldiers had been told they were going to fight for freedom and found instead they were there to kill women and children.

As their constant companion, Muriel developed a great admiration and affection for the three Vietnamese women. She could converse in French with Nguyen Ngoc, who was known by her third name "Dung" (pronounced Zung), and Vo Thi Te, but needed translation for Le Thi who spoke only in a Vietnamese dialect. Muriel would never forget Dung telling her, while sitting next to her on a plane, "you win people over one by one." What impressed Muriel from the beginning was how the Vietnamese women never blamed Canadians or Americans for the actions of their governments. She thought the women handled themselves very well in large gatherings but she felt they were at their best in small groups. Muriel noted the visitors' personal and political independence. They insisted on making their own decisions and establishing their own priorities. Each evening they withdrew to review the day's activities among themselves and examine their own performance. Then they would agree to the next day's agenda.

On one occasion, the local committee in Regina had invited members of the Wheat Board to meet with the Vietnamese women. The Board responded by asking to take the visitors to dinner. The Vietnamese women discussed this invitation far into the night and finally decided to refuse on the grounds that they had come as the guests of the peace groups and they did not wish to accept the hospitality of an organization which they considered capitalist. Later, as a compromise, their host invited a few members of the Wheat Board to meet with them in her home.

Muriel, Cao, Dung and Jack on Mount Royal, Montreal, 1969.

Muriel had taken unusual precautions to assure the safety of their guests by approaching the RCMP to ask for protection. She was told that police protection was not necessary but she felt sure security police covered every public meeting, if only to note who attended. Nevertheless the hosting committees were very careful. The women were never separated, always accompanied by their hosts and were billeted in the homes of Voices. When the women stopped overnight at Muriel's cottage on their way to and from Montreal for the meeting at North Hatley, Muriel was touched to see that young Vietnamese students from Montreal came and slept on the veranda to protect the visitors.

Even with all the security precautions, Muriel became conscious of her guests' enormous personal anxiety. When some Asians, unknown to the Voices, appeared in the dining room at Hart House, University of Toronto, the guests experienced a moment of panic. Another time, while walking at dusk along Spanish Banks beach in Vancouver, between the afternoon and evening meetings, the women wandered far out at low tide. It was so beautiful and peaceful there and the Voices felt their guests needed such a break from the meetings. But suddenly the Vietnamese women became conscious of their isolation, and feeling very vulnerable anxiously turned to Muriel and asked her, "why are you doing this to us?" Muriel was upset at her own thoughtlessness and the group immediately returned to the university.

She came to appreciate how in Vietnam these women's lives were always at risk. Dung told Muriel that en route she had accepted a lift from a truck driver in South Vietnam. He seemed friendly enough, but might easily have shot her in the back as she walked away from his truck. Each of the visitors had lost family members or had family members tortured in the war and one had herself been tortured in prison. All three continued to live under dreadful wartime conditions and both women from the South had risked their lives to come to Canada when they went by foot from South Vietnam to the North in order to fly from Hanoi.

Muriel would always remember the sight of Vo Thi The at Niagara Falls as she stood for a long while looking across to the United States—forbidden territory to her—through a wrought iron fence that resembled prison bars. The expression on her face said, "how can you do this to us?"

The Vietnamese women's visit inspired Muriel to keep a public focus on Vietnam. A press release issued by VOW concerning the two-week visit quoted Muriel:

> If Canada seeks to play a more active part in finding solutions to conflicts, our government can and must take action to end the tragedy of Vietnam. We deeply regret that our country while claiming to be neutral as a member of the International Control Commission, at the same time profits from increasing arms shipments to the United States for use in Vietnam. This traffic must stop.[3]

In letters to the editor, letters to the membership and each time she was called on to speak publicly, Muriel challenged Canadian attitudes and ignorance about the war in Vietnam. She often drew on authoritative sources to give people information not found in daily newspapers. In a letter to the *Advertiser-Guardian* of London, Ontario, Muriel took issue with a columnist, Joan Seager, who had expressed disgust over the criticism of the American government levelled by the famed American pediatrician Dr. Spock:

> There are many errors in her story. It is not true for instance that the Geneva Agreement "gave South Vietnam to the French." It is not true that "the Vietcong swept deep into South Vietnam." The Vietcong ARE South Vietnamese. Miss Seager writes "Vietnam was ORIGINALLY part of French Indo-China." That is a drastically limited view of history.[4]

In a rousing speech which Muriel delivered at a Town Meeting in Halifax, November 14, 1969, arranged by an ad hoc committee of citizens called the Mobilization Committee, Muriel described the visit of the Vietnamese women:

Three times in the last three years, I have spent about two weeks with the Vietnamese women. The last occasion was in July when I travelled across Canada with Mme. Dung from the Mekong River area, Mme. Cao from Saigon, and Mme. The from Hanoi. Everywhere—on a farm in Quebec, in a United Church in Niagara Falls, on University campuses in Toronto, Regina, Vancouver, in a Co-op Union Hall in Nanaimo—these women and their two male interpreters were warmly received. All six of us lived together in private homes, when we weren't living together on airplanes and public platforms.

These are the enemy. They are our sisters and brothers. They stayed one night with us on Lake Memphremagog in Quebec. They write and enquire about "monsieur Jacques" (my husband's) success with his fishing. They want to come again and enjoy the tranquility and beauty of our lake, but it will be only, as so many of their dreams, after the Americans have left Vietnam.

They met hundreds of Americans in Canada who came across the border to talk with them, or who were already here as draft resisters or deserters. I'll tell you about only one of them, Mrs. Boston, a Black woman from New York, whose son had graduated from high school to be drafted to Vietnam, and almost immediately killed. She said, through her tears in a tight embrace with her Vietnamese sisters, "I only hope that he didn't kill anybody before he was killed."

. . . Mme. Dung and Mme. Cao, who met their American sisters in Canada, who stood with Mme. The and their Canadian friends looking across Niagara Falls at the United States, would be shot as traitors to the Thieu-Ky regime if they were caught. Mme. Dung was a medical student before the war. She is now separated by the war from her husband and young children. One of her sisters is a political prisoner. She had a child in jail, and the child was kept in jail too until he was four years old. Mme. Cao was a school teacher. Her husband had to go to North Vietnam under the terms of the Geneva agreements of 1954. He will not be able to come home until after the Americans have left Vietnam. He has a 5 year old son who has never seen his father.

I love these women—and I want for them peace and reunion with their families, and the opportunity to use their great strengths and abilities to rebuild their country instead of having to defend it. And that's why all 500,000 American troops have to leave Vietnam NOW.[5]

A Second Visit from Vietnamese Women

Voices went on organizing public demonstrations through their Vietnam Mobilization Committee. Once again they decided the best public education they could do was to bring women from Indochina to Canada to speak about what was really going on. This time they co-sponsored a visit of six women and three male interpreters from Laos and North and South Vietnam, from March 29 to April 15, 1971. Delegates from Cambodia had also been invited but were unable to attend. VOW held conferences in Vancouver, Toronto, Montreal, and Quebec City with meetings, both formal and informal, in several other Canadian centres. The press paid considerable attention to this tour and published graphic information about the barbaric treatment, particularly of women prisoners. Voices too published supplements, quoting from the women's heartrending stories of torture and imprisonment. Muriel believed the Vietnamese women's tour succeeded in motivating Voice of Women to go on promoting mass actions to protest the war in Southeast Asia.

This second tour was a follow-up organized at the request of the Vietnamese Women's Committee who asked to meet with a wider section of the population. Accordingly, VOW reached out to sister organizations in the US to co-sponsor the tour. Planning and costs were shared by VOW, Women Strike for Peace (WSP), and the US Women's Liberation Movement (which included Native, Black, Asian, Chicano and Metis women).[6]

In Vancouver, Americans from the Women's Liberation Movement insisted on guarding the six guests and their translators everywhere, both outside and inside the meetings and at the private residences where they were billeted. These women were appalled at the minimal security VOW was providing. They thought, "VOW did not know what security was, not having lived in ghettos with the fear of F.B.I. undercover agents who provoke something, or right wing nuts who do something." [7]

As one report on the conference stated:

> There was the "generation-gap" to cope with (80 percent approx. were under 25) but also the racial-gap, attitude-gap and experience-gap. Maybe it was because of their youth, maybe it was because of the excitement of meeting for the first time with so many sisters of such divergent backgrounds; whatever, the atmosphere was electric. There were four different groupings within the women's liberation group itself. (1) Those who work within the system and are generally discounted by the others. They examine the Status of Women Report and make recommendations. (2) Those who think the fate of women all over the world is determined by the "system" they live in. They insist that no improvements will come about unless the system changes. Among these racism is the number one

Muriel with the hosts and Southeast Asian delegation, 1971.

cause of the Third World women. (3) Those who think other women have been sucked into fighting for male defined issues. They feel that even the great women leaders of the suffragette movement after the vote was won were bamboozled into fighting against wars (a male-defined issue) and thus lost all their momentum. And (4) the Gay Liberationists who believe that only when women turn away from men entirely and withdraw their psychological and physical dependence on men, will male supremacy end, and thereby male-defined issues and institutions.[8]

Some women, particularly those from outside the major cities and those on welfare, did not see themselves as being part of any of these groupings. Concluding her article about the six-day Vancouver conference, the reporter said:

> Though the conflicts within the conference were often bitter many of us found it a very useful political experience, partly because the differences within the women's movement were clearly revealed. These differences can no longer be ignored. Hopefully they can be resolved in such a way that we can become a powerful force, as women, in ending the war. The war is an integral part of that which oppresses all of us.[9]

Muriel recalled that the Americans did a good job in getting women to come to the conferences but she acknowledged that the atmosphere was wild. She remembered going into one session where lesbians were singing

love songs to each other—she had not heard that before! She was barred
from entering another session where Black women were meeting and was
"put down" as a white, middle class woman who could not possibly
understand what had happened to the Vietnamese women. The Vietnamese
visitors knew nothing of women's liberation as defined in the US. The male
translators did not really understand it either and when they did not understand they would laugh and this upset the lesbians. One of Muriel's happier
memories was of travelling across the country with the singer, Malvina
Reynolds, who came at her own expense from California to Vancouver and
on to Toronto. Muriel's personally stressful experiences were not reflected
in her account of the tour:

> Because I had the privilege of travelling, living and being with them
> all the time, you have asked me for some overall, and some inside,
> impressions. It does not seem important to the cause to give you
> anecdotes. They came because their organizations thought it was
> important and chose them to come. They did not have the doubts
> in advance, as many of us did, of the value of these conferences and
> face-to-face talks on this continent at this time. All of us who met
> them were moved to a very special feeling of sisterhood. Their lives
> must be saved, their families reunited, the devastation of their
> lands, killing and maiming of their children, corruption of their
> cultures must be stopped.
>
> It is heartbreaking to know that Khemphet must go back to
> living in a cave in Laos with her ten-month-old baby, whose
> chances of escaping rickets, TB or pneumonia are slim. Why?
> Because wave after wave of bombers attack Laos every day when
> the weather is good and the sun shines. It is overwhelming to know
> that Hien and Huong walked for three months carrying forty-pound
> packs on their backs, in constant danger, to get from South Vietnam
> to Hanoi to fly to Canada. Huong, a middle-aged housewife, frail
> after six years of imprisonment and torture, whose nineteen-year-
> old daughter is now in jail; and Hien, a teacher separated by the war
> from her husband and young children whom she sees rarely and for
> very short visits.
>
> I will not forget the bleak looks on the faces of Khampheng and
> Khemphet from Laos while we were in Sheila Young's living room
> in Vancouver with Dr. Inglis, chairman of Canadian Aid to Viet-
> namese Civilians. We were admiring knitted and handmade gar-
> ments and blankets, a whole roomful of them, about to be shipped
> to the children of Vietnam. The presence of women from the
> Laotian Women's Patriotic Association and the certain knowledge
> that we now have of the suffering and the need of clothing and

medicine for hundreds of thousands of their people have speeded up the efforts to find ways of shipping supplies to Laos and Cambodia. (The U.S. Senate Subcommittee on Refugees estimates 300,000 refugees before the recent invasion, of a total population in Laos of 2,000,000. Laos, one of the poorest countries in the world has been bombed by the U.S. since 1964.)

What did I learn, from talks with them, from hearing them talk, laugh, and sing, from just becoming their friend? They told us very directly that we must have unity, flexibility, patience and good organization, if we are to have a part in bringing about fundamental social change—ending the war, doing away with racism, repression, poverty, miseducation. And I would add, from knowing them, that we also must have discipline and courage and a deep understanding of the situation.[10]

Notes

1. Letter to VOW membership, 1969. NAC MG 28 I 218 Vol. 3, File 28.
2. PANS MG 1 Vol. 2910, No. 39.
3. VOW press release, 17 July 1969.
4. *London Advertiser-Guardian*, 28 August 1969.
5. PANS MG 1 Vol. 2932.
6. Letters to VOW from US organizations.*
7. Interview with Lydia Sayle and Kay Inglis.
8. "Indo-Chinese Women's Conference, U.B.C. Vancouver, April 1-6, 1971." NAC MG 28 I 218, Vol. 3.
9. Ibid.
10. "Looking back on the Conference on Indochina," National VOW Newsletter, Vol. 8, No. 2 (June 1971). PANS MG 1 Vol. 2930, No. 35 .

Note: * indicates document awaiting archival deposit.

Chapter 11

Speaking Her Peace

Communicating with the Government

As president of the national Voice of Women/Voix des femmes, Muriel's main task was to communicate with government, with the public and with the VOW membership. Letters, briefs and petitions to the Prime Minister and members of cabinet abounded. Following every interchange with politicians, Muriel would issue media releases informing the public of VOW's views. She would mail copies of the releases to her council members across the country with requests that they in turn distribute them to local media. Similarly, statements and resolutions passed at the executive, council or general meetings were always released to the media across the country.

Voice of Women's National Research Committee produced a spate of briefs to government during Muriel's term as president. In her regular letters to the membership, Muriel invited members to participate in this research and she also encouraged regional members to initiate briefs. Members not only helped one another to prepare the briefs but, whenever possible, several women presented them as a collective effort.

Occasionally VOW got a pat on the back for their communication with government. Freda Hanford, a BC member, wrote to Muriel:

> I think the VOW leaders do the tasks excellently well for which VOW was founded. Tommy Douglas during a recent campaign on Vancouver Island is said to have remarked that the VOW briefs are the best ever presented to the federal government.[1]

In 1968, Muriel and Ursula Franklin presented a brief to the External

Thérèse Casgrain with Muriel presenting vow brief to Minister Mitchell Sharp.

Affairs Committee of the House of Commons entitled, "The Effects of Defense Production and Trade and Commerce Agreements On Canada's Foreign Policy." While pursuing information on military contracts, Ursula came across a couple of very interesting catalogues advertising arms that Canada was prepared to sell duty-free, as free trade in arms sales between Canada and the United States had existed ever since the Second World War. These catalogues were the "bible" of representatives of Canadian business, industry and commerce, and were to be found in many Canadian consulates in the United States and in embassies abroad. The VOW brief stated:

> In looking for constraints that have made it difficult to change our foreign policy with regard to the war in Vietnam we have become increasingly aware that the foreign policy of our government is frequently predetermined by commercial arrangements which the government has entered into over a number of years—without reference to Parliament and without adequate public discussion of the implications.
>   . . . We emphasize that the Defense Production Department actively solicits research contracts for Canadian research establishments and advertises in its publications and circulars the specific competence of various Canadian development and research laboratories. While we regret that Canadian manufacturers find it convenient and profitable to support the U.S. war economy, we insist that the primary responsibility for this lies with our government. The increase in volume and diversity of this trade has occurred because of the considerable advantages that trade with the U.S.A. under the Defense Production Sharing Agreement offers to Canadian manufacturers.[2]

In a lengthy President's Letter to the membership about the use of this brief, Muriel reported:

> On March 7, Jeanne Duval, Ann Gertler and I discussed the brief in Ottawa with M. Dubé, Chairman of the External Affairs Committee, and with M. Pelletier, parliamentary assistant to Paul Martin. . . . We showed M. Dubé and M. Pelletier the two books *Canadian Defense Commodity Index* and *Defense Sharing Handbook* to which Ursula referred in her brief, and we had the distinct impression that neither of them had seen them before.[3]

Unfortunately their findings were not publicized. Ursula and Muriel had called a press conference in Toronto on March 5 to release their brief but no reporters came because the day before Daniel Johnson, the premier of Quebec, had died suddenly. Years later Muriel heard on the CBC radio

Newsmagazine that some reporter had discovered similar catalogues which
were still being circulated abroad and reported it as a brand new discovery.
Looking back, Muriel felt that VOW often had problems being taken seriously by the press.

> We were tearing our hair out and no one was paying any attention.
> People had to wait until some man in authority said so!

The government very often ignored what was said in the VOW briefs as
well. In 1965 and again in 1966, VOW proposed a commission on the rights
of Native people. Then, in their national brief to the Royal Commission on
the Status of Women in 1968, VOW drew attention to the loss of status of
Native women who married non-Native men and called for a change in
policy to give them the same rights as Native men who married non-Native
women. In this brief they quoted Article V of the United Nations Declaration
on the Elimination of Discrimination Against Women which says:

> Women shall have the same rights as men to acquire, change or
> retain their nationality. Marriage to an alien shall not automatically
> affect the nationality of the wife either rendering her stateless or by
> forcing on her the nationality of her husband.[4]

VOW called for the Royal Commission to recommend a change in the
Indian Act. Yet the report of the Royal Commission on the Status of Women
contained no reference to the recommendations of the Voice of Women
concerning Native women. Muriel recalled:

> We were the only women's group that wasn't native that called
> attention to that fact and it didn't get into the final report. I think
> most of the people on that committee had not begun to think of it
> at all.

Muriel was always conscious of the need for resources for Native
people. In a letter of support to Mary Thompson of Vancouver, who was
going as a conference delegate to Ottawa, she stated:

> There is no doubt in my mind that you could speak eloquently in
> the name of the VOW for spending of government money on health,
> welfare and education rather than on arms and I'm sure the VOW
> would support putting emphasis on the tragedy of not increasing
> health services to Indians and Eskimos at this time.[5]

On many occasions Muriel expressed to government her opposition to

Muriel presenting brief to Grace McInnes, only woman in parliament at the time, 1969.

NATO. She insisted that armed defence was no guarantee of peace. The Voice of Women had, for a number of years, been advocating a withdrawal from NORAD, and an independent policy on NATO including a refusal by Canadian Forces to employ nuclear weapons and a refusal to allow them on Canadian soil. In her speeches, Muriel frequently maintained that the money Canada spent on NATO forces in Europe did not contribute to security, but rather kept tensions there alive. She further insisted that NATO, as a military alliance of western powers, was what prevented the United Nations from succeeding in peace-making. To her, NATO, as a regional alliance, offered no security either to Canada or to the world. Muriel maintained that the very existence of NATO and the Warsaw Pact fuelled the arms race.

Just before she attended the women's conference in Paris in the spring of 1968, members in Montreal asked Muriel to take advantage of her trip to Europe to go first to the Hague where the NATO nuclear planning group was meeting in mid-April. Canada was at that time a member of this group. Although she had very recently met the minister of defence, Leo Cadieux, in Ottawa, the Montreal Voices wanted Muriel to follow him to the NATO meeting to register their concerns. The meetings had already begun by the time Muriel arrived, and the minister declined to meet her. Instead he sent an official of the Department of External Affairs. Muriel presented him with a list of strongly worded questions for the NATO foreign ministers, such as:

> Although the UN charter envisioned regional organizations able to deal "with local disputes" by peaceful negotiations (not by armament escalation), how can a political alliance stretching from the

Black Sea across the Atlantic, but excluding more than half the
nations of Europe, masquerade as a peace-keeper?[6]

Later that day, the NATO nuclear planning group announced that they
had decided against an ABM system for Europe at that time. Referring to her
own meeting with the official, Muriel wryly commented in a subsequent
newsletter, "unfortunately, we cannot conclude that these two events are in
any way cause-and-effect!"[7]

On February 19, 1969, Muriel headed a delegation including Thérèse
Casgrain, Kay Macpherson, Ursula Franklin, Louise Gareau, Dorothy Henderson
and Elsie Saumure to present the brief, "Some Aspects of Canada's Foreign
and Defence Policies," to Mitchell Sharp, minister of external affairs.
Quoting Sharp, *The Toronto Star* headline characterized the meeting as "No
Meeting of Minds."[8] Sharp insisted that nobody had yet produced a viable
alternative to NATO while the delegation argued that neither NATO, nor any
other military alliance could defend Canada with its modest population and
enormous land mass. The women rejected the value of Canada playing the
balance-of-power game. They believed that the country's security would be
better assured through non-alignment, disarmament and a stepped-up program of assistance to the poor nations.

Their brief argued for the creation by parliament of a special disarmament agency to be responsible for Canadian disarmament and conversion to
production for peaceful purposes, Canada's withdrawal from NATO, the
termination of the NORAD agreement, Canada remaining outside the Organization of American States, and the immediate diplomatic recognition of the
People's Republic of China.

When the women advocated a special disarmament agency, Sharp
replied with a shocked, "do you mean unilateral disarmament?" as though
Canada were a big power in the same league as the US, the USSR or China.
Muriel was disappointed with the minister and felt he was not really
listening to them. Trying hard to salvage something positive from the
interview, Muriel spoke of VOW's strong approval of the steps being taken
by the government towards the establishment of diplomatic relations with
the People's Republic of China. If Muriel had a *bête noir* it was NATO and
she would continue to oppose this military alliance on many occasions for
many years.

It was not only at the national level that VOW was presenting well-
researched papers. Freda Pryce of Vancouver wrote a strong statement
opposing the proposed underground nuclear tests on Amchitka Island in the
Aleutians.[9] Lille d'Easum, also of Vancouver, published a fine pamphlet,
"Hazards of the Peaceful Atom,"[10] and Solange Vincent prepared an insight-
ful pamphlet, "Quebec After October 1970."[11]

VOW repeatedly protested nuclear tests. Muriel issued a press release

September 3, 1968, on the occasion of France exploding its first H bomb.

> It is with great regret that Voice of Women learned that France had its first H bomb exploded in the Pacific. Voice of Women feels that France should put her scientific potential at the service of progress for humanity instead of contributing to the tragic proliferation of nuclear armament.
>
> The American scientist and Nobel Prize winner Linus Pauling has repeatedly declared that "clean" bombs are not harmless because they have radioactive effects which will remain in the atmosphere for centuries and can cause the birth of retarded children or children suffering from leukaemia, bone cancer and other serious diseases. The French biologist Jean Rostand is also of the opinion that an increase of radioactivity, even in small quantity, will have disastrous effects on genetics.
>
> Voice of Women deplores that France has judged this ephemeral scientific success more important than the physical and mental health of tomorrow's citizens.[12]

Regional branches of VOW undertook careful studies of government policy statements and Muriel would often be called upon to issue national statements reflecting their common analysis. A public commentary she made took issue with the Canadian government's White Paper, "Foreign Policy for Canadians," released in August 1970. She challenged the government's choice of economic growth as a paramount value.

> "Foreign policy," says the paper, "is shaped by the value judgments of the government at any given time." This is a "given time." What values would be appropriate for this government and this people at this time?
>
> Life on this planet is facing extinction. There are limited supplies of everything on this earth, including air, water, wilderness, and places to dump sewage. In an escalating arms race the world spends over $14 million an hour on nuclear, chemical and other weapons which could make it uninhabitable. Governments, to feed the greedy war machine, and private industry, for profit, are willing to deplete our resources and take appalling risks with our environment. Our own country is number five in world arms sales, is the largest supplier of arms to the United States, and wastes millions annually on its contribution to an international program of chemical and biological defence research.
>
> What are the value judgments which permit our government to continue with these programs? What are the vested interests of

government departments, of rapacious industry, of luxury-loving consumers which make it so difficult to feed the hungry—the two-thirds of the world's pre-school children who suffer from malnutrition to the extent that it retards their growth and permanently damages their health? What are the value judgments which allow a foreign power to train its bombers in Canadian skies before they go to kill the people and destroy the present and future natural life of Southeast Asia?

Whatever they are—they are inadequate for this "given time" and they make of this world and of Canada as a part of it a house divided against itself. The way of sanity and survival, along which Canadian foreign policy must go, requires daring, courage, and imagination.

In practical terms, it requires non-alignment, which this report flatly rejects. The polar star of this report is United States as our best friend. So, in spite of all the evidence that our membership in NATO and NORAD make a barrier between us and most of the rest of the world, there we remain. . . . The criteria of peace, independence and quality of life could well have been the framework for the development of specific policies, and they would have aroused the enthusiasm of the Canadian people, especially our disenchanted youth.[13]

Communicating Within Voice of Women

Advice, critiques and complaints from VOW members regularly crossed Muriel's desk either concerning the actions of the executive or the policies and programs VOW was promoting. Her replies to each correspondent illustrated her great skill as a communicator. She was never defensive and admitted responsibility or apologized whenever appropriate. Muriel warmly acknowledged each person's concern and then expressed her own views with tact and clarity. She was careful to straighten out miscommunications and misperceptions among members and welcomed their involvement in issues.

A council member once wrote to Muriel of her concerns over a decision made at a council meeting she had attended.[14] VOW had been asked to circulate a questionnaire which had been developed by the Canadian Peace Research Institute (CPRI), another non-governmental peace organization, and had decided against doing so. This correspondent was uneasy and felt their decision was too hasty and biased. She wanted the matter re-opened at the annual meeting, but had since been told by another council member that this was not possible. She felt this was undemocratic and worried that the negative decision taken at the council meeting was the result of poor relations between VOW and CPRI.

Muriel replied:

> It is hard to begin to write a letter to you which is important and so
> long overdue. This job requires time and energy and imagination
> and sometimes I run out of them. I do appreciate your very kind and
> supportive letter which reached me at the executive meeting,
> particularly in view of your concerns about the way the executive
> has been functioning. Of course I have to share responsibility for
> any weakness....
>
> I would just like to confirm that it is quite proper for you to
> bring up any question that you think is appropriate at either the
> council or the annual meeting. If you plan to re-open the question
> that disturbed you I would appreciate your letting me know in
> advance, but you don't even have to do that. I think this question
> should go to the council rather than to the annual meeting, don't
> you?
>
> As you know, the executive does not make policy decisions but
> it must deal with matters as they come up. Perhaps this question-
> naire does border on a policy decision but we did not think of it in
> those terms at the time. I do trust the competence of the people who
> advised us against participating. You have received contrary advice
> and you should certainly feel free to re-open the question.
>
> As to the relations in general between the VOW and the CPRI,
> as you know, there was quite a crisis in this relationship with fault,
> no doubt, on both sides and a good deal of bitterness. . . . However,
> this happened several years ago, actually in the fall and winter of
> 1962–63, and I assure you it had not the slightest bearing on this
> executive decision. VOW did more than any other group to support
> and raise money for the establishment of the CPRI. When Dr. Alcock
> was in Halifax last year, I helped to plan the public meeting for him
> and entertained him in our home. I'd be glad to tell you more about
> it some time if you want to discuss it with me.[15]

Muriel's letters to the executive and council were models of clear, crisp
communication, generally written in point form. But her efficiency never
disguised her warmth. She constantly invited members to contribute their
views and was very conscious of involving them in policymaking.

In the late sixties VOW became increasingly decentralized and the
executive encouraged grass roots participation. In the early days its leadership promoted national campaigns such as the baby tooth campaign to
measure strontium 90 and the anti-war-toys campaigns, and the national
office sent out educational literature. Later it became evident that women
were more interested in actions and issues promoted by their own branches.

Also, with very limited financial resources it became more and more difficult for the national council and executive itself to meet as often as they would have liked, coming as they did from all parts of the country. As a result, the national executive began encouraging local and regional groups to take on the responsibility for preparing national briefs, and by the early seventies provincial branches even edited and published the national newsletter.

Two problems emerged as branches increasingly initiated their own programs. Firstly, issues proliferated and there was a constant debate about which issues Voice of Women should take up. Secondly, some branches condemned others' actions as inappropriate when these actions generated national publicity which they felt was unfavourable to VOW's image. Some long-term members held that VOW should confine itself to issues of nuclear disarmament and education for peace. At the other end of the spectrum, others felt Voices should speak out on any issue of social injustice and use public protests to get the attention of press and politicians.

Muriel sometimes used letters of complaint from Voices to broaden the dialogue over VOW policies. She received several letters in the summer of 1968 concerning two incidents which disturbed certain BC members. They objected to the presence of some Voices at a noisy demonstration when Prime Minister Trudeau was attending a Liberal fundraising dinner. They further objected to the participation of some Ottawa members in a demonstration on Parliament Hill against Rule 75C, which was to limit the time allowed for parliamentary debate. The Voices had been invited by some young members of the New Democratic Party to join in public opposition to this rule. One Vancouver member wrote to Muriel:

> Some time ago Vancouver branch was opposed to and voted against active participation in "peace" demonstrations by mass groups because of a certain violent and destructive element which seemed to invade these marches and demonstrations, causing more harm than good to the cause being espoused. . . . Urge a directive go out from [the] National [office] requesting that all branches exercise utmost decorum as to how they allow VOW name to be associated with demonstrations and also how members act in an individual capacity where their actions might be interpreted as VOW action and bring about unpleasant experiences.[16]

After checking the facts with the Ottawa members Muriel replied to the Vancouver women. Her letter was direct and tactful. She described the situation through the eyes of the Ottawa members and then agreed with the Vancouver women that representing VOW publicly is a serious matter and encouraged them to raise it for further policy discussion at the annual meeting. However, she did not consent to take any action forcing members to abstain from participating in demonstrations. She wrote:

> Lorraine Chaplin [of Ottawa] wrote on August 24 expressing her distress that you had not checked with Ottawa about what actually happened. She also wrote, "The clipping upon which the letters were based—apparently—makes no reference to violence, lack of restraint or failure to reach a reasoned conclusion on the part of anyone who took part in the demonstration; nor was there. It was a perfectly peaceful demonstration, addressed by representatives of the three opposition Parties. VOW members who were there . . . as individuals, carried no placards at all."
>
> It is true, as I think we would all agree, that any kind of action is open to misrepresentation by the press. An organization such as ours dealing with controversial matters is particularly exposed to that kind of thing.
>
> On the other hand it is important that individual members take seriously their utterances and actions. We all need to be extremely responsible if we are to make any progress towards achieving our objectives.
>
> But we cannot isolate ourselves from other groups and it is in this area that we are all called upon from time to time to make decisions. The point you have raised will certainly be thoroughly discussed at the Annual Meeting which has been set up so that a maximum of time can be given to the development of policy and programs for the coming year. I hope your group will be represented there. You realize that this has been an on-going dialogue within the VOW from the beginning. Perhaps it is becoming more difficult to accommodate various points of view. I doubt whether it can be settled once and for all but it certainly needs to be honestly faced again at this Annual Meeting.[17]

Muriel was always given to consulting with other "wise heads." She wrote to Nellie Peterson, an experienced council member from Mayerthorpe, Alberta, and asked for her thoughts regarding the objections levelled at the Ottawa women and for her opinion on whether Rule 75C was something VOW should be concerned about.[18] Muriel found Nellie's reply so thought-provoking that she circulated it widely. Nellie wrote:

> I can't get very disturbed about whatever activity our members indulge in! There is inevitably a wearying that overtakes people confined to one form only of protest, e.g., the Vietnam war, U.S. arms shipments, ABMs, etc. These seem to many not only far away,

but almost beyond influence. Small wonder then that they turn to actively participating in protests against problems on their own back steps—if they don't do this, they simply tend to drop out.

Perhaps we do need to consider at the annual meeting this whole aspect of the area of VOW concern. There's no doubt in my mind but that the issues of significance in maintaining, or rather obtaining, peace are the main ones. But it is probably necessary to recognize that any organization ceases to function, even in that field which is its major concern, unless it can engage in immediate action on subsidiary issues which are, or even only appear to be of considerable importance.

Rule 75C is as good an illustration of the point I'm trying to make as any other. Used discreetly it possibly could be more useful than harmful but I think it certainly can be successfully argued that repression of democracy begins with just such abrogation of power to the few. The Pentagon—the military-industrial complex of the U.S.A.—has been able to dominate good policies mainly because Congress failed for so long to challenge "cabinet" decisions. It seems to me that Rule 75C could result in passage of government measures without much, or any public knowledge; sometimes governments hesitate when they know a parliamentary (prolonged) debate can lead to news media publicity that arouses public senti-ment. In other words VOW may quite properly be involved if VOW members feel, as I do, that there could quite easily be a connecting link between Rule 75C and government measures that in the interests of peace we would most strongly object to.

I don't know where the line should or could be drawn by executive or council decision; or for that matter by annual meeting without destroying VOW. Issues are involved: housing may not on the surface seem to be a peace organization's concern but the deep internal unrest which wide-spread housing shortage may cause, could be a factor in accepting war contracts to keep the economy booming, taxes coming in and subsidized housing possible! Wars have all too often been the means of taking people's minds off home-made problems. Moon shots may do the trick but only temporarily! Economic depression in the west through failure of grain markets is surely related to the knuckle-headedness of men who can explore outer space but who can't find ways to get food to the starving. In a complicated world VOW can hardly expect to remain simply anti-war and retain the allegiance of people aware of the interrelationship of seemingly disparate events. . . .

Don't let those who protest this or that, that VOW does in various places worry you! You'll get protests whether VOW does or doesn't. Let the ship roll with the waves a bit—it won't go to pieces that way, even if the passengers get a bit sea sick at times.[19]

An Inclusive Approach

During the next two years the debate over which issues and problems ought to be addressed continued within VOW. Several older members, worried over its declining membership, felt that VOW was dissipating its energies. In a thoughtful paper, "A Criticism of the Present VOW Policy," written in 1971, Freda Hanford wrote:

> As an organization the VOW, like a harassed mother, is trying to help many causes, as if they were all children in trouble. We are not pausing to ask if we can help effectively or if we are wasting our limited resources of funds and energy to no purpose.[20]

Another woman wrote:

> At the present time I think VOW is involved in too many projects, and I do not agree with the policy of "doing your own thing." Why belong to a group if you can do it on your own? Discussions of the dangers or calculated risks of the use of nuclear energy for peaceful purposes, or the plight of the minorities and the poor, or pollution, conservation, or Vietnam, are all valuable and important, but not as important as working to rid the world of nuclear weapons and the continuing threat of nuclear war.
>
> . . . One does not have to belong to VOW to protest against pollution or poverty or discrimination; there are already groups to which we could belong. We do need a group and many voices to speak against nuclear war and the arms race and the international traffic in weaponry. We also need far more public awareness and support for the work of the United Nations and its agencies. We should support peace research more vigorously, and press for the establishment of a Ministry for Peace and Disarmament. We should be helping to get less war-oriented text books into the school system, less violence and war glorification into children's books, films and television.[21]

But Muriel and Kay both felt that Voice of Women should not limit itself to a specific set of issues, much less to a program defined by the national executive or council. They recognized the interconnections between the many problems that lead to war. In reply to these members' complaints that VOW was spreading itself too thin, Kay wrote an eloquent memo to "members concerned about VOW/Vdf's multitudinous activities," reflecting her own and Muriel's convictions:

> Many of those who have been in VOW/Vdf for a long time have come to think that everything is inter-related; to obtain peace (unless it is [the Roman historian] Tacitus' kind—"They make a desert and they call it peace") we have to remove the causes of war. The causes of war are in general economic; a fight for markets, spheres of influence, and raw materials on the one hand; and a fight for self-determination, ownership of natural resources, and equality of opportunity on the other. When we look deeper, we find prejudice, social injustice, discrimination, education, propaganda, and power play are all part of the pattern.
>
> Many persons argue that to work for peace is not enough. Social justice and the survival of man must also claim our attention. To remove nuclear weapons but to pollute or populate ourselves out of existence does not make sense either.
>
> If we can, through a wide variety of concerns, bring more people to understand the connections between nuclear weapons and poverty, between war and markets, between Vietnam and black Americans, Portuguese colonial peoples, the Greeks, or the movement for an independent French Canada, then we are contributing to a better understanding of what faces us in working for peace and disarmament.
>
> One final word. We need everyone—but everyone does not have to do the same thing. The strength of VOW/Vdf is that it can combine the efforts of women who write letters, research briefs, walk or picket, interview MPs, support abortion caravans, fast; who sit at home talking on a phone-in radio program, who knit, who act with PTA, ratepayers, and other groups; who help draft dodgers, or house young people, who do dozens of other things with their time and talents, and who do this without worrying too much about what the next VOW/Vdf member is doing—provided our ultimate aim is a peaceful, disarmed and just world for our children and all children.[22]

In retrospect, Muriel was happy that she and the VOW council had taken an inclusive approach to the many issues brought by the membership because it did widen their understanding of the interrelationships between problems and it widened their own network as well. Muriel commented:

> Looking back I feel so much stronger now for having gone along with that and seen the relationship between presenting a brief to the Royal Commission on the Status of Women and the lack of rights

for Native women in Canada. It did have something to do with peace and we quoted the Declaration of Human Rights and said that as members of the UN, Canada had this obligation to its Native women.

Another example . . . was ahead of its time. . . . At a board meeting during the time of the Pipeline Debate we passed a resolution that no development of a pipeline should take place in the north until there was proper testing of the impact on the environment. I took that resolution to a conference sponsored by the Canadian Commission for UNESCO and because of it the Canadian Wildlife Federation looked to us for support.

Muriel understood that as president she was the focus for complaints and she did not take them personally. At least one appreciative Calgary woman recognized Muriel's lot as president of VOW was not an easy one. She wrote:

You are one of the most charming, tactful, conscientious people I have met. Combining all those "firsts" in one person makes you pretty well unique. Secure in the faith that your balance, objectivity and sense of humour will survive my outbursts of petulance, I keep sending off complaints, protests (and goodness knows what else!) in your general direction. Please believe, you are meant to be the reception centre, but not the recipient of my criticism.... As leader and peacemaker among such a group of strong-minded and frequently highly emotional women as VOW members appear to be, you have done much good and no harm at all that I can see. For all of it, thank you. And carry on![23]

Notes

1. Letter from Freda Hanford to Muriel Duckworth, 13 April 1969.*
2. PANS MG 1 Vol. 2932.
3. President's Letter, April 1968.*
4. Brief submitted to the Royal Commission on the Status of Women by Voice of Women. PANS MG 1 Vol. 2918, No. 37.
5. Letter from M. Duckworth to Mary Thompson, 19 March 1968.*
6. "Concerning Nuclear Armament and the Existence of NATO," National VOW Newsletter, Vol. 6, No 2, (June 1968). PANS MG 1 Vol. 2930, No. 34.
7. Ibid.
8. NAC MG 28 I 218 Vol. 9, File 6.
9. PANS MG 1 Vol. 2932.
10. Ibid.
11. Solange, Vincent, "Quebec After October 1970." Toronto: Voice of Women, Fall 1971. PANS MG 1 Vol. 2932.

12. Press Release, Sept. 3, 1968.*
13. Duckworth VOW Correspondence and Papers, June 1969. PANS MG 1 Vol. 2902, No. 4.
14. Duckworth VOW Correspondence and Papers, September 1969. PANS MG 1 Vol. 2902, No. 6.
15. Letter from M. Duckworth to Margaret Fitch. PANS MG 1 Vol. 2902, No. 5.
16. NAC MG 28 I 218 Vol. 21, File 8.
17. Letter to some Vancouver members of VOW. PANS MG 1 Vol. 2902, No. 6.
18. Letter from M. Duckworth to Nellie Peterson, July 1969. PANS MG 1 Vol. 2902, No 4.
19. Letter from Nellie Peterson to M. Duckworth, August 1969. PANS MG 1 Vol. 2902, No. 4.
20. Paper by Freda Hanford, 1971. PANS MG 1 Vol. 2903, No. 1.
21. Letter to M. Duckworth, 16 February 1971. NAC MG 28 I 218 Vol. 21, No. 2.
22. NAC MG 28 I 218 Vol. 15, File 4.
23. NAC MG 28 I 218 Vol. 28, File 5.

Note: * indicates document awaiting archival deposit.

Chapter 12

Putting Pacifism to the Test

The War Measures Act
and the Front de Libération de Québec (FLQ)

At the time of the FLQ crisis in Quebec in 1970, the history of the Voice of Women and Muriel's own personal history compelled her to publicly protest the invocation of the War Measures Act. Having been raised in the province of Quebec, she had an appreciation that few English Canadians outside the province had of the feelings of Quebeckers. She understood how contempt for their language and unequal treatment in government and business could lead to a movement for independence among many ordinary Quebeckers, and she saw the FLQ as the extreme example of this protest.

Muriel had seen an English Protestant minority dominate the French Canadian textile workers in Magog, her home town. She also recalled how very reluctant English farmers were to sell land to French Canadians. But from her formative years positive impressions lingered as well. Her mother had great respect for the local Catholic curé and counted him among her friends. When Muriel graduated, her teacher encouraged her to write her high school valedictory speech in French, and at university she studied French with great enthusiasm and appreciation. Throughout the years when she organized Home and School Associations in Quebec, her goal in that divided school system was to have all parents, French and English, Catholic and Protestant, unite their efforts in a common organization in the interests of the province's children.

Muriel was immensely pleased when VOW members in the early 1960s unanimously declared, "that VOW, proud of its bilingual ties, urges the Canadian government to adopt legislation to establish Canada as a bilingual and bicultural nation, in order that our two cultures may flourish together in peace and mutual respect."[1] Jeanne Duval, a delegate from Quebec, spoke prophetically to this resolution:

> You will forgive me, but the Quebec delegation is most anxious that this resolution be passed unanimously, if possible. The situation in Quebec is much more serious and alarming than many people realize. There is tension and anxiety and those in responsibility are a little afraid.
>
> . . . I am completely convinced as . . . are so many French

Canadians, that if something is not done there may be no such thing as the Canada we now know in four years.[2]

In 1962 Solange Chaput-Rolland and Gwenthalyn Graham, both members of the Voice of Women, first met on a train when a coachload of Voices went from Montreal to Ottawa to meet with Prime Minister Lester Pearson. The two women engaged in an animated discussion about the political situation of French Canadians and the result of this exchange of views was their subsequent joint book, *Dear Enemies*. When it was published in January 1964, two hundred Voices and their guests gathered to fete the two authors in Toronto at a luncheon.[3]

Muriel recalled the lengths to which VOW went to make their organization bilingual, even before the "Bi and Bi" commission. In a background paper prepared for a council meeting in 1969, Ann Gertler described their struggle:

> For those who have attempted to live it [bilingualism] in Voice of Women/La Voix des Femmes, it has been a learning experience which contrasts with the delays and exasperations of trying to do the job with inadequate time, energy and money. And it should be pointed out that bilingualism in VOW began in 1961, years before André Laurendeau made it fashionable, not only because of the need for a Toronto-founded organization to communicate with seven million Canadians, but because we felt that the practice of bilingualism was part of our work in building a more peaceful world. It was for this reason that we testified before the Bi and Bi Commission. . . . The responsibility for meeting the press and public in French has been a heavy task for few hands—Thérèse Casgrain, Elsie Saumure, Louise Gareau, to name some.[4]

With this history, it was not surprising that VOW came out so strongly against the War Measures Act. Muriel was at a council meeting in Toronto at the time of its proclamation. The women were horrified to hear that Prime Minister Trudeau had called out the troops, and that many people were being arrested without charges being laid. Immediately, Quebec members issued a press release:

> To fight against violence in all its forms is the reason our peace organization was formed. It therefore goes without saying that VOW/Vdf supports effective measures to apprehend the murderers and kidnappers. We feel nevertheless that this is only part of the task to bring justice to Quebec. We feel that the violence that has come to Quebec is a symptom of serious problems, and that until

these are faced up to and resolved the danger of more violence remains. We fear that the military-police regime now in effect will provoke rather than prevent more violence. . . . We feel that the War Measures Act was too harsh a measure to bring into force, that it multiplies injustices, and creates a climate of suspicion and repression unfavourable for finding the terrorists or for resolving the problems that led up to these events.[5]

But some of the western Voices objected to their organization's involvement and position on the War Measure's Act. One wrote:

> I think Voice of Women could help to provide a steadying influence by continuing to work for peace and disarmament and by not being diverted by the injustices and tragedies in Quebec. Violence is upon us, and if we are drawn in to supporting it, we shall only help to bring harsher repressive measures upon us all.[6]

Such sentiments only caused Muriel and her colleagues to redouble their efforts to encourage Canadians to communicate their opposition to the War Measures Act which had been proclaimed in October 1970. To help this happen they published and widely distributed a special broadsheet which reproduced the text of the emergency regulations; outlined what the act meant to the public; and quoted articles and statements by the Canadian Civil Liberties Union, the Canadian Council of Churches, the three largest labour organizations in Quebec, Jacques Hébert (president of the Quebec Human Rights League) and Professor James Eayrs of Toronto.[7] VOW advocated that independent observers be allowed access to the detainees to insure fair and humane treatment of prisoners and that any new legislation replacing the War Measures Act be temporary, subject to review by parliament.

Finally, in March 1972, VOW submitted a brief to the Citizens' Commission of Inquiry into the War Measures Act, and pointed out that the government had never stated a valid reason for the use of the act, and that there was no evidence of "real or apprehended insurrection" against the elected government. The Voice of Women blamed both the government and the media during the FLQ crisis for the reaction of the people of Canada. They objected that news and commentary were censored across the country and that the media sensationalized the news in ways that played on the fear of revolution in Canada. Muriel felt that many people in Canada failed to see that the government's arbitrary method of handling the FLQ crisis was counter to the concept of democracy and that it threatened youth groups, leftist organizations and private individuals.

A Pacifist Leader

Muriel's feelings, understanding and reactions were tempered and enriched by her own efforts to live as a pacifist and by the experience she had gained over many years of working with people in organizations and in adult education. Her negotiating skills were so well developed that they appeared second nature. Muriel had an aptitude for putting people at ease. Her manner was very informal and she talked in a simple and straightforward way. Because she was such a good listener and showed such personal interest in everyone she met, people readily felt drawn to her. She laughed or cried very spontaneously. The personal tragedies of others struck her deeply and she would weep openly as she listened or talked of their sorrows. While her manner was gentle, she learned to project an image of tenacity and strength whenever she challenged politicians or officials.

Questions of violence and social justice preoccupied Muriel. Whenever she saw people violently rebelling against social injustice either in Canada or in other countries she would harken back to a distinction Ursula Franklin made between violence as the response of those who are without power—the "resourceless"—and the violence of aggressive powers. During her President's Report at the eighth AGM in Calgary, September 20 to 23, 1968, Muriel talked about violence:

> Ursula Franklin writes, "Where do we stand on violence? Person-ally, I believe so firmly that the means are the end, that I cannot see a just end coming through unjust means. But I wish to distinguish the violence of resourcelessness, which is forced upon those who are deprived of constructive means to security, their basic human right, from the violence of organized force as a tool of power (à la Chicago police), the terror of the status quo.
>
> "It must be our task to point out how lack of practical response to the constructive challenges for change creates the violence of resourcelessness, and that real changes in the social organization can reduce or eliminate the violence of resourcelessness. It is the drift to the violence of aggressive power, however, that gives me the greatest sense of urgency. I am afraid of the drift towards fascism under the guise of 'law and order.' VOW has refused to accept the use of force or the threat of force as a tool for settling disputes among nations. We cannot accept the same tool for settling disputes within our own countries."[8]

While Muriel believed in non-violent resistance for the Voice of Women, even as a pacifist she would not condemn those who were engaged in the violent overthrow of repressive regimes. Though she believed that peace was, in the end, impossible without justice, she also recognized that there could be tensions between the demands of pacificism and the demands of justice. One way to resolve those tensions, she believed, was for women in unison to use their voices to empower those without resources. Both pacifist and egalitarian, Muriel articulated her vision of a peaceful world and she lived this radical vision in a very civilized way.

In her day-to-day experience within the Voice of Women, pacifism never meant negating or smothering conflict. She recognized that VOW had never gone smoothly since it was founded. But she attributed the differences between women to their passionate search for peace and saw their disagreements as a creative form of tension. She felt she had never belonged to any organization whose members were so passionately committed to their cause. Their anxiety over international crises was immediate and their desire for peace profound; this intensity, not to mention their different political perspectives, created problems. At times, every woman was sure she was right and when different solutions were proposed, feelings ran high. Muriel commented:

> There were people who joined the Voice of Women who dropped out because they did not think we were radical enough. There were those who expected of us that we would accept the far left agenda. Others were concerned that we were getting too political and that we would turn out to be partisan. At the Annual General Meetings there was a lot of debate over resolutions, and we were often the basket for a lot of women's concerns. There was no other place in Canada for women to express them. Later, with the establishment of the National Action Committee for the Status of Women (NAC), the pressure was off us to support what every woman had on her mind.
>
> I probably had an idealized notion that you could keep people together with the same objectives even though they saw such different paths to meeting their objectives. I had never been involved in anything where people had such passionate feelings. They really felt that it was a matter of life and death. When you feel that it is a matter of life and death you're bound to be passionate, to make sure that life triumphs and death doesn't.[9]

Comparing her work in VOW to her efforts in other organizations, Muriel felt that almost everything she had previously done had gone along calmly and smoothly, except perhaps the time during the Duplessis era in Quebec, when she had insisted at a large meeting of the Home and School that they not give in an inch to his government. While trying to keep the web of relationships intact within VOW, Muriel trod some delicate ground. She was sometimes caught between supporting the women who sought more radical expression of opposition and those who felt that such measures would never win over mainstream Canadians.

> I had a lot of self-doubts over my ability to do it. At the same time I had this feeling that you go along with people as long as you are going in the same direction. There may be issues over which you may not agree but on a particular issue you may well agree. That of course got us into some trouble because we were going along demonstrating with people on the far left. That bothered some of the membership. And some people just can't function that way. I thought it was my job to keep together as many women as we could in the VOW, working for peace, knowing that there was a tremendous range. We didn't have a very clearly defined feminist perspective. We were still willing to accept Man and His World [the theme of EXPO '67].

Muriel thought they often fumbled as they tried to break new ground. In her leadership role, Muriel was never highly confident that her way was the right way to do things or that her opinions were necessarily correct. She felt she stood on firm ground only when discussing issues that concerned children, race relations or human rights. On other topics, if people said she was wrong she assumed she probably was wrong. She was never inclined to defend her opinions. If others took the time to inquire or consult with her they would find that Muriel had a great store of information, a luminous intelligence and a remarkable memory. Whenever she lacked vital information she did not hesitate to do research. Muriel was always more interested in consulting and negotiating with other women in the peace movement than in leading them in a single direction. As a result Muriel retained the loyalties of many women of disparate views.

As a pacifist, Muriel felt that she should try to respond to differences among the Voices in a way that did not further antagonize, and that she should be looking for "another way." She knew that few Voices were pacifists, and for this reason she expected more of herself. She quite consciously drew on her inner convictions as a pacifist for the courage to face issues that seemed beyond her, even when she felt she had a tenuous hold on these same convictions. Her leadership lay in promoting the search to resolve the tensions between pacifism and justice.

> I was trying to be a pacifist, knowing most of the Voices were not, and not even being too sure of my own ground, of what were the implications of being a pacifist. (I still have a lot to learn, though I am now sure of my pacifism.) Knowing some Voices would say, "I don't believe in disarming like that. I believe we have to have a Defence Department. We have to have arms." I needed to keep

encouraging the Voices to think in terms of non-violence in all aspects of life. I was not an outstanding leader. I was not clear enough about where VOW ought to go or where I was going. On the other hand, I did have the feeling that that's okay because I did have faith in the group and the group process and that it's not up to just me to know. It's up to everybody. I was always sure of that. The outside world's pressures had a lot to do with determining where we went and what we did. The fact that we saw the FLQ crisis as demanding something of us, that itself is significant. A lot of organizations would have thought it didn't demand anything of them. It was a very strong group process all across the country. We may not always have come to a good conclusion but this consultation went on.

Muriel's faith in the ability of a group to come to the right decision served as a strong guiding principle in her work. In turn, her presence was an equally strong motivating force for others. It is unlikely that Muriel was aware of the extent to which her presence was often what propelled women to give their best effort. While she may have felt hesitant about her own abilities, her enthusiasm and warm approval clearly inspired self-confidence in those around her.

Muriel often found she was thrust into situations for which she was unprepared, or put in the position of acting because no one else was prepared to act and something had to be done. Her modesty protected her from thinking she was doing the absolutely right thing or that she was the best person to be responding. She simply recognized that she was there and a response was needed. Muriel's saving grace was her sense of humour. She did not take herself very seriously. Whenever she took on responsibilities for which she felt ill-prepared, Muriel would repeat the wry axiom, "anything that's worth doing is worth doing badly."

> Not that you don't try to do your best, but if it's terribly important that it be done and it falls in your lap, you do it even if you don't know enough to do it very well. I found that a very releasing sort of motto . . . instead of "it's worth doing well." Because you might have to do it badly!
>
> . . . There's another one I liked a lot from a book I once read and it goes:
>
> > They told him it couldn't be done
> > But he smiled and went to it
> > He tackled the thing that couldn't be done
> > And he couldn't do it. . . .
>
> And that always comforted me too!

Muriel loved to joke about herself. One of the members from Vancouver remembered how, at a reception given to welcome Muriel, she had complimented Muriel for looking so nice, especially since she was wearing the very same suit that she had worn two years previously, on her last trip west. Muriel laughed with great delight and told the women, "and my suit was second-hand even then!"

While she gave and received much support from the Voices, Muriel's attempts to hold the organization together, to lead the opposition to the war in Vietnam and to take on the government took their toll on her health. She was subject to laryngitis and to heavy colds and no doubt was run down. After suffering from a cold that hung on for several months, she wrote to a friend:

> My throat is bad again right now and I am seeing a specialist next week. The doctor in Montreal told me that I had nodules on the vocal chords and I would have to keep quiet! I am still looking for some other form of treatment. I am sure the problem is partly psychosomatic, related to the national meetings I have to run, but I have had trouble with my throat for a long time and I hope it can be corrected.[10]

In the spring of 1970 Muriel undertook another tour of the West Coast branches of VOW. Just as she was given to carting around educational materials in the days when she worked for the Adult Education Division, she carried with her a big suitcase full of documents and papers from the national office to distribute as she went. By the time she got home to Halifax, her back was giving her severe trouble and shortly afterwards she was hospitalized for two weeks. Muriel was hardly home from the hospital when she was forced to return due to severe bleeding. She required a hysterectomy. Kay Macpherson held the fort at the national office in Toronto. She warned the council that Muriel's health was delicate and that she could not undertake VOW work for two or three months.

The personal stress in Muriel's family that year was also very great. Martin had a near fatal accident while driving in Mexico. Eleanor also was involved in a serious car accident driving from Montreal to Vermont. In their Christmas letter to friends in December 1970, Jack and Muriel said:

> As for us, we're happy to leave 1970 behind and contemplate the possibilities of 1971. Too many brushes with death and disaster dominate our rear-window view of our own family, and yet here we are—all of us at the end of the year fully alive and in good health.[11]

The following year, when Muriel travelled to Ottawa to council meet-

ings in the spring, Jack was still concerned about her stamina. He wrote to
her:

> I hope that you arrived safe and well in Ottawa last night, without
> turbulence, and that your room in the YWCA is a comfortable one.
> . . . Promise me you will not shout through bull horns; nor strain
> your voice at meetings and don't lift bags, chairs, valises or bundles
> of anything. Lift nothing. I hope you get rest enough to keep you
> fit for your VOW meetings. Much love darling.   Jack[12]

Muriel had been urging the council members during the past two years
to find someone to replace her. However, in this era when women were going
back into the work force or taking on other status of women issues, no one
wanted to fill her shoes. As Nellie Peterson put it in a letter to Muriel:

> My own opinion (which for a change coincides with that of our own
> active members) is that you have brought to the Presidency a new
> dimension, specifically a personal warmth which has created mem-
> bership involvement in the sense of being really interested in VOW.
> That this interest doesn't extend to wanting to take on your job (or
> any of a dozen other jobs) [indicates] perhaps no more than an
> appreciation of just how much work you do—and a grave doubt that
> you can be adequately replaced! But also, I fear there is the feeling
> of disillusionment that comes to the good-intentioned fold who
> once thought the world could be changed by gathering together
> Voices to say, "there shall be war no more." Those who have
> remained to work are those who either have learned the lesson that
> it's a long hard pull not just on one rope, but on many—or those who
> knew it before VOW came on the scene.[13]

After four years as national president Muriel resigned at the AGM at the
Banff School of Fine Arts in September 1971. The women presented her
with a lovely Nova Scotia agate pendant designed and made by Nancy
Pocock, her long time friend in VOW. Kay Macpherson agreed to take on the
presidency for an interim of six months during which time the organization
restructured and at length hired a coordinator. Muriel's daughter, Eleanor,
read (on tape) a poem composed by Hattie Prentice, a Halifax VOW member,
and sent it to Muriel with love from the Nova Scotia VOW.

> The World is her family
> and she is a devoted mother.
> Caring—with courage always,
> always with compassion

for the wounds and beauties
the desperations of humanity.

With tears, yes.
Never with despair.

She can confront, comfort, enlighten
all of us:
      War-torn refugees, hate-torn kids,
      timid well-wishers, the hopeful people
      and sometimes, even, the spite-filled ones
      with no hope at all.
All of us,
from her own inner well
of tranquility and strength.
Her self-found peace.

We have much to learn.
None of it easy.

She glows from within
like a candle lit
for a big high holy holiday,
the celebration of life.

Dedicated with love and admiration to Muriel Duckworth, on the occasion of her retirement as National President of the Voice of Women.

Jack, whose letters, phone calls and flowers followed her around the country wherever she went, wrote on September 30, 1971:

Dearest Muriel:
    It was great to learn on the phone last night that you are feeling a lot better. I hope your usual vigour will be returned to you for your annual meeting in Banff—and that they will all get the clear impression of how great the energy resources within you, kept the VOW ably led during the past four years. You have been great in so many ways for that important organization. I do hope your final sessions will have rewarding moments through important decisions, and that your retirement will give you a definite joyous feeling of accomplishment. . . . Lots of love my dear, and may you be endowed with much wisdom and skill as you preside at your final VOW national meetings. I love you, support you and hope for your acclaim. All good wishes. Jack[14]

Muriel's retirement from VOW was only partial. She would continue to be active with the national Voice of Women for many years, and her lifetime involvement in the Nova Scotia branch, in particular, continued to attract women. With increased free time, Muriel could now return to community leadership in Halifax in the Movement for Citizens' Voice and Action (known as MOVE).

Notes

1. "French-English Relations," National VOW Newsletter, Vol. 1, No. 28 (July 1963). PANS MG 1 Vol. 2930, No. 32.
2. Ibid.
3. "Dear Enemies: Gwenthalyn Graham and Solange Chaput-Rolland," National VOW Newsletter, Vol. 2, No. 1 (June 1964). PANS MG 1 Vol. 2930, No. 33. Gwenthalyn Graham and Solange Chaput-Rolland, *Dear Enemies: A Dialogue on French and English Canada*. Toronto: Macmillan, 1963.
4. Ann Gertler, "Notes on Bi-lingualism and VOW/Vdf for Council, 1969." NAC MG 28 I 218 Vol. 23, No. 2. See also, "Brief to the Royal Commission on Bilingualism and Biculturalism submitted by Voice of Women/Voix de femmes." PANS MG 1 Vol. 2932.
5. Voice of Women Newsletters, Montreal, PQ. PANS MG 1 Vol. 2931, No. 9.
6. Correspondence, 1965–71. NAC MG 28 I 218 Vol. 21, File 2.
7. Special Issue, National VOW Newsletter. PANS MG 1 Vol. 2912, No. 16.
8. President's Report to VOW Eighth Annual Meeting, Calgary, 20–23 September 1968. PANS MG 1 Vol. 2932.
9. This and subsequent quotations from Muriel in this chapter are, unless other-wise specified, from interviews with the author.
10. Letter from M. Duckworth.*
11. Personal collection of M. Duckworth.
12. Letter to M. Duckworth from Jack Duckworth.*
13. Letter to M. Duckworth from N. Peterson. NAC MG 28 1 218 Vol. 21, No. 8.
14. Letter to M. Duckworth from Jack Duckworth. PANS MG 1 Vol. 2941.

Note: * indicates document awaiting archival deposit.

Chapter 13

Forming a Citizens' Coalition

*I*n the late 1960s the twin cities of Halifax and Dartmouth were under immense pressure from the federal government to become the centre of the Atlantic economy. To facilitate regional development the government appointed a Metropolitan Area Planning Committee (MAPC) in 1969 to draw up a regional plan. While the public was promised a chance to participate, the government was slow to consult with anybody besides the Voluntary Economic Planning Board (VEP) which consisted of a few business and establishment interests. Eventually some far-sighted bureaucrats persuaded VEP to sponsor a public forum. This week-long public planning exercise was called Encounter On Urban Environment.

Each day a team of twelve urban experts conducted a detailed examination of the cities and region as they met successively with a great variety of public officials at all levels of government, and with business, professional and community groups. Then in the evening at a public meeting the experts would discuss their findings and their analyses. In an effort to jolt people into reaction, the visiting experts' comments were sometimes abrasive; one described Halifax as "a society dedicated to underachievement"; another remarked, "I have very much the sense that I am in a southern Mississippi town"; a third called the housing shortage "the worst kept guilty secret I've ever come across in my life." They made public the great lack of coordination amongst officials at every level of government, and the abysmal job creation record of Industrial Estates Limited (the province's economic development agency). They also exposed the media's failure to cover the uprooting of Blacks from their homes in Africville carried out by the City. Public expressions of anger and dissatisfaction with the status quo were the immediate results.

Members of the local VOW group saw the importance of the week-long exercise and took part in many of the meetings. Muriel attended all of Encounter's public events and during one large meeting she went to the mike to protest that there were no women among the experts. She told them that she was sure that with a little effort they could have found five or six equally competent women to sit on the panel so that there would be a balance between women and men. A burst of applause followed her remarks, which were captured on film by the National Film Board. While Muriel looked and sounded highly self-confident, she found speaking out very difficult. It marked the first time in a mixed group that she had publicly protested the inequality of women—their experience and knowledge being completely ignored in this forum. Linda Christiansen-Ruffman, a professor of sociology at St. Mary's University, remembered how delighted women in the audience were with Muriel's comments. Johanna Oosterveld, who emerged as a community leader during the months after Encounter, thought that Muriel's intervention was typical of her. Muriel always held that people have different views on things, and she would have asked herself how these problems affected women, why they were not represented on the panel and why the public was not invited to see things through women's eyes.

Following Encounter came months of silence from the government. Voters, in their anger, turfed out the Conservative provincial government that same year. However, the new government set up no mechanism to follow up on Encounter and to allow the public to participate more fully in MAPC's planning process. In fact the new government disbanded the very secretariat that had brought about Encounter. This inactivity was both frustrating and puzzling because at Encounter, the Voluntary Economic Planning Board had made much of the need for leadership training of citizens who wished to participate in the planning process. They had passed around forms for people to complete, with the expectation that VEP would provide training. Muriel suspected that training grassroots people was not what they had in mind, but rather they had expected to recruit volunteers like themselves from the middle and upper middle class.

Muriel and other members of the Nova Scotia Voice of Women finally took matters into their own hands. They got on the phone to talk with others who had expected action and they met with an enthusiastic response. A delegation was chosen to meet with Allan O'Brien, mayor of Halifax, to find out why VEP did not follow up on Encounter and why the anticipated MAPC hearings had not been held. The group was determined to get answers to their questions, to open up the system and to have some part in the decisions affecting their lives.

Finally, MAPC called a public meeting for December 14, 1970, nearly a year after Encounter, to outline the new MAPC plan and process for public participation.[1] The people who attended were highly critical. An alternate group that had already come together to form its own ad hoc committee held several smaller meetings open to anyone interested. On several occasions these meetings occurred at Muriel's home on South Street. As a result of their efforts, ninety groups and individuals signed a request asking the government to fund the founding conference of a citizens' coalition. They succeeded in obtaining a grant of $6000 from MAPC.[2]

Muriel recalled the hours the ad hoc committee spent in her living room, combing through lists of 1300 organizations in the region trying to decide which should be invited. At length they decided the coalition should be composed of groups that were trying to get something for themselves as opposed to groups that wanted to do things for other people (such as social workers). Linda Christiansen-Ruffman felt that this distinction was an extremely important part of the coalition that later emerged (the Movement for Citizens' Voice and Action). It meant that the citizens' coalition would be controlled by people who had a stake in making changes; and it allowed for an incredible diversity in terms of class and race. Linda felt that Muriel was attracted to working across class, gender and race lines and saw a coalition of this kind as very important. Some of the groups invited included the Africville Action Committee, Halifax Welfare Rights, Heritage Trust of Nova Scotia, the Downtown Businessmen's Association, Ecology Action Centre, the Nova Scotia Housing Tenants' Association, the Nova Scotia Association for the Advancement of Coloured People, Ward Five Resources Council, Union of Nova Scotia Indians, the One Parent Family Association and the Voice of Women.[3]

Forty organizations each sent a representative to a three-day conference in Kentville, Nova Scotia, in February 1971. Initially there was much tension at the gathering. Low income groups needed to vent their frustrations and test out whether they could build alliances with middle-class groups. The animator, Reverend Lucius Walker from New York, who had demonstrated his remarkable ability during the Encounter exercise, skilfully guided the difficult discussions.

By the end of three days of feverish work the conference had elected an interim board; decided the criteria for membership (groups had to be action-oriented, self-help in approach and grass roots, with little power or access to power); defined three classes of membership (regular, supporting and individual); developed a statement on the necessity for a coalition with independent resources and training opportunities; and wrote a funding proposal for $216,000 to establish a staffed centre.[4]

People at the conference recognized Muriel's leadership abilities and wanted her on the first board. She declined since her responsibilities as national chairperson of Voice of Women were too heavy. However, she became active right from the outset of MOVE, representing VOW. In 1972, when no longer the president of VOW, she was elected to the MOVE board and in 1973 she became the chairperson of MOVE for a one-year term. Muriel continued on the board until its final days in 1976.[5]

Muriel found this coalition of citizens' groups very exciting since it represented a genuine attempt at grassroots democracy. MOVE's main committees on planning, environment, education and housing raised issues of great concern to her. The MOVE offices were a beehive of activity and information with people constantly dropping by. A biweekly newsletter, *INFLO*, circulated all the news.[6]

MOVE gained much publicity over the issue of Harbour Drive North. In 1972 the City of Halifax proposed a six-lane expressway, to be called Harbour Drive, that would have been detrimental to low-income neighbourhoods through which it would pass. Middle-class groups such as Heritage Trust also felt it would endanger some of the city's prized older buildings. MOVE organized a very effective and well-attended public meeting at which numerous well-researched briefs were presented by both its own member groups and other civic groups. People were furious. Where were all the cars to be parked that would be driven into Halifax's small downtown area? Did the City alderpeople think this was New York? In turn, the City's ire was raised by MOVE's role in rallying such strong public opposition. Later they withdrew their grant to MOVE.[7] Muriel's presence and influence must have irked the politicians too because some of them once again attacked Voice of Women as comprising communist and socialist rabble rousers.

An editorial in MOVE's newsletter also brought the organization a good deal of negative publicity. It criticized the Catholic archdiocese for having sold a large Quinpool Road property for high profits with no regard for appropriate land use. The bible was quoted:"it is easier for a camel to get through the eye of the needle than for a rich man to enter the kingdom of Heaven"—churchfolk took great exception to that! As a result, Dartmouth city council voted to demand that MOVE's funds be cut off.[8]

For Muriel, a seasoned adult educator, one of the most satisfying aspects of MOVE was the way in which the staff organized training projects for member groups, including workshops on writing press releases, dealing with the media and gaining access to information. Staff developed a resource library and were available to help member groups prepare budgets, do bookkeeping and use video equipment. The staff's continual "hands on" teaching approach proved most effective. They showed people how to run the Gestetner printing machine, prepare newsletters and notices of meetings, draw up agendas, distribute minutes and so on.

The MOVE board spent a great deal of energy trying to get ongoing government funding.[9] In 1971 they obtained a federal Manpower grant for $61,000 under the Local Initiatives Program (LIP) to enable them to hire nineteen workers. It was decided by the membership that twelve member groups would be enabled to employ a worker, and MOVE itself would have a staff of seven. Throughout the next year they made exhaustive efforts to obtain a three-year grant from provincial and federal government departments, but to no avail.[10] Muriel thought they had trouble obtaining funding because the provincial bureaucrats did not like the direction in which MOVE was going. They had expected it to be a nice respectable middle-class organization and were not prepared to deal with lower-income groups. Linda Christiansen-Ruffman also thought that MOVE had difficulty because its members challenged the government power structure.

Board members grew discouraged over how much time was taken up with unsuccessful efforts to get funding. Michael Bradfield, one of the original members, recalled that Muriel was always a great morale booster.

She would continually point out all they had accomplished in spite of the lack of funding. Michael felt that were it not for Muriel's encouragement they would have "thrown in the sponge."

Whenever citizens who were critical appeared before city council some alderpeople considered them "foreign" to Halifax and would enquire where they were born and even where their parents were born. Johanna Oosterveld recalled Muriel's righteous indignation whenever politicians or bureaucrats treated people with less than full respect. "She would never treat people with less than utmost respect and many of these people did that all the time." Some politicians thought that people involved in MOVE were using it as a political base for their own self-interest. Some bureaucrats were concerned that MOVE was taking over some of their functions, particularly around social planning. But Muriel felt that most groups and people who became involved at MOVE did so out of concern for community issues. However, whenever certain members occasionally became obstreperous Muriel was not beyond confronting them privately. She would simply tell them that they made her very angry.

As a coalition, MOVE had its own internal difficulties. Its very successes raised expectations among its members and some felt it did not carry through with challenging city hall. Some members faulted MOVE for developing policy without enough consultation with its member groups. Others felt that as MOVE gained ground planning issues that affected the whole city, such as Harbour Drive, it did not emphasize sufficiently particular neighbour-hood issues. An articulate doctrinaire Marxist led a faction that insisted middle-class people or groups should not belong in the coalition at all; she insisted they would always successfully defend their interests against those of the low-income members. Muriel disagreed; she felt everyone should have an opportunity to participate in decisions that affected their lives. However, she demonstrated her democratic convictions when she encour-aged the board to pay for a pamphlet advocating that middle-class groups be excluded from the coalition. She felt that all members had the right to express their views and be heard.

Recalling the class struggle between groups in MOVE, Muriel said:

> The feeling I've had for a long time is that the world is divided, and in between is the middle class and we've got to decide which side we're on. I think there is a great difference, in general, between the position taken by the rich and powerful and the position taken by the poor and working class.

Muriel was never fuzzy on where she stood as a white, middle-class woman. She identified with the poor and working class. She recognized the dilemma this posed for a pacifist as she went on to say,

That's kind of contrary to the idea of negotiating and reconciling, but you have to start from some position and then do whatever reconciling can be done from that position.

She was clear about fundamental principles and this grounding gave her the patience to seek solutions. Johanna remarked:

> [Muriel] came to everything out of a certainty of what she was and what she stood for. That didn't mean that she always had her mind made up and she wouldn't change her opinion but that centredness—knowing who you are, knowing what you believe in and knowing what you stand for, basically—that was absolutely unshakeable. Out of that she always could find a solution. There never wasn't a solution. That was always clear with Muriel. Everyone always knew that. You would not come to a meeting and find that Muriel would change her mind about something fundamental. She just wouldn't. She might compromise. She would go a long way to find solutions and make compromises but she spoke from a basic conviction.

Muriel agreed to become the MOVE chairperson in 1973 because no one else was willing to take it on. She seemed the obvious person because she had worked closely with the previous president, Beth Boutilier, but there was resistance from some of the low-income people and also some middle-class members who felt MOVE should be led by its low-income members. Muriel worked hard at building trust among the groups so that they could work out procedures to accommodate one another. Norma Scott, a member of the board from the Ward Five Resource Council said of Muriel,

> she was such a voice of reason—helping people to focus, bringing it back from the rambling we would get into. She never cut people off, she was just really calm and helped people look at the issues.

Johanna Oosterveld said that in the face of MOVE's own internal divisions, Muriel's role always was that of conciliator. According to Johanna, she would bring people together, saying

> we have a common interest here and if we can't take a position because we don't agree let's try to get the information out so that people can make up their own minds and represent their own positions.

Johanna described how Muriel conducted herself at meetings.

> She never got angry. She never got offensive. She never got
> defensive. . . she was always willing to hear and listen to criticism
> and come up with constructive solutions. She never said "well
> you're wrong and I don't want to hear it." She always said, "Well
> if that's how you feel then we must find a solution." That's not to
> say that she always agreed with people but she always insisted that
> we find solutions. And she may have been perfectly conscious of
> the fact that she was right but she never said that. She always
> accepted when people voiced criticism of problems that we must
> find a solution for them. That was a very useful contribution. When
> people got discouraged and upset and angry, she was always the one
> who would say it's part of working through those things. If you had
> a committee with Muriel on it you knew it would work well. People
> might not always agree but you would know it would never dete-
> riorate into back-biting because she wouldn't let it.

Linda Christiansen-Ruffman felt that Muriel's understanding of some of
the tensions among members and groups at MOVE and her ability to foresee
potential conflict was the reason she invested so much energy in overcoming
the interpersonal barriers that often arise from class and race differences.
According to Linda, Muriel's real secret lay in the ways in which she headed
off many potential conflicts and organized things so that conflicts did not
happen or were mitigated. Maureen Vine recalled that talking with people
between meetings was one of Muriel's constant practices.

According to Maureen, Muriel's facilitating seemed effortless.

> She was constantly asking for our ideas and opinions and would
> give information about what was going on or what we might be
> interested in. She got on the phone and told people about what was
> happening that needed to be challenged. Her role was outstand-
> ing—especially for people like me. [She] prepared one for the head-
> on battles that we involved ourselves in with government and with
> bureaucrats at various levels. We needed a lot of encouragement.
> I can remember times when I would feel terribly upset about some
> way I might have behaved at meetings, the anger that would come
> out of me and some of the things I would say. Afterwards I would
> go home and I would sweat it. I would think, "how could I have said
> that?" I would be mortified at my behaviour. The next day I would
> get a phone call from Muriel saying, "look, you were dead right
> about that. It was important that somebody say it." I would tell her
> about how I felt and she would give me reassurance that I had done
> the right thing. I'm sure she did it for others. She never ever
> criticized my style. She only encouraged me to continue on. Fre-
> quently when I was going through a period of self-doubt I would

get a phone call or a note or post card from Muriel quite unexpect-
edly, and it would give me that assurance to continue on.

Through her outreach and her support, Muriel succeeded in involving
many women and keeping them involved. Johanna found that Muriel was
perceived by the young women around MOVE as their Halifax mother in
many ways. Johanna recalled:

> She had the ability to project that kind of warmth to people. She was
> always there. You could always go talk to Muriel. Although she was
> a very busy woman you would never know [it]. She would always
> have time for you. She always did. My impression, and I am quite
> convinced of this, is that everyone respected Muriel. They may not
> always have agreed with her but they always respected her. She didn't
> manipulate and she was always straightforward. You always knew
> where she stood with people. . . . I have since talked to people and
> Muriel occupies a soft spot in all their hearts. I think that that partly
> comes from the fact that she's well-known and she has been involved
> in a lot of different things, but it comes primarily from a very special
> quality that she does have. It's the ability to make you feel that you
> are the most important person in the world when she talks to you.
> She's right there for you—completely—not thinking about some-
> thing else while she's talking to you. . . . And I think it's not something
> she puts on. I think it's really true—that's the way she operates as a
> person . . . she focuses her attention on whatever she is doing at that
> particular time. It's a very useful way to be. It makes for very
> important interpersonal relationships. She is very, very good at that.

According to Maureen, some people at MOVE thought

> VOW was a bit airy fairy—this peace thing didn't fit in a coalition
> of planning groups concerned with the environment. They were
> seen as a lot of pinkos, crazy women concerned about peace and far
> from the concerns of the poor people.

But Maureen Vine remembered Muriel as

> one of those persons who tried to help people see the connections.
> . . . You could see her own life growing in that way. She went from
> peace activity to developing this whole range of concerns in the
> community right down to the grass roots people. . . . [and to] people
> [who] are going hungry and the effect bureaucracies and their
> decisions are having on their lives . . . she made all these connec-
> tions so quickly.

While some members of MOVE never thought that urban planning and peace issues had anything to do with poverty, others saw Muriel and the Voice of Women as very important allies. Johanna said:

> Muriel always knew that the money we spend on armaments is where the real problem was—that you couldn't have the social and economic development without stopping the arms race coupled with the nuclear capacities. That tells it all.

After MOVE's heyday from 1971 to 1973, the organization's demise was a slow death which its participants had seen coming for some time. MOVE succeeded only too well in challenging government. It was highly evident that the government did not want to see it continue. After the initial grants no further funding came from LIP, although for a couple of years grants from the federal Secretariat for Urban Affairs and the Department of the Secretary of State enabled it to continue with a core staff.

Looking back over MOVE's six-year experiment, Muriel reflected that coalitions are probably more viable if they are focussed on specific, short-term objectives. Yet MOVE had a long string of credits, which included causing the City of Halifax to appoint a Municipal Planning Committee and to have citizen representatives sit on the MAPC committees. Groups learned how to use legislated regional planning principles as part of their strategy to fight specific battles. MOVE clearly helped the city's North End groups to put the spotlight on social issues. Many individuals learned how to run meetings, how to search for consensus and pay attention to dissenting opinions. Many community groups felt strengthened because of their representation in MOVE.[11] Linda Christiansen-Ruffman thought that it was incredible that such a diverse coalition stayed together for so long and she felt that Muriel was one of the main ingredients which it made this possible.

Notes

1. *Halifax Mail-Star*, 15 December 1970.
2. PANS MG 1 Vol. 2907, No. 1.
3. MOVE Collection. Dalhousie University Archives (DUA), Box 14.
4. Ibid.
5. MOVE Collection. DUA, Box 12.
6. MOVE Information: Reports, Newsletters. DUA, Box 41.
7. Ibid.
8. Ibid.
9. MOVE Funding Proposals. PANS MG 1 Vol . 2907, No. 1.
10. MOVE Collection. DUA, Box 6.
11. MOVE Collection, Study Prepared by David Smith and Linda Christiansen-Ruffman. DUA, Box 5.

Chapter 14

A New Democratic Party Candidate

The 1974 Campaign

*M*aureen Vine never admired Muriel more than when she followed-up on her municipal involvements at MOVE by running as a candidate for the New Democratic Party (NDP) in the provincial election of 1974. Maureen saw this as a very logical step for a person who had the kind of knowledge Muriel had and who had such a profound understanding of the connections among issues. But Muriel felt that once again life was pushing her to the limit. The pattern was repeating itself. She had been asked to be national president of Voice of Women before she had finished working for the Adult Education Division, then she had become deeply involved in MOVE before her term with VOW was over. Now with the provincial election coming up she was being asked to run while her work load with MOVE and several other national organizations was still heavy.

The Halifax Cornwallis riding where Muriel lived, in the south end of the city, was generally identified as an affluent area, although parts of the riding contained poor and overcrowded housing. Many university students,

NDP headquarters for Muriel's 1974 campaign.

staff and faculty lived there, as did student nurses. Still, it was essentially a very conservative area of the city.

Doris Dyke, the head of the department of education at Dalhousie University, had recently arrived in Halifax from Saskatchewan. In her home province, an NDP nomination meeting was as hotly contested as an election; she was surprised by the lack of this NDP tradition in Nova Scotia, where it was a challenge to even find a candidate. Finally, three weeks before the election was held, Michael Link, a student at Dalhousie who was president of the Halifax Cornwallis riding, approached Muriel. She was feeling very tired from her work in MOVE and was resting when Michael came by. Because she had three immediate commitments, including one in Europe and one in Toronto, she felt free to turn him down. However, within two or three days all of these obligations fell through, so she called Michael back and said she would run. Even though her nomination was uncontested and the meeting appeared tame in Doris's view, Muriel was surprised and delighted to find that many people instantly appeared, wanting to help, as soon as they found out she was running.

Muriel scarcely expected to be supported in her own neighbourhood. However, the very first time she rang a doorbell, Val Aikens answered and wrapped her arms around Muriel, quite overwhelming her. It pleased Muriel to see that many women immediately supported her. Women on the street whom she did not know came up and hugged her. Muriel was the first woman in Halifax ever to run in a provincial or federal election.

The CBC carried an announcement that a sixty-five-year-old housewife was the NDP candidate for Halifax Cornwallis. Immediately Johanna Oosterveld fired off a letter to the *Halifax Mail Star*:

> A 65-year old housewife indeed! Muriel Duckworth is no more a 65-year old housewife than George Mitchell is an x-year old father! I'm sure the CBC would not describe as such George Mitchell or George Cooper who are running for the Liberals and Conservatives respectively in that constituency. They would not even think of them in that way.
>
> Muriel Duckworth is an experienced educator and an internationally known and respected representative of women's rights. She is knowledgeable and concerned about many issues and has and is spending a great deal of time working with community groups in Halifax.
>
> She is a housewife and mother just as much as men are gardeners or repairmen and fathers—no more, no less. I am disturbed enough that no more women are running in this campaign. It's disgraceful to have the CBC dismiss them as housewives.[1]

The party publicity stressed Muriel's community work with MOVE, VOW and the Halifax Children's Foundation, and her former job as secretary of the Adult Education Division of the Nova Scotia Department of Education.

Politicians are known for making rhetorical statements and promises during election campaigns which they have no intention of keeping. But anyone who knew Muriel Duckworth recognized that she was holding to the same principles and saying the same things that she had always said during her many years of community work. On the subjects of education, foreign affairs and the status of women she was clearly a leader in shaping NDP policy. Even though she was an informed speaker on many issues, running for a political party was a great challenge to her. Not only was her age a factor (campaigning is a very arduous activity), but as a woman she had to work very hard in order to be taken seriously, even within the party, by men such as the Nova Scotia party leader, Jeremy Akerman.

Halifax Cornwallis was not seen as a strong NDP riding and Doris Dyke felt that Muriel was undervalued by the provincial organization. She recalled how Jeremy Akerman referred to all the candidates as "men" at a large David Lewis-Akerman rally in support of all candidates in the Halifax area, and how Muriel responded humorously to this. Muriel must have captured the audience, for Alexa McDonough, then a member of the Halifax Cornwallis riding, wrote a note at the bottom of a notice of this public meeting and kept it in her scrapbook: "Of the eight candidates Muriel Duckworth was the only one given a standing ovation! She was great and looked beautiful."

Alexa loved accompanying Muriel as they campaigned door to door. Alexa's favourite story about Muriel was about the time they encountered a very hostile old man who raged at Muriel, "you should be at home looking after your family!" Muriel countered that her children were all grown up and had left home. "Then," he said, "you should be helping to look after your grandchildren." "But," she protested, "none of them live in Halifax. They live in Montreal." For the most part, though, Alexa remembered that Muriel generally won people over. Muriel was very successful on the doorstep; her optimism appealed to people. Alexa described Muriel as a little bit like the Pied Piper in the way she forthrightly drew people into her campaign. She would ask people, "are you willing to help?" This was how she addressed Dennis Theman at the door, the first time she met him, and he promptly became very active in support of her candidacy.

Doris Dyke, as the campaign manager, was amazed that so many young people wanted to work for Muriel. One student told her: "Muriel is the neatest person I know." Doris and Muriel put the emphasis on morale building at their meetings. Each Sunday evening, Muriel would have an open house at the always-hospitable "Hive." Muriel and Doris would begin by encouraging canvassers to relate how things were going and made a point of learning from and supporting them. Doris described it as a personal campaign. I would say now it was a different style of leadership—a feminist style. People were valued and were never pushed into doing more work than they could do. Whatever they could do was valued.

And there were no jobs that women could not do. In their campaign committee there was no hierarchy—those who made cookies could also write promotional material or answer the phone. Doris felt the campaign style bore Muriel's imprint. Things were done in a cooperative way. While the atmosphere was informal, the accuracy of records and organizational efficiency were not sacrificed.

The committee shared sparse office quarters on Brunswick Street with Michael Bradfield who was running for the adjoining riding of Halifax Citadel. Muriel and Doris were at one end of the room and Michael and Pat Kerans, his manager, at the other end. Each had a desk, a table and a telephone. Doris noted that the party leader Jeremy was prone to keeping decision-making in his own hands. For example, she noticed that the NDP headquarters would send far more publicity materials to Michael Bradfield than to Muriel. To one of the women workers in the Bradfield campaign, all the fun and excitement seemed to be at the other end of the room. Things were much more spontaneous there. Finally, irked by being told her job was not to answer the phone, she threatened to "go over to the other side" if the men did not let her take more responsibility.[2]

Muriel was surrounded by a wealth of talent in her campaign. People were only too glad to contribute their expertise because she so evidently welcomed their input and used their knowledge. The publicity committee put out well-designed broadsheets for door-to-door distribution by the canvassers that cited Muriel's position on a host of issues. Alexa discovered her own flair for writing political statements, press releases and campaign literature. Jack, who had greatly encouraged Muriel to run, rang doorbells, distributed flyers and poured over press releases. He, too, often accompanied her as she canvassed. It was he who put up the striking orange flower-like NDP posters all along the white fence around their home.

Throughout her campaign, Muriel gave rousing speeches and media interviews about economic development, education, day care, health care, the Election Act, equality for women and comprehensive social security for the aged.[3] Muriel's platform contained many measures for the improvement of the status of women. She promised to work towards the creation of a women's bureau within the provincial government. This office would pressure the government to fully implement the recommendations of the Royal Commission on the Status of Women, to enforce existing legislation against discrimination on the basis of sex, and to equalize the legal position of women. If she were elected, Muriel planned to work for the appointment

of women to all lev-
els of management
and government, to
improve the status
of particular jobs
that are generally
filled by women and
to improve career
opportunities for
women.

It was in the
education policy
field that Muriel
shone in the NDP.
She was able to draw
on her vast experi-
ence in this area.
Improving the edu-
cation system for

Muriel canvassing with Jack in 1974 election.

everyone was a focus of her campaign and she had ideas for every level of
schooling. Although some of these were not established NDP policy, she was
not afraid to advocate them. Muriel had been pushing the idea of free
university education since her Home and School days in the forties, probably inspired by the free higher education provisions for war veterans after
1945. She called for free post-secondary education to remove the barrier of
high costs that prevented many people from attending post-secondary
institutions. She wanted more emphasis on continuing education, part-time
degree courses, technical and vocational training and community colleges,
as well as on giving adult education the same status as all other educational
programs in the province.[4] Muriel also made the education of blind and deaf
children an issue in her campaign.

Muriel was not your usual politician. She herself remained primarily an
educator throughout her campaign. As a political figure, Muriel used every
occasion possible to broaden people's understanding of issues. Doris Dyke
said of her speaking style:

> Muriel, even in town hall meetings, could not resort to the quick
> laugh or the cheap shot. She showed that the NDP understanding was
> different—[it featured] an educational thrust rather than a political
> confrontation, or excessive use of power. She emphasized a rational
> understanding of the conditions of life. Muriel had a teaching style
> in her speeches. She didn't tell her listeners everything they needed
> to know. She presented her material in a way that enabled people

to think and enabled them to go on thinking. She asked questions rather than gave answers. She presented information and she asked questions herself and dealt with other people's questions. I never heard her put anybody down who asked questions publicly. She had a style where she was not just holding onto the platform but sharing it.

Doris found that even though Muriel was so beloved and so well known, her popularity did not necessarily translate into votes. Some people told Doris that they would have voted for Muriel if she were running for non-partisan municipal elections, because they respected her and knew she would have committed herself to the work, but since they could not bring themselves to vote NDP they could not support her.

Doris also recalled how Muriel antagonized people like Henry Hicks, president of Dalhousie University. Hicks told Doris that he thought it was quite admirable of Doris that she had involved herself in Nova Scotia politics. In turn, Doris told Hicks how wonderful it was to be working with Muriel and he replied, "yes she is a wonderful person, but just think what a disaster it would be if she got in." Doris asked him why and he said Muriel did not know anything about fiscal politics and she was too strong a pacifist. It was alright to have that dimension in the campaign but not, he thought, in office. Doris asked whether he thought Muriel might win. He replied, "I do notice that it is the strongest NDP campaign I've ever seen."

Others gave her their unequivocal support. A letter from J.K. Bell, long time secretary of the Nova Scotia Federation of Labour, which accompanied a financial contribution to her campaign, stated:

> You have the enviable record of fighting social issues on behalf of the common people, locally, nationally and internationally, which compels anyone calling themselves progressive to support you in your efforts to carry these issues in higher political forums. Best wishes from a fellow rebel. J.K. Bell[5]

Muriel's son John, who had many Liberal friends, had promised to support George Mitchell before he knew his mother was running. He too was amazed to find how much support Muriel was getting in the riding and would tease her about this whenever he dropped by to visit.

On election night so many workers gathered for a party in a private home that it was a wonder the building's foundations survived. Everybody was singing from specially prepared song sheets, familiar old tunes with new lyrics about Muriel's exploits. Resplendent in a black dress with silver jewelry, Muriel stood before her supporters and announced that they had obtained between 19 and 20 percent of the vote, which was the NDP's best results to date in that constituency. She asked the campaign workers to see the results as a success. Even though George Mitchell had won the riding, Muriel declared their campaign a victory.

A letter from a young canvasser summed up sentiments typical of Muriel's election workers.

> Last night I was quite despondent until you pointed out how the NDP had fared last time in Cornwallis and what a truly conservative riding the south end is. It appears now that our efforts of the last month were largely for the future; certainly you have given the NDP lasting respectability in the south end. I enjoyed working for you, regret you do not have a new career this morning; and would gladly do it again.[6]

Jack's Death

Jack became ill in October 1974. Muriel was due to go to a conference at Mount St. Vincent University on Thanksgiving weekend. On Saturday night there was a terrible snow storm and she decided not to go out on Sunday because she did not want Jack to shovel out their circular driveway. Nevertheless, on Monday morning Jack did try to clear the snow instead of waiting for help. Shortly afterwards he felt pain. Some days later he went for an examination during which he had a further heart attack and was hospitalized for a couple of weeks. He and Muriel then spent a quiet Christmas season at home and he continued to recuperate. In February, when he was approaching the time when he was to have a heart check-up, he developed a bad cough and felt rapidly worse. He returned to hospital for tests on his heart in early March and never left the hospital. Doctors informed Muriel that Jack had cancer of the lung. She found this difficult to accept as Jack had never smoked and had always kept himself fit. He had even run a mile and a half on his seventy-sixth birthday, the previous August.

All the children came home, Martin coming from Montreal and Eleanor from Geneva. John was living in Halifax. Muriel was in a state of turmoil but she could not bring herself to talk with Jack about his impending death as she felt that it would be an invasion of his privacy. Martin did ask his father what he would like to have done as a memorial and he replied, "something for peace." Jack died in the Camp Hill Hospital on May 17, 1975. He was in his seventy-seventh year and Muriel was sixty-six.

The Jack Duckworth Peace Fund (later changed to the Jack and Muriel Duckworth Peace Foundation) was established in his memory by the Halifax Society of Friends. Three young men from the Halifax Quaker community lovingly made the arrangements for his cremation. One of them made his coffin. The Quakers held a memorial service for him at the CNIB in Halifax, and the following summer the family gathered at the cottage and spread his

ashes over their beloved Lake Memphremagog which had meant so much
to him and to the whole family.

The Voice of Women national newsletter remembered him fondly:

> Jack and Muriel worked together and yet supported each other
> completely in their separate fields of work. Jack "retired" several
> times, but since age meant little to him he would soon be giving his
> time to yet another good cause needing his talents.
>
> Many Voice of Women members remember his boundless
> energy as he acted as baggage master, tour organizer and general
> trouble shooter for the cross-country visit of the Vietnamese women
> in 1971. Many times when Muriel was far from home on VOW
> business, a phone call, flowers or letters always arrived. He was a
> devoted husband and father.
>
> Members are happy for having known Jack and offer their love
> and sympathy to Muriel and her family.[7]

Muriel carried on with her work in the community, in national and
international organizations, and at the political level, feeling that her best
tribute to Jack was to continue being active in all those areas that meant so
much to them both. She continued to live in "the Hive" for the next three
years and felt that her activism helped her to cope with her sorrow.

The 1978 Campaign

Having survived the 1974 campaign, Muriel was persuaded to stand for
renomination in the spring of 1976, well in advance of the next provincial
election. By now she knew the ropes of an election campaign. As she was
primarily interested in public education, she felt she could engender a wider
debate over public issues by running early for the next election which was
not called until the summer of 1978.

During these two years she went on giving speeches and interviews, and
issuing press releases critiquing government policies, particularly those
concerning housing, economic development, day care and electric power
rates. She called for legislation that guaranteed people's rights and freedoms.
Through the many issues she addressed ran a common theme of social
justice. Her vision of the role of government was that it should provide equal
opportunities for all. Whether she was talking about jobs, health or education, Muriel drew on her deep understanding of what ordinary people need
to develop to their full potential. She championed the rights of the poor,
Blacks, Native people, women and children in clear, unequivocal language
and she laid before the public very concrete ways to bring the government
nearer to her vision of equality.

Questioning the huge investments of foreign capital that would be required for the development in the Bay of Fundy of tidal power for export to the United States, she said:

> Enterprises are "free" to come into Nova Scotia, the government of Nova Scotia is "free" to take all the risks, and the people of Nova Scotia are "free" to lose millions of dollars of tax money when these companies go bankrupt.
>
> The principle of autonomous, self-induced growth is as important for the people of Nova Scotia as it is for the people of any Third World country.[8]

Muriel described Canada's tax structure as a

> hidden welfare system for the non-poor . . . [in which] ordinary citizens are unaware that it is they who bear the greatest burden of this cost, while it is the wealthy who reap the greatest benefits.[9]

Muriel continued to critique government fiscal practices and policies. She pointed out that a chief factor that allowed things to balance so neatly for the Liberal government was the way it transferred expenditures from the current account to the capital account. She kept bringing before the electorate the rising unemployment figures, cutbacks in equalization payments to the province and the reduction in the level of unemployment insurance payments.[10]

Muriel called for the amendment of human rights legislation, for safeguards so that no person would be afraid to seek redress of grievances and for access to information. She called for an even closer monitoring of textbooks and curriculum content in the light of human rights legislation. And she called attention to the way history is taught, or not taught, in the schools.

> Ms. Duckworth . . . argues that not nearly enough emphasis is placed upon the role of the "ordinary person" in history; that history is too concerned with "leaders" and insufficiently concerned with the people who made history—the people who do the jobs. "Lack of working-class history is a major curriculum problem," she said.[11]

Muriel particularly opposed cuts in spending for continuing education and she pointed out discriminating barriers to women's equality. She highlighted the lack of women in educational administration at all levels and she called attention to how access to higher education benefited the elites. She called for student aid policies to help people wishing to pursue part-time or non-degree studies. Muriel attacked the government's meagre day care subsidy program and its policy of keeping day care as a part of the welfare system rather than part of the education system. She decried the low salaries (some as low as $7500 a year) paid to day care workers, that resulted in a scandalously low standard of living for the workers and high staff turnover at the centres.[12]

Muriel emphasized that the NDP was prepared to ensure equality for women. They planned to introduce legislation amending the marital property act for the protection of both partners, and legislation granting the courts power to collect maintenance payments quickly and efficiently so that those requiring support would not suffer needlessly. In the workplace the NDP would initiate amendments to the Labour Standards Code to ensure equal pay for work of equal value. The Trade Union Act would be amended to encourage the unification of working women for their common good.

Muriel continued to emphasize that health care must change to make greater resources available for the prevention of illness. She advocated better nutrition, education, fitness programs, early screening procedures for breast cancer, and better living and working conditions as essential ways to prevent early death from heart disease, respiratory disease and cancer.[13]

Helpful as Muriel's campaign team proved to be under the management of Giff Gifford (founder of Veterans Against Nuclear Arms and an old family friend), the personal climb was even more uphill during this second election. Her ever-supportive Jack was no longer there to cheer her on. Then, in the middle of the campaign she had to move out of her home to a nearby flat. "The Hive," home to so many community meetings, had been sold by its owners to Dalhousie University and just at this time the university wanted the property vacant in order to develop student residences. Muriel had known for some time that it was likely that she would have to vacate the house, but the actual notice came at an inconvenient time. Yet, despite having to take time out to move to a small apartment, she focussed her attention on the campaign.

This time election day yielded even better results for the NDP in Halifax Cornwallis than in 1974. The votes cast for Muriel Duckworth increased from 19 percent to 23 percent.[14]

Speaking on a panel devoted to issues affecting women in politics at the NDP annual convention, Muriel shared her experiences of campaigning as a woman. She spoke alongside Jane Strange and Susan Holtz. The three of them comprised half of the women candidates in the 1978 election.

Strange maintained that there was absolutely no difference between being a man and being a woman in an election campaign. She felt women had to be more aggressive, had to work actively for change, but had only themselves to blame for their failure to make an equal showing with men. Muriel expressed a very different view:

Duckworth says blaming women is an argument which is "totally unacceptable, as unacceptable as it would be to blame women because they are battered, or blame them because they're raped. It's like blaming the unemployed for the unemployment situation in this country. . . . There are several myths about women in politics that need to be seriously examined. One is that women don't support women. I think we have to be careful that such anecdotes don't cloud the issue of real support that exists for women from other women. Another is that women are to blame for their position in this society. In our society, the majority of women are still poor and unorganized. Women's salaries are still only 60 percent of men's. In Nova Scotia's history, there have only been two women in the legislature. It's okay to say that women have to stand up and do these things, but we can never lose sight of the real position of women in this society."[15]

Participation on Federal NDP Committees

Muriel was the representative from Nova Scotia on the NDP Federal Participation of Women Committee from 1975 when it was established to 1977.[16] This committee was set up in order to encourage women to run for office, to keep women's issues in the public eye and no doubt to combat sexism within the party as well. Muriel recalled how difficult it was for women who sat on NDP councils that were dominated by men. Usually more attention was paid to the opinions of men than of the few women on the councils. The issues women brought up, of interest to them, were often overlooked. The Participation of Women Committee was formed to change these practices. For her contributions, Muriel was named an honorary member of the NDP Participation of Women Committee of Nova Scotia.

Muriel played an important role on another federal committee of the NDP, the Committee on International Affairs Committee, co-chaired by Pauline Jewett and Bob White. They produced a report on "Peace, Security and Justice" for the 1981 NDP convention in Vancouver. Their policy paper was designed to respond to the global emergency—the threat of nuclear war. It proposed a democratic socialist alternative of a world order based on social justice and freedom. The paper dealt with North-South relations, human rights, refugees, peace and security issues, bilateral and regional concerns, the environment and space.[17]

As a long-standing member of VOW, Muriel was accustomed to arguing against NATO and NORAD. VOW had long insisted that Canada should get out of NATO, believing that the only defense for Canada was peace. VOW argued that a stance of genuine neutrality was Canada's best defence and that participation in collective security arrangements outside the United Nations threatened rather than protected Canada's survival as a sovereign and

economically independent nation. VOW maintained that NATO provided no
defence against nuclear attack from the sea or the sky and that Canada's
membership in NATO led the country away from peace.

In the debate within the NDP Committee on International Affairs there
were two strongly held views. Those in favour of NATO thought that
membership meant that Canada could exert influence on the other members
of the alliance to reduce tensions that could lead to nuclear war. When NATO
was first created it was thought by some statespeople, including Mike
Pearson who was one of its architects, to be a potential force for peace and
disarmament given the possibility of political, economic and cultural cooperation.

The other side argued that NATO was primarily a military alliance.
Canada's influence on NATO policy had never been significant and would
never be, given the American dominance of the alliance. They insisted that
tax money could be put to better use cleaning up the oceans, modernizing
fisheries and equalizing opportunities in Canada and abroad. They argued
for countering the real enemies—poverty, pollution, over-population, repression, famine and war. They felt that once apart from NATO Canada would
have more freedom to pursue cooperation with other small and middle
powers both inside and outside NATO and Canadians could more easily
broaden their international perspectives and interests beyond Western Europe and the "North Atlantic Triangle." Muriel argued strongly on this side.
At one point, when some of the members were adamant that Canada had to
maintain a strong military defence against invasion, Muriel expostulated,
"and who do you think is going to invade us, except the United States?" One
of the members glared at her and she countered, "And don't you look at me
as if I'm some foolish old woman!"

After reading a draft of the committee report, Muriel wrote back:

> There is no naiveté in showing some understanding of the history
> of military alliances and particularly that of NATO, NORAD, and the
> DPSA [Defence Production Sharing Arrangement]. Alliances do not
> go on forever. The NDP needs to show that we understand this, and
> to lead the Canadian people in understanding what life after NATO,
> NORAD and DPSA would be like. We cannot base a defense policy
> on the lies or misapprehensions, to use a gentler word, which have
> come to be regarded as truth. We have firm grounds for withdraw-
> ing from military alliances and taking a more appropriate and useful
> place in the world community. . . . The paper needs most of all to
> be written in contemporary terms. Of course there is a historic
> perspective but the paper as it now stands does not show enough
> movement in thought and perspective over the last 40 years, [it]
> does not truly, I think, represent thinking within the party. . . . Why

do we write about deterrence as if it were a policy for Canada? Why do we pretend not to know that so-called "conventional" weapons in Europe are horrific, close to nuclear weapons in their effect and meant for first use? . . . Please don't use phrases like "commitment capability gap" or "Windows of opportunity." It makes me shudder. I like the bottom of page six re Canada's military presence in Europe: "It is simply expensive symbolism."[18]

To her great satisfaction, Muriel's view won the day and the resolution that came before the NDP convention in Vancouver in 1981 and which was passed read:

At this time, recognizing the grave concerns about the current operation and strategies of NATO, a New Democratic Party government would not participate in the NATO alliance.[19]

Notes

1. *Halifax Mail Star*, 7 March 1974.
2. The author is telling this story about herself.
3. Press releases by Muriel Duckworth, candidate for Halifax Cornwallis, 1974–1976, PANS MG 1 Vol. 2908, No. 15.
4. Press release, 22 March 1974. PANS MG 1 Vol. 2908, No. 15.
5. During her second campaign, letter to M. Duckworth from J.K. Bell, 6 September 1978. PANS MG 1 Vol. 2908, No. 41.
6. Letter from a canvasser, Denise Loiselle, 3 April 1974. PANS MG 1 Vol. 2908, No. 40.
7. National VOW Newsletter, Vol. 11, No. 1 (June 1975). PANS MG 1 Vol. 2930, No. 36.
8. Press release, 10 March 1976.
9. Press release, NDP. PANS MG 1 Vol. 2908, No. 18.
10. Press release, NDP. Undated. PANS MG 1 Vol. 2908, No. 16
11. Press release, NDP. Undated. PANS MG 1 Vol. 2908, No. 15.
12. Press release, 11 September 1978. PANS MG 1 Vol. 2908, No. 16.
13. Press release, 6 September 1978. PANS MG 1 Vol. 2908, No. 1.
14. Letter from M. Duckworth to friends and supporters. PANS MG 1 Vol. 2908, No. 16.
15. *The Barometer*, 7 December 1978. PANS MG 2 Vol. 1397, No. 9.
16. Papers of the NDP Participation of Women Committee. PANS MG 1 Vol. 2909, No. 5.
17. PANS MG 1 Vol. 1209, No. 5.
18. Letter to National Committee. PANS MG 1 Vol. 2944, No. 20.
19. Papers of the federal NDP convention 1981, Vancouver. PANS MG 1 Vol. 2909, No. 24.

Chapter 15

A Pacifist Feminist

*M*uriel brought a very particular dimension to feminist thinking in Canada. She gained this perspective from her international work in the Voice of Women. She saw war—with its violence against women and children, the rape of women in war, the millions of refugees, most of whom were women and children, and the threat of nuclear destruction—as what stood in the way of women's advancement in every country. She helped to make Canadian women think about war as the ultimate instrument of violence against them and about the cost of the arms race as the siphon that stood in the way of women meeting their needs. Muriel insisted on disarmament. And she did not just think about the larger international picture, but focussed on specific injustices at home. For example, Muriel grasped the importance of exposing racism towards Native women in Canada as violence towards these women.

Six short weeks following Jack's death Muriel was asked by the Voice of Women to represent them at the United Nations International Conference on Women in June 1975, in Mexico City. Still in shock over Jack's loss, she protested that it was too soon for her to go, but Kay Macpherson persuaded her that the trip away would be good for her. The conference which Muriel went to was the unofficial parallel conference to the first United Nations conference introducing the UN's decade of women. It was called the Tribune. Thousands of women from non-governmental organizations (NGOs) attended it.

On her return home, Muriel's remarks about the conference showed how conscious she was of applying the themes of equality, development and peace to all women, everywhere. These were the stated purposes of the United Nations conference and have remained the purposes of all UN conferences on women since 1980, including the conference in Copenhagen in 1985 and Beijing in 1995. Muriel could readily illustrate the contradictions between the federal government's words and women's reality. The views of the official national delegates did not necessarily correspond to the views of the NGO women at the Tribune.

> I want to give you the illustration of Canada's failure to give women an equal vote. Coline Campbell [MP speaking for Marc Lalonde, minister responsible for the Status of Women] made the big announcement at Mexico that from now on Canada would give high priority to needs of women in its development programs abroad.

That sounded great. But I've been checking up ever since. Nothing has been done about it in Ottawa, absolutely nothing. Nor have they put any women in decision-making positions in Ottawa or CIDA and, until they do it in Ottawa, they're not very likely to do it in one of their receiving countries. . . .

Another thing I want to talk about is disarmament which was an important issue at the conference. The Canadian government decided they wouldn't mention the word peace. And the three purposes of International Women's Year were equality, development and peace. Coline Campbell didn't mention it because it could be used for political purposes. (Development—of course, Canada's happy to talk about development but that raises another question. A lot of Canadian and American women had no idea what development meant. They thought of it in terms of personal development and had no idea what the United Nations meant by [the] development of women's role in developing countries, which may be desirable or undesirable depending on what you mean by development of the country.)

On the whole, I didn't feel that the people from North America had the same sense of urgency about disarmament as the people did from the developing countries to whom armament means wars. . . . They are just destroyed by wars. Their progress gets set back by armament. . . .

There's still one other thing I should mention and that is the question of women prisoners. Rape was discussed and recognized both as an act of war and a general act of violence against women prisoners. But, of course, from the beginning of time it's been an act of war and is only beginning to be talked about, really, as a thing that happens to women during wartime. But there were several women there from Chile—and that marks one of the big differences between the Tribune and the other conference. The Chilean women at the Tribune were women who had been in jail. And, of course, at the other conference they were an official delegation from the present government. And it was just about that time that the UN was going to send a team into Chile to investigate charges of torture and of unreasonable imprisonment. . . . That was an important point for me because women in prisons are at the lowest level of society wherever they are. It's usually worse for them—wherever it's bad it's worse for the women than it is for the men.[1]

Margaret Fulton, who later became the president of Mount St. Vincent University in Halifax, first met Muriel at this conference and she noted what a useful contribution Muriel made. Although she was living through a period

Betty Peterson, Rita Joe and Muriel at Antigonish Women's conference, 1986.

of personal grief following Jack's death, Muriel gathered Canadian women together to plan an action in support of a Native woman from Canada, Mary Two-axe Early. This was the only matter that the Canadian women addressed together as a delegation.

Mary Two-axe Early had been threatened with eviction from her home in the Caughnawaga Reserve (now known as Kahnawake) because, according to Canadian law, she had lost her status as an Indian upon her marriage to a white man. The Voice of Women in Toronto received money from the Women for Political Action to bring Mary to Mexico; VOW felt that it was important to publicize her case outside Canada. One night during the conference Mary phoned home because she was so worried only to discover that her own son-in-law, a police officer, had just conducted the eviction. This prompted the Canadian women at the conference to act. Muriel called the meeting at which they planned their strategy.

The position the Canadian women took was that Native women who married white men should retain their Native status in the same way as do Native men who married white women. The children of these Native women should retain their Native status as well. They got a young Native lawyer to read relevant provisions from the Indian Act. Mary then spoke about what it was like to lose her home. Then the vice-chairperson of the Fédération des Femmes de Québec spoke. She read a telegram in French to Prime Minister Trudeau, to Premier Bourassa and to the chief of the reserve stating that this was a terrible thing to happen while Canada was sitting on the United Nations Commission for Human Rights and while the Indian Act was under review by Natives. This appeal for immediate help received world-wide support for the cause of Native women in Canada and good coverage in the Canadian press. With world attention focussed on Mary's plight, the Canadian government could not defend such an action.[2]

A Feminist Leader

In 1975 the government of Nova Scotia set up an International Women's Year Committee and called for nominations. Because Muriel received nominations from all over the province, the government had to appoint her even though she was the only one on the committee who was not a Liberal supporter. After the committee had been named, a radio reporter asked the chairperson if these were political appointments and she said, "oh no, we've got Muriel Duckworth from the NDP."

Throughout the seventies, Muriel was increasingly recognized by women throughout Canada as a leader in the women's movement. Her own evolving consciousness of the need to take leadership as a woman came out of her experiences in the early days of the Home and School, in the Voice of Women, in MOVE and as a candidate for the NDP. Tracing her emergence as a feminist, Muriel gave credit to each of these organizations for the insights she gained about the role of women in the community and in politics.

> I don't know how much the experience of VOW had to do with [becoming a feminist] because I always say I came to the women's movement from the peace movement not vice versa. . . . There must have been some kind of response because I did not say, as other women were saying, "why a separate women's peace organization? Why women—why not the Voice of Humanity?" I had to keep on working that one out. There are a lot of things in my life that I never could be finally clear on, so that I could say, "this is it! This is true!" Only about a few things have I been able to say that. The trend towards feminism goes back to my Home and School years. I think I gradually saw that it was pretty silly the way we were behaving, that we were always pushing men up front and saying, "we have to get a man to be the president or we won't have any credibility." I was probably just getting pretty tired of that.
>
> It was exciting to see what women could do when the Voice of Women got going and you knew the women could do it. Before that I had not really belonged to women only organizations. I had belonged to a women's reading group because our husbands were all occupied working at night. And it was nice and comfortable. I had not thought at all whether it would be any different if there were men in it. It just happened to be all women. But in VOW there was that experience that women were competent and able to do it and

that was different from the Home and School. Women did things in
the Home and School, actions like getting a kindergarten, getting
a library, getting children's art classes. Although women did it I
didn't think of it [as being] particularly women. . . . During the VOW
experience there was an editorial in the local paper saying, who do
these women think they are? What do they think they know about
international affairs? They don't know anything! That sort of thing
makes you feel very angry. How can they write that? . . . Then there
was Encounter Week in Halifax. That was a point when it really hit
me. Twelve men on the platform analyzing what was wrong with
Halifax and not a single woman involved!

When Muriel issued public statements as national president of the Voice
of Women or from the executives of the Home and School or MOVE, or when
she was a candidate for the NDP, she was conscious that people reacted to
her. They were either strongly opposed to or supportive of her as a leader
who represented women's rising aspirations.

Along with her considerable public profile, Muriel's leadership was
acknowledged by many women because of their personal relationships with
her. Women from every walk of life would come to see her or make
appointments to talk things over that were bothering them. A young woman
who lived with Muriel for some time became aware of the constant procession to her front door, and felt sure that Muriel was completely trusted by
the women who came to pour their hearts out to her. They knew their secrets
were safe with her. When Muriel spoke publicly about issues of concern to
women she communicated an authority that was grounded in real lives.
Whenever she challenged opponents to the women's movement on radio or
television many women recognized that she was speaking out of their own
experience.

Muriel's strength was not only that she spoke out on behalf of women,
it was how she involved women in feminist issues, how she dealt with
differences within the feminist movement and the attitudes she displayed
towards those with whom she did not agree that marked her as a special kind
of feminist leader. For Muriel, integrating the personal and the political
meant integrating pacifism and feminism.

Doris Dyke described Muriel as a "natural feminist." Doris went on to
say:

She has a curious combination of self-esteem and of modesty. So
often those are seen as opposites but my own understanding is that
persons love their neighbours as they love themselves. It was as if
she didn't ever believe that women ought not hope to take a public
position or have a public life or that women ought not to be well

read, well educated, to be competent and skilled. At the same time she had all the valuable characteristics that society has assigned to women—she was caring, had a tremendous listening capacity, not given to an adversarial understanding of life but a negotiating, mediating one. She valued relationships over the rules of playing the game. I would see her life as an example of what many women would hope for and struggle for and have to learn to practice. . . . That's why I say that Muriel was a natural feminist.

Sylvia Hamilton, Marie Hamilton and Muriel at Halifax CRIAW conference, 1981.

Muriel had a gift for reaching out to include other women. Single-handedly she got many women involved in a host of issues. Initially women found it was easy to respond to her charismatic personality, but sometimes what she asked proved too challenging. One person felt that Muriel had incredible expectations of what others were capable of doing. In her view, some women feared they could not live up to Muriel's expectations or to the role model she offered. Internally they sometimes felt judged by her or that she triggered their own feelings of insecurity. Some women of her own generation felt threatened by Muriel's independence and freedom to say publicly what she felt. Perhaps they envied her, perhaps they too might have liked to have had the same independence. One good friend of Muriel's acknowledged, "Muriel is a hard model to follow. A lot of us look at ourselves in comparison to Muriel." A not untypical comment about Muriel was, "sometimes I regret it when I am being pushed by her when she wants me to do something and I don't want to do it. But I know how to resist her a little bit more than I used to." Another woman said, "she will continue to push until you say 'No.'" Perhaps a number of women also felt that, given their jobs and their family responsibilities, it was too much to get involved in voluntary activities fighting for women's concerns.

Others counted on Muriel to draw them into her activism. One woman reported that whenever she got a phone call from Muriel she would think,

> oh my God! Muriel's calling! What do I have to do? . . . It is almost absolute shame that makes me get moving again and it was a darn good thing that she did. We got a lot of good publicity and it brought some people together that needed to get together.

A close friend on whom Muriel relied acknowledged that Muriel never held it against one if one could not do what she asked. But she felt that Muriel's single-mindedness made her call on people persistently. Because she was highly respected, women generally tended to respond to her requests for their help. One woman observed that women who felt that they could not do what Muriel was doing no longer felt that way once Muriel talked with them because she created such a sense of community that one felt immediately included. "The magic of being with Muriel made you part of it. The closer you got to Muriel the less you felt you were part of the audience and that she was the speaker. There was such a sense of community, of oneness."

Muriel's Influence on Other Women Leaders

Margaret Fulton had a great appreciation for Muriel's leadership in the Halifax community. Having previously received an honorary doctorate from Mount St. Vincent, Muriel was present when Margaret was installed as president of the university and the two quickly became friends. Margaret was quite surprised that a woman like Muriel, with her outspoken views and her commitment to feminism, would have received an honorary degree from Mount St. Vincent University. It soon became apparent to Margaret, from talking with Muriel and with faculty, that the university was a very complex community. In no way did it reflect only a conservative Catholic tradition. Margaret thought Muriel understood very well that the Mount's purpose could no longer be to turn out young women who would be the wives of the elite and who were expected to influence society through their husbands. Muriel knew women had to be educated for their own careers and had to make their own contribution.

Margaret received support and encouragement from Muriel when she found herself in hot water over an article in the *Halifax Mail Star* which misrepresented Margaret's remarks to a *Toronto Star* reporter. She was cited as claiming that she would remove men from the university. What Margaret had said was that she had had no say in the original decision to admit men as students, but if she had she would have said no. Naturally male faculty of the Mount were upset. Margaret felt that what she learned from Muriel was the art of taking risks while being careful to preserve a public image such that she could not be easily discounted.

Margaret also felt that Muriel was able to challenge her to accept the authority of her job. Soon after coming to Halifax, the two women attended a meeting of the Canadian Research Institute for the Advancement of Women (CRIAW) at Dalhousie University. It was mentioned that another women's organization, the Canadian Congress for Learning Opportunities for Women (CCLOW), was looking for a place to have their annual conference in Halifax. Muriel quietly turned to Margaret and said, "why don't you offer the Mount?" Margaret felt rather stunned and replied, "I wouldn't have the authority!" To which Muriel countered, "but you're the president!" And Margaret found herself on her feet saying, "it would give me great pleasure . . ." and later bringing her staff on side to make the necessary arrangements. This marked the first of a great number of important women's local, regional and national meetings that were held at the Mount during Margaret's term as president, culminating with the Women's International Peace Conference in 1985.

Margaret recognized Muriel as "the quintessential networker" who was forever connecting people to one another and making them feel at home. Soon after Margaret's arrival, Muriel had her to tea to meet people Muriel knew were interested in the Mount. Countless times Muriel would pick up the phone and tell Margaret about particular functions or speakers coming to Halifax that might be of interest to her. Margaret came to realize that Muriel served many other persons in the same way. The two women had frequent tête-à-têtes over tea or dinner, went to movies together, and Muriel took to inviting Margaret to VOW functions, including peace marches. Margaret saw Muriel as both a doer and a catalyst. She got other people organized.

Gillian Thomas, an English professor at St. Mary's University and a peace activist, said of Muriel:

> Her great gift is to bring people together and to get projects rolling. She also has the ability to just put people in touch. Her assumption is that if you put two or three people together with progressive ideas, something worthwhile will come of it and it's worth doing in itself. She doesn't then have to go on and direct the project and influence exactly what they do. She'll enquire about it, no doubt, but she won't make all sorts of assumptions about what will come out of it. I think that's quite unusual because most people want to direct it once they have initiated it.

Muriel influenced young people early in their careers. Alexa McDonough attributed her joining the NDP to Muriel. Although Alexa's father was a staunch member of the CCF and later the NDP, in her early political life Alexa did not understand how her family's values translated politically. Alexa herself was a Liberal for a short time in the early 1970s. She worked to have Gerald Regan elected, thinking the promises he made for reform were important. She was soon disillusioned. By 1971 she became very angry over how the federal Liberal government had decided to use unemployment to fight inflation. All the decisionmakers cared about was economic growth and not the effects of unemployment on the poor. She was also angered by the use of patronage. Finally, what really liberated Alexa from Liberal thinking was hearing Muriel speak. Alexa saw her as a woman for whom the personal was political. "She had the guts to speak out about what she saw, publicly. I came to recognize 'I think exactly what she thinks!'" Previously Alexa had thought of Muriel as some kind of radical. Alexa joined the NDP at the time of the 1972 federal election. She soon became president of the Halifax Cornwallis constituency. During the provincial election Alexa noticed that Muriel took in her stride the different party politics within her own family. This reassured Alexa that families with different political affiliations could survive.

Alexa found that Muriel was a steady, ongoing influence. From time to time Muriel would send notes to Alexa from Magog that might seem like random greetings, but there was always a calculated reason for a communique from Muriel. She would write if, for instance, she saw things going astray in the women's movement or to critique some defence issue. Alexa observed that Muriel always understood that while you had to be willing to stick your neck out, it was also important to keep peace in the family within the women's movement. She hated to see fights develop that could be avoided and tried to bring women along in their thinking.

Support for women characterized Muriel's leadership. Muriel was known to remain at a public meeting all day to support an inexperienced woman who was to make a statement or give a brief. Muriel took women seriously and gave careful attention to everyone with whom she came into contact. She never dismissed women just because she could not agree with their views. Nor would she approve of a woman's tactics just because she was known as a feminist. Doris Dyke remarked:

> There were women who were feminists with whom Muriel found it difficult to get along. She could usually understand why at times women were angry or strident. But Muriel did not have unrealistic expectations of herself. There were women whose experience was such she would have to recognize that she was not able to work with them. I cannot remember Muriel ever confronting. I have heard her

say that she didn't share those opinions, that "that is different." She would recognize inconsistencies in life. . . . She is a pacifist but not a cheap peacemaker. It was not peace at any cost . . . I have seen her saddened. I have seen tears in her eyes because of the behaviour of women who were not acting in accordance with what they said they stood for. I have seen a certain kind of resignation or recognition that there was nothing she could do about that.

I have also seen her with some of her close women friends who were doing really self-destructive things and I have seen the same attitude in her. But I have seen something of the same response to women politically, who were acting out in the public sphere things that Muriel would see as destructive to the women's movement or to the good of people. . . . Far beyond the issues that Muriel was involved in was the way she was a feminist who never distinguished between the personal and the political.

Muriel came to the understanding that for the status of women to improve and for women's views to be valued, research by and for women was essential. Because of this she became involved in a new women's organization to which she devoted a great deal of time and energy over the next decade.

Women and Research

In 1976 Muriel became a founding member of an organization formed to encourage, coordinate and disseminate research into women's experience, and to bring together women who do research and women who make use of research. CRIAW was begun primarily by academic women. When Muriel was first invited to its inaugural conference she was not inclined to go as she felt she did not have a role to play in such an organization. However, she was persuaded by a bright young activist lawyer, Judy Wouk, that this was a very important opportunity for women who were community activists as well as for academic women. As a result of this founding meeting Muriel became an enthusiastic supporter of the notion of community-based research by and for women; she saw CRIAW as a bridge between academic researchers and community activists.

Muriel was elected as the representative from Nova Scotia to the first board of directors and became the treasurer.[3] She remained on the national board from 1977 to 1981 and was elected president for the term of 1979 to 1980.[4]

At first the board had a hard struggle because the sizeable grants they expected from the federal government never materialized. Research up until then was largely male-oriented and the women at CRIAW innocently thought they would get grants comparable to those given to academic institutions such as the Social Sciences and Humanities Research Council (SSHRC). It was hoped that Pauline Jewett, the first president, would attract funding, but since she had left the Liberal party and gone over to the NDP, her previous contacts were unhelpful. At the first AGM in Winnipeg in 1977 it was "touch and go" whether the organization would continue to exist. Nevertheless, CRIAW attracted five hundred members in its first ten months of existence. As treasurer, Muriel kept the members informed and urged them to get after the government for support.

While CRIAW was still trying to get off the ground, an early conference at Mount St. Vincent University on Women and Research was called in the fall of 1976 by three professors of sociology, Linda Christiansen-Ruffman of St. Mary's, Susan Clark of Mount St. Vincent and Lynn McDonald of Dalhousie. It attracted fifty presenters and six hundred participants. The enthusiasm shown for the idea of CRIAW at this conference greatly encouraged Muriel and Pauline Jewett.[5]

The Nova Scotia Chapter of CRIAW

Muriel took seriously her responsibility to recruit members from her region. Fifty women from Nova Scotia joined CRIAW in its first year and Nova Scotia is the only province which still has an active provincial organization.[6] The Maritime membership reflected Muriel's own style and interests. Donna Smyth, a professor of English from Acadia University, recalled that right from the start the character of the Nova Scotia chapter was unique:

> It is much more rooted in the community and the academic women are involved in the community too. It tends to have a character that is not fast-track academic. It tends to be a liaison, an interaction between women of learning whether they are of the community or academic women, rather than institutionally-based.

This model, which resembled adult education and community action approaches, suited Muriel. Later, when participatory research gained credibility, the notion of community involvement became important to CRIAW at the national level.

Early on, members in the Metro area of Halifax began holding informal monthly meetings in each other's homes and in community places such as the Unitarian Church. Women would present their work and learn about one another's research. Not all the research was done by women in university settings. CRIAW made small grants available to women who were not members of university faculties. Kathy Muggeridge presented her work on "Women and Work." In 1978 the Nova Scotia CRIAW organized and produced an excellent thirteen-part television series which presented a wide cross-section of Nova Scotia women, especially those women whose lives were seldom profiled. Muriel conducted several of the interviews in the first series and did many of the arrangements for the telecasts. Donna Smyth and Toni Laidlaw produced a second series in 1979 which was telecast all over the country.

The Nova Scotia chapter also made a practice of sponsoring public meetings and organizing provincial conferences on the same themes as the annual national conferences. This was done to satisfy the interest of women who could not attend national annual meetings in other parts of Canada.

The National President Speaks Out

At the national level, Muriel continued her efforts to raise funds for CRIAW. At the fourth AGM in November 1980 in Toronto, Muriel, as president, thanked the Ontario and the federal governments for their partial funding of the conference, and went on to give the governments a gentle slap on the wrist:

> In this euphoric atmosphere it doesn't seem quite appropriate to be critical, to hint that all is not well in the garden. But we cannot honestly ignore the message of many of our speakers and discussants and the evidence of our experience that the interests of the women of Canada are neither understood nor served by their governments. . . . We have primarily to bring feminist scholarship to bear on women's experience and vice versa.[7]

Muriel's experience within the NDP and the Voice of Women enriched her contribution to CRIAW. In a speech she gave later at the same conference, entitled "Making a Difference, Women in Politics," Muriel called upon her audience to:

> Imagine if you can a House of Commons and a Senate where 50 percent of the members are women. Imagine provincial legislatures, municipal councils, school boards where 50 percent of the members are women. Imagine that these women are feminists, and that a sizeable proportion of them are members of the Feminist Party of Canada. Imagine that you might be sitting in Parliament next to or across the aisle from a nursing mother, perhaps several of them scattered across the House. If you can ever imagine any of these circumstances, do you think that would make a difference? . . . The real question is how do women change society so that there can be a genuine expectation of a partnership for us in government, and an environment in which reproduction is seen for what it is, a central fact of life, and not a side issue to the main business which is, as of now, production. . . . Do we want to make a difference and how much time are we willing to spend on understanding with other women and feminist men the differences we need to bring about

what Elise Boulding calls "The Gentle Society."

In my own experience I would not have felt like running, would not have been asked to run without the experience I had in VOW and before that in Home and School, largely women though male-dominated. In 1974, I was the first woman to run above municipal level in the Halifax area. . . .

[During] International Women's year [the theme] was equality, development and peace. The head of our delegation to Mexico City didn't mention the word "Peace." . . . Will it be like that in Copenhagen at the mid-decade conference in June?[8]

Muriel made sure that she emphasized peace as a major theme of the United Nations decade of women when she reported on the 1980 parallel UN conference on women in Copenhagen, where she had represented both CRIAW and the Voice of Women Canada. She made it known that on the opening day of the conference, Nordic women presented to Kurt Waldheim, secretary general of the United Nations, a statement with 500,000 signatures which concluded: "We demand Disarmament for lasting world peace! The millions spent on weapons to be used for providing food. No to war!"

Muriel spoke of how the same demands were made in workshop after workshop and speech after speech by women who realized that war means violence against women and brings suffering to millions of refugees, most of whom are women and children. Women everywhere at this conference talked about the threat of a nuclear holocaust and saw the prevention of war as essential to the advancement of women throughout the world.

At the forum that paralleled the official UN conference, Muriel valued the chance to discuss many of the concerns of women. It was very unlike the strict and formal governments' conference where the agenda was rigidly controlled. She loved meeting informally with many different women as she walked around university buildings where the conference took place. Yet she was very conscious that she, like most of the women there, were from a privileged class and that the points of view they represented might not reflect sufficiently or accurately many of the women in their respective countries. She noted some of the serious differences among the national groups. In one meeting there was a highly charged atmosphere when the subject of clitorectomy was raised. At that time many African women were not inclined to debate in an international forum the sexual disfiguration practiced on young girls. After four hundred years of cultural imperialism, they refused to accept the criticism of Europeans and Americans, and some protested that Americans, with their high divorce rate, were not fit to criticize them.

A subsequent letter to CRIAW members described some of Muriel's impressions of this mammoth conference.

The Forum was at Copenhagen in July, where I represented you. Media coverage there was feeble, though 8,000 women were there, and 40 of them were Canadians. It's a most difficult conference to report. An overwhelming impression is of energy, mutual support and a few angry confrontations. A big women's festival in a park, conversations in the crowded corridors, hundreds of exhibits, thousands of posters, over 1,000 sessions of organized workshops, an exhibit of African women's tapestries, another of women's paintings from all over the world.

Every day there were workshops on women's research. I was impressed with a session run by African women sociologists and anthropologists on their research. They spoke of the special oppression of women under colonialism and under apartheid, [and] the difficulty of getting universities and governments to support research by and about women. Research is an orphan—thought of as a luxury—but it is necessary in order to provide documentation to policy-makers and other women. Laws alone don't change the status of women. Research can be consciousness-raising so that women will fight for their rights.

These African women were strongly aware of the impact of the outside world, of neo-colonialism and imperialism, translated through their own patriarchal systems into special oppression and both urban and rural poverty for their women. The politicization they brought to the conference was more than justified. Their message to us was: If you really want to help African women, get your governments to stop their economic and military support of the government of South Africa. It will collapse without that outside support. Meantime, apartheid is the ultimate in racism and sexism, and it rests on the backs of black women.

Of the huge quantities of statistics available, the one set that will stick in all our minds, and influence all our actions in future in solidarity with the women of the world, was this one provided by the United Nations and quoted in one of the sessions on Women and Politics: 77 percent of women are illiterate. They constitute 33 percent of the work force, spend 66 percent of the total hours at work, receive 10 percent of the income, and own 1 percent of the property. In general, the relative status of women has deteriorated in the last five years, since the beginning of the UN decade of women. Without political power, women cannot change the social and economic conditions that oppress them. Women speak now with a very small voice. Governments of men decide the outcome. The Forum was like the elephant and the blind men of Hindustan. I have read and heard several reports and they are all quite different because the conference was too big and varied and physically scattered for any one person to get a total picture.[9]

A Halifax-based committee of CRIAW planned the fifth annual general meeting and conference held at Dalhousie University, November 13–15, 1981, and chose as a theme women's culture.[10] CRIAW had a preponderance of social scientists and historians among its members and the conference planners wanted to widen its scope. For the first time the accent would be on the arts. There was an exhibit of nine women artists at Mount St. Vincent. On the Dalhousie campus, Henson College held a showing of traditional women's crafts including weaving and sculpture. A dramatic piece of sculpture entitled "The Crucified Woman"[11] was brought for display from Toronto. A panel discussed women's culture and at a memorable mother and daughter session, three sets of mothers and their daughters talked about their relationships. There were also folk singers, plays and films by women, as well as Maritime entertainers. The usual paraphernalia of conferences reflected women's culture too. Instead of brief cases for their papers, delegates were provided with plastic shopping bags with the conference's insignia. And the committee paid special attention to planning menus of very attractive food. Following the banquet in the spacious Great Hall there was a play on scenes from women's lives.

The planning of the conference was particularly collegial. The close-knit committee often rotated their functions and dispensed with a coordinator. All of them helped each other out. Donna Smyth worked with Muriel on the conference budget and found her to be one of the best persons she had ever worked with on finances. Muriel kept the budget right on target. She invited artists and guests to the opening ceremonies, raised funds, met with local Nova Scotia business leaders, and spent many hours at her cottage writing to Canadian firms to request funds for the conference.

At the conclusion of the conference, Muriel was honoured by the inauguration of the Muriel Duckworth Award, to be presented annually to a feminist woman who had contributed significantly to the advancement of women within Canada through action-research in the field of social justice, including peace. It was first awarded to Kay Macpherson.

Linda Christiansen-Ruffman made a very moving speech and presented a loaf of home-made bread and a bouquet of roses to Muriel. Several hundred women (with few dry eyes) then serenaded her with the song, "Bread and Roses." In her remarks, Linda said:

> Muriel always wants to get the latest political issue on the agenda. She always has a political, a social and a personal dimension and all three are a part of her way of presenting herself and are part of her political, social and community practice.

Muriel herself was named an honorary member of CRIAW in 1983.

Notes

1. M. Duckworth, "Report on World Conference on International Women's Year, Mexico, June 19–July 2, 1975." PANS MG 1 Vol. 2932, No. 6.
2. In June 1985 the Canadian parliament passed Bill C-31, ending more than one hundred years of legislated sexual discrimination against Native women. Deborah Kaetz, "IWY Conferences in Mexico City: An Interview with Muriel Duckworth." Atlantis Vol. 1, No. 2.
3. PANS MG 1 Vol. 2905, No. 20.
4. PANS MG 1 Vol. 2906, No. 18.
5. "CRIAW Celebrates 10 Years of Growth as a Research Institute." Obtained from CRIAW national office, Ottawa.
6. Ibid.
7. PANS MG 1 Vol. 2905, No. 25.
8. Ibid.
9. "Some Thoughts from the President to Members, Lapsed Members and Future Members of CRIAW—Report on the Copenhagen Conference." Letter of October 1980, obtained from CRIAW national office, Ottawa.
10. PANS MG 1 Vol. 2905, No. 26.
11. The sculptor was Almuth Lutkenhaus-Lackey.

Chapter 16

An Ambassador for Peace

Two Havens

C oburg House affectionately replaced "the Hive" when Muriel moved
there in the fall of 1980, along with her friend Betty Peterson and two
Dalhousie women students. This had been her son John's home for several
years but when he moved away from Halifax and began to travel he wanted
her to live there. She and her friends proceeded to live co-operatively. Their
large old friendly house became a meeting place each Sunday for the
Quakers of Halifax/Dartmouth and for many meetings of women in the
peace movement and the women's movement. Abundant green plants
thrived in the spacious sunny living room and a lovely, huge old pine hutch
housed Quaker reading materials. Running along the front hall, a long table
contained the latest "alternative" periodicals for ready borrowing. Often a
peace march or a rally would begin with a rendezvous and a bite at Coburg
House. Numerous potluck suppers, committee meetings and sometimes the
monthly meetings of the Voice of Women and CRIAW were held there. A
great many persons came to consult Muriel at home and she somehow
always managed to find the time to take them into her study and give them
her undivided attention. She would extend the same friendly welcome to a
high school student as to a visiting dignitary.

Then in the late spring Muriel would return to "Maple Crest," her

Coburg House, 1985.

beloved cottage in Austin, Quebec. There she prized her solitude and renewed her energy by getting in touch with nature and visiting lifelong friends along the lake and in Magog. She relished the chance to be with people in a more leisurely way, as family and friends frequently came for weekends or holidays to see her. It was such a relaxed setting, whether outdoors on the big wrap-around veranda at the top of a hill overlooking the lake or indoors gathered around the old stone fireplace.

Between these two idyllic settings Muriel considered herself very fortunate. People knew whenever they visited her that she was delighted to share her home. Her son Martin, a film-maker, felt that if he could only stay one whole summer at the cottage he would be able to film the world at Muriel's doorstep because so many people found their way to her from all corners of the earth. Many came to enjoy themselves and to draw on the wisdom of this pacifist, feminist humanitarian.

Once back in Halifax, at an age when most women would have been content to bask in the appreciation of an admiring circle, Muriel carried on working to initiate public actions on issues at local, provincial and national levels. She gave equal support to the efforts of others to organize in the community. Muriel regularly spent hours on the telephone getting people to turn up for meetings or events. A telephone call from her was invariably personal, cheerful and efficient. The media consulted Muriel regularly whenever international

Betty Peterson and Muriel.   Muriel and Virgie Noanea, Coburg House.

Betty Peterson

peace or women's issues were in the news. She could be counted upon to speak at any youth or women's conference and, because she was so appealing to children and young people, often teachers called on her to meet with their classes.

Already past seventy years of age, Muriel took every opportunity she got to travel to other countries as an informal ambassador for peace. During the 1980s she attended the second United Nations Special Session on Disarmament (UNSSOD 2) in New York city, visited the Hiroshima Peace Park in Japan, and travelled to the Soviet Union, Mexico, Nicaragua, El Salvador, Honduras and to Quaker communities in New Zealand. And she was a moving force in bringing women from around the world to the Women's International Peace Conference in Halifax in 1985.

A Visit to NATO

In 1982 Muriel represented CRIAW at the invitation of the Department of External Affairs on a Canadian Women's Study Tour. The tour included visits to NATO in Brussels, to the Supreme Headquarters of Allied Powers in Europe in Mons, to the Organization for Economic Cooperation and Development (OECD) in Paris and to the Canadian Forces Base in Lahr, Germany.[1]

Each year the government sent five or six groups of people deemed to represent significant segments of society for the stated purpose of informing the Canadian public (i.e., engaging in public relations on behalf of the government) about Canada's foreign policy. Up until then the study tours had been for mayors, labour leaders, journalists, academics, high school teachers and parliamentarians; this was the first and only occasion when women's groups were invited. Twelve national women's organizations were included.[2]

Muriel was not to be taken in. In her report back to CRIAW she stated:

> There is no escaping the propagandist nature of the enterprise—to build up faith in the deterrent, complete distrust of the Warsaw Pact countries, support for the horrendous notion that the future deployment of Cruise and Pershing missiles is essential to maintain the balance of terror in Europe. One needs to check everything, especially the recurring story of "gaps" to be filled and the perception of the present balance of weaponry, both nuclear and conventional, between the Warsaw Pact and NATO, against other sources of information. Perhaps the fact that at least this dozen Canadian women will now be more concerned and pay more attention to sources does make this trip worth while.[3]

Muriel provided a powerful role model during the NATO briefings on how to go after information and how to challenge the received wisdom. The Voice of Women had prepared a kit of information containing articles critical of NATO, as a service to the women going, and Muriel distributed these at the first informal gathering in one of the hotel rooms. As she said in her report for CRIAW, "we did a lot of talking on buses and trains and in hotel rooms."

Later at a briefing, when a military official gave statistics showing the outstanding strength of the Warsaw Pact, she asked for his sources. He cited several and said that the rest were classified. As Muriel pointed out, this meant that it was impossible to verify his statistics. She also commented on the fact that NATO did not quote the Stockholm International Peace Research Institute (SIPRI), a well respected source of statistics about arms.

The NATO personnel, possibly thinking that the women would not be too interested in military activity, offered for their edification session after session on obscure non-military agencies of NATO. Finally Muriel asked the speaker what percentage of NATO's total budget was consumed by these agencies. He confessed to not knowing. Later when the ambassador was rounding off the meetings he asked whether the women had had all their questions satisfactorily answered. Muriel immediately repeated her question about the amount of money spent on NATO's non-military activities. The ambassador sent an official off to get the answer—less than 1 percent! The effect of that lesson was not lost on the delegation.[4]

Speaking Truth to Power

While Muriel relished being a national and an international communicator of good will and loved playing a supportive role to many women and women's organizations, her passion for truth and justice remained undiminished. She never missed an opportunity to "speak truth to power" and she was a challenging communicator.

Muriel and Ann Gertler presented a lengthy statement on behalf of the Voice of Women/La Voix des Femmes to the House of Commons Standing Committee for External Affairs and National Defense on February 16, 1982. These seasoned peacemakers stated:

> There is some feeling among us that war preparations and plans, and the actions that flow from the tunnel vision of professional involvement in the military definition of security come from the traditionally male-dominated world of the politics of power. There is no guarantee that women could prevent world destruction. However, we think that already there exist in communities, at many levels, alternative models and social skills. They should be employed by men and women together to change the disastrous course of events.
>
> We would like to take a moment to say that as women, we are

particularly aware that "conventional" wars that have ravaged the Third World in the second half of the 20th century killing an estimated 25 million people have not been wars between armies in the historic mode, but wars in which women and children, not to mention old people, have been victims. Furthermore, in every country of the world, but especially in the non-OPEC developing world, militarism is depriving women of funds to meet daily human needs. It is women who have to bear the greatest burden in coping with life in the growing refugee camps of the world. In Canada militarism contributes to our difficulties from inflation, unemployment and restricted budgets for social services.[5]

Women's Petition for Peace Presented at UNSSOD 2

A committee of Voices in Halifax took the lead in organizing and circulating the only peace petition originating in Canada for presentation to the United Nations second Special Session on Disarmament held in New York in June 1982. Betty Peterson and Pat Kipping had brought back to Canada from a European disarmament conference in 1980 a strong petition first circulated by Norwegian women demanding an end to nuclear arms. Over the next fifteen months VOW members collected 125,000 signatures from Blubber Bay, BC, to Come-by-Chance, Newfoundland, and from the Yukon and North West Territories. The petition was printed in newspapers, circulated in English and French, and translated into Cree and Innuk. VOW began by having the petition endorsed by known political figures, church women,

Betty Peterson, Kay Macpherson, Muriel, New York City, UNSSOD II, 1982.

Betty Peterson

Peace Petition entering Parliament, 1982.

writers, artists and women in labour organizations and education, and then encouraged women everywhere to sign it as evidence of their determination to have governments stop the madness of nuclear armament and pay attention to human needs. Women from a multitude of settings—the Ladies' Aid Society in a little fishing village, the staff of a hospital, an educational centre and the Atlantic Symphony Orchestra—signed their names. Muriel's good friend Betty Peterson assembled the signatures. She and Muriel organized their presentations for maximum publicity.[6]

Before going to New York for UNSSOD 2, the two women led a delegation of twenty Voices from around Canada to Ottawa where they were welcomed on May 27 by Mayor Marion Dewar at a breakfast in city hall. The women then proceeded to Parliament Hill where they were met at the eternal flame by a colourful procession. Women with little children in strollers and prams, accompanied by clowns, pranced up to the House of Commons carrying balloons, posters and blowing bubbles in the sparkling sunshine. They sang peace songs and heard speeches, and then the twenty representatives, led by Pat Kipping and her little daughter Tara, were received by women senators and women members of parliament. That afternoon Pauline Jewett introduced a resolution to the House and presented the petition calling for nuclear disarmament.[7] Writing about the event afterwards in the VOW national newsletter, Betty Peterson said: "[Muriel's] persistent phone calls, invitational letters and superb media presence and coverage paved the way for it to happen."

Muriel and Mary Two-Axe Early, VOW Petition in Ottawa, 1982.

Muriel and Betty also arranged to have the petition presented at the United Nations in New York, where a busload of women from Halifax joined them. Muriel and Kay Macpherson had left a few days beforehand, thinking they would take in a Women's International League for Peace and Freedom (WILPF) conference in New York before UNSSOD 2. However, when they reached the US border, Kay, who had been delegated as the speaker to represent the peace groups in Canada at the major rally, was stopped and refused entry. No explanation was given; Kay was simply refused. Muriel wanted to remain back with her but Kay insisted she carry on and bring pressure to bear from New York while Kay returned home to inform the world about this extraordinary situation. A flurry of telephone calls resulted in much political pressure being mobilized in Canada, and the US decision to bar Kay was rescinded. Muriel could never figure out why Kay was stopped and not herself. They had equally opposed the US war in Vietnam, and each had often spoken out against US foreign policy.

The excitement of Kay's exclusion did not quite eclipse the VOW presentation event. On June 10, 1982, two hundred Canadians, mostly VOW members, joined Betty and Muriel for the presentation of the petitions in the auditorium of the Dag Hammarskjold Library to Gerard Pelletier, Canadian ambassador to the UN, and Arthur Menzies, ambassador for disarmament, at a ceremony chaired by Muriel.

The NGOs at the UN organized a giant rally. On June 12, one million people marched for peace from the UN buildings to Central Park. Muriel was caught up in the contagious spirit of the massive rally. She was especially pleased to hear Kay's voice over the loudspeakers calling for a freeze, a reversal of the arms race and the reallocation of resources from military spending to meet human needs.

The Peace Park, Hiroshima, Japan, 1983

After Muriel returned to Austin from UNSSOD 2 she was suddenly struck on the night of August 4 with the Guillaume-Barre virus, a sometimes fatal illness. She was hospitalized in Sherbrooke, Quebec, for six weeks with Eleanor and Martin at her bedside. When she returned to Halifax in a very weakened condition she could only walk with support on both sides. During that fall and winter she had to learn to walk again with the help of daily physiotherapy. Corrie Douma organized a committee of Quakers and friends who saw to her transportation to the rehabilitation centre and provided loving care. Her convalescence throughout the spring was so remarkable that that summer she decided to make a trip to Japan for Hiroshima Day, August 6. She had always wanted to visit the Peace Park in Hiroshima and to take part in the ceremonies on Hiroshima Day, and this year the opportunity presented itself. Her son John and Anne Fouillard, his fiancée, were planning to go there on their return from a lengthy trip to Southeast Asia, and Martin was also going for the premiere in Japan of his new film, "No More Hibakusha," about survivors of the atomic bomb. Muriel's good friends Suellen and Michael Bradfield from Halifax were also planning a trip to Japan that summer and Suellen agreed to travel with Muriel.

VOW members made necklaces of gold foil cranes, a Japanese peace symbol, for Suellen and Muriel to wear. They collected letters from school children and folded hundreds of little paper peace cranes into necklaces for them to take along. They also collected from government offices Canadian maple leaf pins for distribution to Japanese citizens. Muriel herself visited the mayors of Halifax and Dartmouth to receive their letters of greeting and friendship to the mayors and citizens of Hiroshima and Nagasaki. A peace group organized by Kay Leslie from Georgeville, Quebec, a community across the lake from Muriel's summer cottage, sent a very special gift. They had a banner designed by an artist in their group. A red Japanese sun had a maple leaf superimposed on it and a message in Japanese calligraphy read: "to the people of Hiroshima and Nagasaki from the people of Georgeville, Quebec, Canada, Peace." They made twelve such banners for Muriel to take to peace groups and the mayors of the two Japanese cities.[8]

When they arrived in Tokyo, Suellen and Muriel met Martin, John and Anne, and spent several days there. Ms. Seyaki, a leading volunteer in the YWCA who was very active in the peace movement, met them and Suellen and Muriel stayed at the YWCA. Ms. Seyaki took them to the Maruki museum where they met and had tea with a gentle woman artist who had depicted the Hiroshima experience. Twelve floor-to-ceiling panels displayed horrific scenes of ghosts, fire and water following the explosion. They attended a series of meetings with grassroots peace groups and union groups where Muriel spoke.

Along with six other Canadians, including Setsuko Thurlow, a Toronto

Muriel speaking at International Peace Conference in Tokyo, 1983.

VOW member, Muriel and Suellen attended the 1983 World Conference Against Atomic and Hydrogen Bombs which began in Tokyo, continued in Hiroshima and ended in Nagasaki. At the convention, Muriel gave a speech and met a Quaker who was a survivor of Hiroshima. He had been a child of seven at the time of the bombing and he gave them a book he had written about it. Muriel and Suellen also had a very interesting conversation with a Japanese single mother who worked as an editor in a textbook publishing firm. She told them about the difficult lot of single women in Japan and shared much of her life with them even though she never expected to see them again.

Muriel communicated great sympathy towards the people she and Suellen met. A Japanese man who saw them in a restaurant insisted on paying for their meal because she reminded him of his mother. When they visited a hospital for survivors in Hiroshima, a beautiful old woman sup-

Muriel, a local girl and Suellen Bradfield at the Sadako Memorial, Hiroshima, 1983.

ported by a walker moved towards Muriel as though she were drawn to a magnet. The two women embraced and wept even though the one could not speak English and the other spoke no Japanese. Three elderly patients shared their experiences through an interpreter. They spoke with dignity of the unimaginable horror that the A-bomb had brought into their lives, and presented Muriel and Suellen with gifts of a beautiful quilted doll and paper flowers.

At the end of each day the women would return to their quarters physically and emotionally exhausted. With the extreme heat, Muriel was often very tired in Japan. Nevertheless she took in everything possible.

On August 5 they took the five-hour train trip to Hiroshima. They met that day with Mr. Takeshi Araki, mayor of Hiroshima, who told them about the appeal sent out by himself and Mr. Motoshima, the mayor of Nagasaki, to promote solidarity among cities, towns and villages throughout the world for the total abolition of nuclear weapons.

On August 6, the anniversary of the bombing, Muriel and Suellen were on their way by 6:00 a.m. As they arrived at the Peace Park they were met by young Japanese boy scouts who gave each person a bouquet to lay before the cenotaph. Two hundred thousand names were recorded there and each year new names were added as people died from the effects of the bomb. That year over five thousand new names were added to the list.

Solemn music played as they were ushered to the seats reserved for foreign guests. At precisely 8:15 a.m., the moment of the bomb's explosion, there was complete silence. Then hundreds of doves—symbols of peace—were released to fly above the cenotaph, across the city and towards the hills. Muriel thought of the pictures she had seen of the thousands of birds and butterflies with their

Anne Fouillard, Muriel, John Duckworth, Martin Duckworth at Sadako Memorial, Peace Park, Hiroshima, 1983.

wings aflame, killed by the bomb; dropped from the sky. Mr. Araki, himself a survivor, read a peace declaration and told them, "today's hesitation leads to tomorrow's destruction." He urged the US and the USSR "to rise above their military and strategic considerations and with a global citizens' perspective, to make a decision that shall bring hope to the world."[9] A great number of women all in black came solemnly up to the cenotaph to lay flowers.

Martin, John and Anne met up with Muriel and Suellen at the Peace Park. Martin filmed throughout the ceremony. They remained there most of the day joining in the peace crane walk in the afternoon. Muriel and Suellen carried the crane necklaces made by the Halifax children to the memorial statue of Sadako, a symbol of all the children who died from the bomb. They placed the paper cranes at the foot of the statue of this Japanese school girl who was exposed to radiation and who died several years later of leukaemia. Sadako tried unsuccessfully to fold a thousand cranes before she died, in keeping with the legend which claimed that if one folded a thousand paper cranes one would have a long life. John encountered Yukio Matsoura, a former teacher of Sadako, and brought him to meet Suellen and Muriel. They told him how moving children found her story whenever they did peace education and taught them to fold cranes. Mr. Matsoura then took them by car to his daughter's home and showed them pictures he had of Sadako. He had organized the campaign to raise money for the memorial statue.

In the evening they attended the lighting of candles service for the spirits of the dead. People floated memorial lanterns down the river on which were written the names of loved ones who had passed away. Muriel, John and Martin's thoughts were with Jack as their candle joined the others in a stream of light. Before leaving the Peace Park they returned to Sadako's statue and held their own private Quaker ceremony and sang peace songs. Suellen led them in "We Are a Gentle Angry People."

They travelled to Nagasaki for the ceremonies on August 9, and they presented Mayor Motoshima with one of the banners they had brought with them. Japanese people's eyes would light up whenever they read the message from the people of Georgeville. Muriel spoke to a Buddhist priest on one of the parades and she gave him a banner for their head priest which he agreed to deliver. Later Muriel received a touching letter from the head Buddhist monk thanking her and conveying his message of peace.

Lunch with the Prime Minister, January 16, 1984
"Lunch with the Prime Minister was not an occasion for witty repartee," Muriel reported in the national Voice of Women newsletter. Ten leaders from peace groups had been invited to 24 Sussex Drive to say what they thought about various models for a peace research institute which the government was thinking of setting up. Over lunch each in turn spoke of

their own organization's concerns and the prime minister responded.

Muriel was not about to let an occasion such as this pass without persistently putting some hard questions to Trudeau. As she reported:

> I raised the question of the Cruise missile testing which is about to take place in Canada. My question was not related to the fact of the testing but to the deceit involved. I asked the Prime Minister how he could justify telling the Canadian people, as he and his Ministers have repeatedly, that the testing of Cruise missiles in Canada was an obligation to NATO. I reminded him that the missiles to be tested in Canada are air-launched, to be used by the U.S. Air Force and that they are being tested at the request of the United States, not at the request of NATO. . . .
>
> Mr. Trudeau did not immediately reply, and so later I put the question again. "The missiles being tested in Canada are not for NATO, are they?" and he replied, "No, they are not for NATO." He then justified the tests on the grounds that the air-launched Cruise missiles are not "destabilizing." The statement, though certainly open to question, is in itself an admission that the NATO (Pershing) missiles are "destabilizing," that is, they upset the balance in Europe.[10]

Muriel also took Trudeau to task for Canada's voting record at the United Nations questioning, for example, Canada's vote against the nuclear freeze. She pointed out inconsistencies in the Speech from the Throne. How he could reconcile including in the budget a 3 percent increase in real money terms in the defense budget with his stand on peace and disarmament in another paragraph? She objected that his reference to Canadians being armed with only "conventional weapons" did not convey that a conventional bomb was being developed with the destructive power (except for the fallout) equal to that of a two- or three-megaton atomic bomb.

Person to Person in the Soviet Union

Muriel valued no role more than that of bearing good will between parties. In 1984, when she was asked by Bonnie Klein of Studio D of the National Film Board to go with her to the Soviet Union, she accepted eagerly. Bonnie was making a film called "Speaking Our Peace." In her customary style Muriel began to involve everyone she knew in the preparations so that by the time she left she carried many symbols of friendship, more than a hundred letters from school children, pins, peace posters, prints, buttons and pictures to give to the people she would visit. As she reported in the VOW national newsletter:

> The great thing about these gifts was the spontaneity of the giving
> and the genuine warmth and smiles on the faces of those who
> brought them to my door. Even the provincial and federal govern-
> ment people from whom I got pins as gifts to take were enthusiastic
> about taking part in this peace mission and asked me a lot of
> questions about it.[11]

She described the response she met—the surprise and delight on the
faces of the women selling cheese and flowers and pickled garlic in the
market, and the children she taught to make paper cranes and who sent her
back with their own beautiful paintings and continued to correspond with
the children in Halifax and Vancouver who had written to them.

In the film, Muriel appears as a seventy-five-year-old grandmother with
Kathleen Wallace Deering, a young Ploughshares researcher who was fifty
years younger. The two of them interview Soviet citizens, most of whom are
women and children. Their role was to have a frank discussion about the
differences between the governments of the East and West while retaining
and promoting friendship between their peoples. They met with the official
Soviet Women's Committee and discussed with them how each side fur-
thered the arms race using the rhetoric of defence. Muriel was able to soften
the tone of this difficult exchange when she discovered one of the Soviet
women had been to the same conference that she had attended in Moscow
in 1967.

They spent thirteen days in Moscow and three in Leningrad. In Leningrad Studio D filmed a very touching scene of Muriel and an older woman,
Olga, who had been a pilot during the Second World War and had ferried
children out of the starving, besieged city of Leningrad. The two women
discussed these tragic times as they overlooked the memorial park where lie
buried 450,000 of the 750,000 men, women and children who died during
the seige of Leningrad. Olga told her that people still remembered these
times of starvation when they came to the graves to place cake, pastry and
candy on them. With tears in her eyes Muriel embraced Olga and the camera
zoomed in on their tightly clasped hands.

The films "Speaking Our Peace" and "Russian Diary" by Bonnie Klein
and Terry Nash of Studio D were made during the pre-glasnost days. There
were occasional uncomfortable moments when the film crew members were
sure they were being followed. Nevertheless they proceeded according to
plan. There was a close call while they were visiting the one remaining
Moscow synagogue. In front of the synagogue they spoke to a "Refusenik"
whose words were later erased from the tape at the insistence of the
authorities who came to their rooms following this conversation. They were
told the entire film would be confiscated if this was not done. Muriel felt
nervous when three days later they quietly met and exchanged gifts with a

few citizens who were part of the independent Group to Establish Trust Between the U.S.S.R. and the U.S.A. One of their members, Olga Medvedkova, who was four months pregnant, was tried on a trumped-up charge of beating up a police officer. When Muriel met with people from the official peace movement she asked about this woman who was on trial and they denied that this was so. She insisted that it was true and the women with whom she spoke became very angry. Later, on the plane from Moscow to Norway, Muriel read in a newspaper that the woman was released due to her pregnancy but the court did not say that she was not guilty.

For Muriel, speaking her peace meant meeting and supporting the dissidents who formed their own peace group, just as much as it meant folding peace cranes with Soviet school children or talking with the officially sanctioned peace groups. She agreed with Ursula Franklin who said in the film, "peace is not the absence of war but the absence of fear."

The Women's International Peace Conference, Halifax, 1985

One weekend in February 1984, at Mount St. Vincent University, Muriel and Betty Peterson had an exciting conversation with two other peace activists, Berit Ås, a visiting professor of social psychology from Norway, and Dorothy Goldin Rosenberg, an environmentalist and longtime member of VOW in Montreal. They began by asking themselves, "where are the peace women at the negotiating table?"[12] The effects of their dialogue were to ripple out across Canada and throughout the world. They considered that it was time for a women's international conference to talk about how women would negotiate peace. They wanted to find alternative strategies to militarism and new techniques to solve conflict through non-violent means, and they wanted women at the negotiating tables. Their idea met with an enthusiastic response from the national and regional Voice of Women, who

UN Diplomat, Inga Thorsson, Muriel and Berit Ås, 1983.

Women's International Peace Conference, Halifax, 1985.

also wanted to come up with a way of involving women in their own communities.

By June of that year a VOW committee had reached out to numerous Canadian women's organizations and invited them to a weekend conference at York University in Toronto to consider co-sponsoring an international conference. Twenty-six Canadian women's groups decided that weekend to join together to hold the Women's International Peace Conference on the theme of The Urgency for True Security: Women's Alternatives for Negotiating Peace. Local conferences on the same theme were also organized in different cities throughout the country in preparation for the international event. Mount St. Vincent University was chosen as the location for the international conference because Muriel had had the foresight to interest Margaret Fulton in it. Muriel had also interested Nancy Jackman of Toronto in providing start-up funding.

Once again Muriel was selected as chairperson of the national planning committee and helped the staff with the thousand and one details involved in preparing for the five day conference, held June 5–10, 1985. Local planning committees of women's groups organized mini conferences (some had as many as three hundred women in attendance) in fourteen cities across Canada. Educational materials were prepared for all of them by the four women organizing the international conference. Muriel helped to obtain generous funding from private donations and government grants that enabled the conference committee to invite women from every continent. Even in her personal Christmas letter that year Muriel solicited donations from her

Muriel with founding members celebrating vow 25th Anniversary, 1985.

many friends. On numerous occasions she stayed up late at night to have telephone conversations with women on the other side of the globe to interest them in coming. And she made sure that groups of Canadian women of colour were represented in good numbers. Staff members recalled how Muriel assisted them sometimes late into the night to meet their deadlines.

Muriel had a particular genius for ensuring that people who came to the conference would be at ease and want to participate. It was her idea that every panel of speakers should be a rainbow of colours so that everyone in the audience could see her own race on stage. She suggested "buzz" groups immediately following plenary sessions, preceding the question period, so that women in the audience would be comfortable in putting questions to the speakers. Muriel was particularly successful in involving more than a hundred Halifax volunteers to form a myriad of committees to ensure the conference's success. However, one of Muriel's ideas backfired. Having been to countless conferences in her lifetime that concluded with the passing of resolutions that were often not acted upon, she suggested to the planning committee that this conference follow a different format. She suggested that they dispense with resolution-making and instead focus on ways to have women demonstrate negotiating peaceful solutions. This was exactly what was to happen but not in the way pictured by the planning committee. What Muriel and her committee had not bargained on was that women from several countries who came to the conference were counting on an expression of worldwide opinion to sway their governments back home, particularly on issues of human rights abuse. They wanted ringing resolutions to come from the conference in defence of the right of women to security in their particular countries. Generalities were not enough for them. At the final plenary this was a sticking point. The conference had achieved an astonishing consensus on a common statement that had been through a long and careful process. And now there was danger of this solidarity being ripped apart. Muriel, as the chair, encouraged a full debate and allowed women full rein to express their passionate convictions.

Eventually an acceptable arrangement was arrived at whereby women agreed to "affirm" the findings of the small group discussions and the conference was extended by several hours for every concern of each group to be brought to the floor and voted upon. Throughout the entire meeting Muriel remained calm and warmly facilitated the process. Although unplanned and unforeseen, this demonstration of women negotiating a peaceful resolution became a memorable event for every woman there.

/Mission for Peace to Central America

Little did Muriel realize at the time of the Women's International Peace Conference how soon she would again be travelling as a peacemaker. Within a few weeks of returning to the cottage for a well-deserved rest she was asked by an organization known as Non Intervention in Central America: Canadians for Self-Determination (NICA), to join a Mission for Peace to Central America during August 1985. Muriel thought she could not turn down this request. She felt that it was important to go in order to gain more first-hand information about a region that was in turmoil and to try to have an effect on Canadian policy.

In the mid-eighties levels of militarization in Central America were rising and all the economic indicators were in critical decline, fostering social and political unrest. US military involvement was very worrisome. Many Canadians were afraid that the region was likely to become a flash point, as border incidents between Honduras and Nicaragua were increasing with Contra mercenary forces being trained in Honduras with US backing. The military governments of both El Salvador and Honduras continued to perpetrate atrocities and human rights abuses on their civilian populations. A Gallup poll in September 1984 found that two-thirds of Canadians interviewed were opposed to expanded US military involvement in Central America.

NICA, formed by the Canadian Labour Congress, the United Automobile Workers, CUSO and Oxfam, decided to send a fact finding delegation to Central America as a "Mission for Peace." Their purpose was to analyze the current regional crises, to evaluate the role of peace initiatives, including the Contadora Plan—drafted by the leaders of the region and rejected by the US—and to examine the current and potential role for Canada in promoting political negotiations which would lead to long-term reconciliation and equitable solutions.

Originally there were six men going but when the Halifax Oxfam office heard this they objected that there were no women. NICA then tried to include Margaret Fulton. She was not free to go, but suggested Muriel, who had been on the national board of Oxfam for several years. There were times when Muriel was asked to be the token woman at public events that she declined, on principle, but she felt this was an exception. The mission also included Daniel Benedict, an academic and former labour leader; Timothy Draimin, the delegation coordinator and a Central America specialist who worked out of the Jesuit Centre for Social Faith and Justice; Maurice Dupras, a former Liberal MP; Karl Friedmann, the first ombudsperson of BC; Leonard Johnson, a retired major-general and member of Generals for Peace; and Jack McNie, a former Liberal minister for the province of Ontario.[13]

Mission for Peace delegates were required to raise their own funds for the trip. Muriel, with the help of the Oxfam staff in Halifax, wrote to many of her personal friends and met with a tremendous response. Her trip was oversubscribed. It did not occur to Muriel at seventy-six that this might be too onerous a trip for her. She still thought of herself as more like a person in her fifties. The tour was somewhat of a forced march with few creature comforts in the simple hotels where they stayed. During two weeks, from August 26 to September 11, 1985, they visited five countries, Mexico, El Salvador, Honduras, Nicaragua and Costa Rica, as well as Washington, New York and Ottawa. The delegates interviewed over one hundred persons, including military commanders, heads of state and foreign affairs members, as well as a dozen groups including human rights and humanitarian organizations.

Upon her return to Halifax Muriel described what she had seen on the trip at a public meeting held at the Archives of Nova Scotia. The mission had not gone to Guatemala since they were told at an earlier briefing in Mexico that it would be too dangerous for the people they would visit. In El Salvador they had to be very careful. They met secretly with NGO representatives who themselves never talked openly to each other. Muriel found El Salvador frightening. Her first cultural shock was stepping out of the plane at San Salvador and being surrounded by the military. From the airport they drove up the main road past the spot where four nuns had been murdered not long before, and they saw the hotel where Americans had recently been killed. Later they saw where Archbishop Oscar Romero had been assassinated. When they met with government officials at Defence Headquarters they found it hard to ask polite questions.

Evidence of the military regime was even more painful when they went to visit people at the Human Rights Commission, a non-governmental organization supported by the late Archbishop Romero. The young volunteers showed the mission visitors pictures covering the walls, and albums of photographs of people who had been shot and mutilated. They saw charts of the numbers of civilians assassinated since 1979, amounting to more than

1 percent of the total population. They were told of people killed and in prison. The young volunteers who ran the office were all under thirty years of age; they had a rapid turnover because they were obliged to look for paid jobs and because their lives were frequently threatened. The office was intensely hot and noisy with the exhaust of cars rising from the street below.

Afterwards they went to visit several members of the Committee of Mothers of the Disappeared who worked from a busy and cluttered room next door to the Human Rights Commission.

When they were in Honduras, members of the mission visited a human rights protest vigil in front of the cathedral in downtown Tegucigalpa, and spoke with relatives of the disappeared. Dr. Ramon Custodjo Lopez, president of the Committee for the Defence of Human Rights of Honduras told them torture was systematically employed against political prisoners. People were also "picked off" secretly, but the government never admitted it.

Muriel was really impressed by the sincerity and the concern of all the NGOs they met. Those they met in Costa Rica were upset that they could not do anything valuable in El Salvador because they were not allowed to do any development work with the people there. All they could do was relief work. The mission also met NGOs from several European countries, the US and Canada. Many were from religious groups, some from agencies. In Nicaragua they had an evening with fifteen Canadians working in various NGOs. They told Muriel that they found it easy to work with the full cooperation of the Sandinista government and she contrasted their lot with the unhappy NGOs in El Salvador.

In Managua she met an NGO worker called Joe Gunn whose nickname was "Pepe Pistoles." He accompanied them to meet a family in a Christian base community who were living in a newly built home. Muriel heard their story and saw how committed they were to the revolution. Music was what kept them alive during the revolution and often it was all they had to sustain them. The family sang and danced for the guests. Muriel carried away in her notebook a Spanish inscription which said "Without the Participation of Women There Can Be No Revolution," and the signatures of five women she met that day. Muriel thought that if people such as these were called upon again to take up arms they most likely would. Although she would never condemn them for supporting the Sandinistas, she still thought there was an important role for people who were looking for non-violent solutions. She was impressed when she heard that the Peace Brigades planned to go to Guatemala. Peace Brigades International is a grassroots organization exploring and implementing non-violent approaches to peacekeeping and support for basic human rights. Muriel also thought that the role played by the international NGOs working in Nicaragua would do as much to deter or contain the United States as anything else would.

When they were in Costa Rica the delegation interviewed the former president, Jose Figueres, in his home. He had a month earlier joined three other former presidents to publicly urge a dialogue with Nicaragua to resolve the border tensions. Figueres insisted that if the US wanted to avoid carnage it must stop supplying arms and supplies. Muriel noted that in Costa Rica, despite the country's official peace policy, the press incited the people to oppose the Sandinistas in Nicaragua. She expressed the hope that Costa Rica, a country without a standing army, would provide another alternative.

The mission delegates worked at a feverish pace, meeting together on the planes and early in the mornings to decide on the questions to raise and to review their findings. They kept copious notes of their interviews for the report they later issued and the media conferences they held in seven cities they visited during their travels.

On their return from Central America the delegation met with members of the American senate in Washington, with officials of the United Nations in New York and with members of parliament in Ottawa to present their findings.

Muriel reported that the delegation felt the major stumbling block to the peace process was the US administration of President Ronald Reagan. US policies were aggressively undermining the chance for peace. The heart of the mission's message was that, in their opinion, the Contadora Plan was the only alternative to war in the region. Muriel urged Canadians to use all diplomatic and political pressure to get the Central American countries, the US and the European nations to sign and back the Contadora agreement.

When Muriel landed in Ottawa from Washington, I met her. Muriel looked ashen and she could scarcely talk. The temperature in Washington had been near 100°F and the humidity was very high. Although exhausted, she refused to go to lie down at a friend's apartment; she only wanted to sit on a park bench for a while. The two of us sat in silence for an hour while Muriel gathered her forces. Although she was clearly on the point of collapse she was not about to give in. Rather than think about herself, her thoughts lingered with some of the desperate people she had seen or heard about in the past two weeks.

Some time later Muriel spoke at an outdoor rally organized by Oxfam and a local Latin American Information Group. In front of the Halifax Library Muriel passionately proclaimed:

> The men in power in the United States have got it all wrong and I grieve for the consequences.
> I grieve for the war in Nicaragua.
> I grieve that they have betrayed their own revolution by causing the deaths of thousands of Nicaraguan citizens.
> I grieve that they cannot see that the Sandinistas have been trying since 1979 to give meaning in Nicaragua to Emma Lazarus's

moving poem quoted on the Statue of Liberty, 1886, "Give us
your tired, your poor, your huddled masses yearning to be free."
I grieve that they will not accept the verdict of the World Court as
to their guilt.
I grieve that they have guaranteed more and more cruelty and death
by voting $100 million in continued military support for the
Contras.
I grieve at the hypocrisy which makes it possible for congressmen
to grab at concessions granted to them by the President in
exchange for their crucial support of this bill. They have sold
their integrity for a "mess of pottage."
I grieve that the sanctuary movement of churches in the United
States is punished for trying to end the suffering of real political
refugees from El Salvador and Guatemala.
I grieve for the lies which are told and repeated and make their way
into editorials.
And most of all I grieve for the completely unjustifiable, and
therefore wholly tragic deaths of these men, women, and children, health workers, teachers, farmers, friends and families of
people I met in Nicaragua—death from the hills that look so
friendly until you know that at any moment, a band of murderers
trained and armed by the United States may come down on your
village or your school, or hospital or health centre. These are the
tired, the poor, the huddled masses yearning to be free.[14]

Leading Protests Against Militarism

Betty Peterson had been very active for several years in involving the Voice
of Women in opposition to the low flying military jets in Labrador. Having
visited the Innu people at Sheshashit and Davis Inlet she knew first hand the
harmful effects of low flying planes on the Native people. During 1986,
5000 military sorties were made from Goose Bay airfield to two massive
flight ranges covering 100,000 square miles. The jets left in their wake ear
shattering sonic booms that terrorized Innu hunters (and still do) and their
families, as well as the Caribou herds and other wildlife on which the Innu
depend. The frequent flights often caused frightened animals to leave the
area, creating food shortages for the Innu communities. Voices helped to
form the Atlantic Peace Coalition (APC), a body of fifty-two Atlantic area
groups, to register a public protest at the time of the NATO foreign ministers'
meeting in Halifax in June 1986. APC protested against the training of NATO
countries' pilots in low level high speed "assault" manoeuvres in Labrador.
Muriel was a great inspiration to this coalition because of her well known
stand against NATO. She spent many hours encouraging APC's members to
produce a strong joint statement to the NATO foreign ministers. At the time

Betty Peterson
Muriel and David Nook at Coburg House, 1986.

Canada was considering enlarging the military base at Happy Valley-Goose Bay to permit more NATO countries to train pilots there.

Muriel headed a delegation from the Atlantic Peace Coalition that met with Joe Clark, the minister of external affairs, to discuss APC's objections to the bilateral agreements allowing low level military test flights and the proposed establishment of a NATO Tactical Fighter and Weapons Training Centre in Goose Bay. Muriel made the opening remarks and turned to a young Innu, David Nook, who was part of the delegation. David told the minister of the dangers of low level flights to his people. Later that week a huge rally was also held in Halifax. An Innu family who attended visited Muriel and Betty at Coburg House.

The struggle against low level flying continues. The Voice of Women, with the encouragement and support of Betty and Muriel, submitted two briefs to the Environmental Impact Study conducted by the government in the nineties. VOW was the only peace group and the only women's group given the status of intervenors. VOW withdrew from the second hearing in support of the Innu who had decided to boycott the hearings as they viewed them as false and unjust.

Objecting to "War Taxes"

While Muriel never had to go to jail for her pacifist beliefs, they did land her in a federal tax court in Halifax on April 5, 1989, when she was eighty years of age and a recipient of the Order of Canada and the Persons Award.

For nine years Muriel had been withholding about 9 percent of her federal income tax—the portion she figured the country used for war preparations. She did this as a member of Conscience Canada, a group of over 475 Canadians who put their "war tax" into a special fund each year rather than give it to the government. Annually she wrote a letter to the minister of national revenue to explain why she was not paying her full tax bill and she sent a photocopy of the cheque she forwarded to the Conscience Canada trust fund. However, she had not sent the tax department a "notice of objection" form in response to the "notice of assessment" form for the years 1983 to 1986. For this reason, the Taxation Division, with no prior notification, garnisheed $1395.81 from her bank account, an amount equal to what she had sent to Conscience Canada between 1983 and 1986, plus interest, and she was called before the Tax Court.

At the same time, one of the other members of Conscience Canada, Dr. Jerilynn Prior of Vancouver, was arguing in the courts that under the Canadian constitution, the individual's right to freedom of conscience should take precedence over their duty to pay taxes. Revenue Canada had agreed not to proceed against the members of Conscience Canada until the courts had ruled on Dr. Prior's case. Muriel objected that she had been treated differently.

With dignity and assurance Muriel stood before Judge W. Kempo and stated:

> I am an honest person, not trying to evade responsibility but rather attempting to be guided by my conscience, after the manner of Quakers since the 17th century. I am 80 years old. I joined the Society of Friends (Quakers) 14 years ago, after a lifetime as a member of another church. The Quakers' peace witness and their reliance on inner conscience rather than on outside authority as the guide to one's life decisions—these I hold in deep respect. With my husband, I had been strongly opposed to war and the threat of war as a means of dealing with international affairs since I was 20 years old.
>
> Finally I realized that to be consistent with my religious belief, I could not allow my money to be conscripted for war. I must instead withhold it, in the spirit in which I myself would not take up arms. How could I sit comfortably at home writing cheques to make it possible for others to do the killing?
>
> I know, now, with a certainty that, in order to keep up the technological preparations for horrendous conflict and to support an increasingly militarized economy, our government needs cold cash even more than it needs warm bodies.[15]

At this point the judge interrupted Muriel, but she did have a sympathetic ear as she granted Muriel more time to serve a notice of objection to the minister for the 1986 tax year. However she also ruled that Ms. Duckworth had waited too long to try to launch a formal objection to federal taxes assessed in the years 1983 to 1985. Regardless of the outcome, Muriel had issued a press release stating that she would continue to refuse to pay taxes to support war preparations.

> For two hundred years Canada has allowed young men not to be conscripted if they objected on conscientious grounds. . . . she said. I feel that neither should my money be conscripted for this purpose.[16]

Supporting Women's Actions during the Gulf War

During the Gulf war the Voices were extremely active both in initiating actions and in joining with other peace groups to express their opposition. Muriel spent her time in her customary fashion, on the phone, going to meetings and participating in the vigils, rallies and marches and picketing the US Consulate. Before the war was declared the Nova Scotia Voices expressed their total discouragement at their annual Day of Renewal. Betty Peterson soon mobilized them as she announced that she intended to undertake a noontime one-hour vigil outdoors in front of the Halifax Library, seven days a week, to witness against the impending war and to hand out educational material. This vigil continued throughout the winter. Muriel joined Betty one day each week throughout the war as did other Voices. Other citizens too stood with them to show their protest.

The Voices helped to organize a series of protest actions in Halifax and Dartmouth during the week of January 12, 1991, including a large scale rally, a public forum, a "rage in" at the Halifax Citadel, a candle light harbour vigil and a rally in solidarity with Minority Groups Dartmouth. Muriel participated with them as they marched up over the Citadel with the women banging pots and pans to acclaim their rage.

Protesting Rape in War

When Muriel heard the terrible news of the atrocities committed against women during the war in Yugoslavia she felt called upon to protest. She had always decried the rape of women by soldiers during wartime and it was happening again. Muriel felt that rape should be recognized as a war crime.

VOW had learned that Women in Black in Belgrade, Serbia, were holding a weekly vigil every Wednesday in downtown Belgrade as a demonstration against war and nationalism and in solidarity with the women and children victims of the war. At a large public meeting concerning the war the Voices announced their intention of conducting a weekly noon hour vigil each Wednesday for eight weeks in front of the Halifax Library, in solidarity with the Women in Black. They conducted this vigil in the late winter of 1993. Betty and Muriel handed out information sheets while eight Voices dressed in black stood for a silent hour, holding placards explaining their action. Other women joined the Voices in their silent vigil with placards and handouts of information.

On the last day, May 5, the Wednesday preceding Mother's Day, Muriel publicly presented a letter of petition to the president of the United Nations Association of Canada, Geoffrey Granville Wood. He had come from Ottawa to receive the letter and had agreed to convey it to Boutros Boutros-Ghali, secretary general of the United Nations. The letter read:

> We are petitioning you on behalf of the Voice of Women, one of Canada's oldest peace groups, regarding the continuing violence against women and children. Specifically, we are concerned about the use of rape as a means of genocide ("ethnic cleansing") and as a strategy of war in the former republic of Yugoslavia. We are also concerned, however, about reports of Somali women being raped in their own villages and in the refugee camps on the border with Kenya . . . . Putting an end to war means creating the conditions in which peace can flourish. It does not mean military intervention nor the sale of more arms to regions already in conflict. These responses to violence by more violence reflect a poverty of thought which the world cannot afford. They also reflect the old, male-dominated world order where women's bodies become battlefields and children become the hostages of history.

The letter put forth seven resolutions including:

> Establish a permanent War Crimes Tribunal with a fair representation of women and a mandate to give central attention to gender-specific violations, including rape and forced pregnancy, in all contexts of war and military occupations, including those by peacekeeping forces.[17]

VOW kept in touch with two of the women's groups, one in Belgrade and one in Zagreb. Donna Smyth and Gillian Thomas helped to sponsor the visit of an academic woman, Vesna Nicolic Ristanovic, to Montreal and to Halifax. Muriel chaired a meeting in Montreal where Vesna spoke and afterwards she visited Muriel at her cottage. The Voices tried to bring together Croatian and Serbian women without much success, but Muriel remained convinced that it was important keep in touch with women inside countries that are at war—especially if there are peace movements there— in order to support them.

Notes

1. Notes kept by M. Duckworth while attending the Canadian Women's Study Tour of Europe. PANS MG 1 Vol. 2945, No. 16.
2. The twelve organizations were: CRIAW, l'Association des Femmes pour Education et Action Sociale, Canadian Congress on Learning Opportunities for Women, Canadian Federation of University Women, Federation des Femmes de Québec, Federated Women's Institutes of Canada, National Action Committee on the Status of Women, National Association of Women and the Law, National Council of Jewish Women of Canada, National Council of Women, Voice of Women, Women's Interchurch Council.
3. Notes kept by M. Duckworth while attending the Canadian Women's Study Tour of Europe. PANS MG 1 Vol. 2945, No. 16.
4. Details of this trip are from the author's own observations as the delegate of the Canadian Voice of Women for Peace.
5. "Atlantic Voices of Women," 14 April 1982. PANS MG 1 Vol. 2930, No. 39.
6. PANS MG 1 Vol. 2904, No. 14.
7. PANS MG 1 Vol. 2904, No. 13.
8. Accounts of the trip to Japan are from the author's interview with Suellen Bradfield, 18 August 1983, Halifax, and "Hiroshima August 6, 1983," National VOW Newsletter, Vol. 3, No. 3 (October 1983). PANS MG 1 Vol. 2930, No. 37.
9. Peace Declaration printed in the program for the Hiroshima Peace Memorial Ceremony. Personal scrapbook of M. Duckworth.
10. National VOW Newsletter. PANS MG 1 Vol. 2930, No. 37.
11. National VOW Newsletter, Vol. 4, No. 2 (June 1984). PANS MG 1 Vol. 2930, No. 37.
12. "Where are the Peace Women at the Negotiating Table?" National VOW Newsletter, Vol. 4, No. 1 (February 1984). PANS MG 1 Vol. 2930, No. 37.
13. "Report Mission for Peace 1985–86." PANS MG 1 Vol. 2946, No. 23.
14. Notes for speech. PANS MG 1 Vol. 2946, No. 23.
15. Letter to family and friends, 16 April 1989 containing the article, "Muriel Duckworth in Tax Court Halifax, April 5, 1989."*
16. Ibid.
17. *Atlantic Voice of Women Peaceletter*, Spring 1993. The Canadian Voice of Women for Peace, Toronto, ON.

Note: * indicates document awaiting archival deposit.

Muriel celebrating with "Pentagon Protestors" after their day in court, Halifax, 1985.

Muriel protesting War Tax, 1992.

Muriel with Raging Grannies, Peoples' Summit, Halifax, 1995

Chapter 17

The Spirit of Muriel

Honours and Awards

In 1978 Mount Saint Vincent University was the first university to confer an honorary doctorate on Muriel. She was named Honorary Doctor of Humane Letters. By 1993 she had received six more honorary doctorates from Canadian universities from coast to coast. Eight in all, if one counted a delightful degree conferred May 6, 1986, tongue-in-cheek by the fictitious People's University of Nova Scotia (PUNS) at Coburg House, during a party for Ursula Franklin. Ursula was in Halifax to receive an honorary degree from Mount St. Vincent and that same spring word was out that Dalhousie University had refused to accept Muriel as a candidate for a doctorate from Dalhousie. An article in the university paper, *The Gazette*, for March 20, 1986, quoted a student senator:

> When someone brought up that she had 60 signatures on her nomination form, they were told [by the committee] that it was not a popularity contest, but rather a measure of the good someone did for society. Then it was suggested that the committee just didn't have a category for an elderly, socialist woman in the peace movement.

So her friends decided to confer their own doctoral degree and their citation read:

> In recognition of Muriel Duckworth's years of apprenticeship in the fine art of weaving lives together and providing truly subversive leadership in all the communities associated with PUNS; in honour of her status as Uppity Woman of the First Order; in appreciation of her life, generosity, and grace of soul, we hereby declare her a Honorary Doctor of Humane Letters and a Mistress Weaver of People.

The sequel to the story is that Dalhousie granted Muriel an Honorary Doctor of Laws the following year. By then, faculty members of the senate had come to realize what had happened the year before, and threatened to vote against any doctoral candidate proposed by the committee who had refused her, until her candidacy was fairly treated.

Presentation to Muriel of "People's University Honorary Degree."

Muriel turned each award she received, whether it was the Person's Award in 1980, the Order of Canada in June 1983, the Lester B. Pearson Peace Medal in 1991 or several honorary life memberships, into an occasion for honouring all the women who worked to bring about a peaceful society. She saw herself as a symbol of the honours that were long due to women and which they so seldom received. Muriel reminded her audience of this in the convocation speech which she gave when she and Florence I. Wall, a well known and respected Nova Scotia educator, received their honorary degrees from Mount St. Vincent University in 1978.

> I cannot refrain from mentioning, just in case you in this audience might be feeling unjustifiably happy about the present status of women, that you have before you the only three women who will be receiving honorary degrees in Nova Scotia this year. My con- gratulations to Kings University for having the good sense to choose Sister Albertus [president of Mount St. Vincent University]. It makes the proportion of men to women being so honoured about nine to one.[1]

Contrasting the year of her graduation from McGill (1929) when students were ill-prepared for the depression and war years ahead, with the understanding of present students, she said:

> You know you may not be able to get jobs for which you are qualified, that the idea that you will have a range of attractive jobs to choose from would be laughable if it were not so tragic.
> You women know that you are a reserve army of labour, that myths abound as to why you should leave the paid work of the world to men, that you are even blamed for unemployment. You need to know that in over half the families where both parents are working

their total income is less that $15,000 or in other words, 60 percent of families would have incomes below the poverty line if only one parent were earning.

She went on to relate the economy to war preparations and to talk about poverty in the Third World, racism and the horrendous consequences of living in an age which had split the atom. Implicitly she urged upon students her own personal recipe for turning the world around:

> Seek out and join in community with your sisters and brothers who are forces for change, who have found their own inner sources of power, who are together moving the world. . . . They have turned their outrage at the status quo not to self-destructive isolation but to intelligent, disciplined, loving work which they do joyously.

When Muriel received an Honorary Doctor of Laws at Concordia University in Montreal in June 1983, she talked about "reconstituting the world" and "reweaving the web of life." She read a favourite stanza from a poem by Adrienne Rich:

> My heart is moved by all I cannot save:
> so much has been destroyed
>
> I have to cast my lot with those
> who age after age, perversely,
>
> with no extraordinary power,
> reconstitute the world.[2]

Muriel told her audience how the expression "reweaving the web of life" was invented by a group of Vermont women to describe their street theatre. On March 30, 1980, they began spinning their symbolic web of many colours in support of a week-long occupation at the Vermont Yankee Nuclear Power Plant. In their handout they said: "We will meet, all of us women of every land, we will meet in the centre, make a circle, we will weave a world web to entangle the powers that bury our children."

Muriel described patriarchy and militarism as two expressions of the same social ill. To her, "reconstituting the world" meant, at the very least, getting rid of both of them. "Reweaving the web of life" meant empowering ourselves by taking part in protest action with others. She quoted Dr. Rosalie Bertell who had been a witness at the Nuremburg trials, where individuals responsible for the Second World War including the Holocaust, were on trial for genocide:

We are at a point of termination of a primitive stage in human development, the stage of national sovereignty. . . . The nation's right to destroy its own people or those of other nations for some political advantages is as outrageous today as was the old custom establishing a male's right over the life of his spouse and children.

Muriel repeated this same theme when she received an Honorary Doctor of Laws from Dalhousie in 1987 and gave the law students examples of people who were "reconstituting the world": judges and prosecutors in Germany publicly opposing government policy over nuclear armaments; Lawyers for Social Responsibility in Halifax who were studying the legality of nuclear armed submarines coming into the Halifax Harbour; Dr. Jerilynn Prior of Vancouver who was appealing to the Supreme Court of Canada the decision of a lower court that she did not have the right under the freedom of conscience and religion clause of the constitution to withhold that part of her taxes which went to the armed forces for destructive purposes. Then Muriel went on to challenge the graduates:

You, in your conscious, I, in mine, need to be clear on how we feel about such actions and whose side we are on. And the best way, maybe the only way to be clear, is to be a part of the action holding on to our vision of a world where forests flourish, where the water is clean, and where each person knows she matters to all the others.

The Lester B. Pearson Peace Medal, October 1991

A gala party awaited Muriel when she returned from Government House in Ottawa after being awarded the Lester B. Pearson Peace Medal. Evelyne Meltzer of the United Nations Association in Halifax invited Muriel's many friends in the peace movement to the Waegwoltic Club. Since Muriel had been confined to a few brief remarks when she received the award in Ottawa she was delighted to have saved her longer speech for Halifax. She used the opportunity to inform her audience about the history of the founding of the UN and its agencies. The lighting was not very bright and when Muriel went to read quotes she realized she could not see them. With great aplomb she called on three women in the audience to read them for her. This was just before she had successful cataract operations on both eyes.

Maxine Tynes read some of her lovely poems and Emily Purdy sang beautiful peace songs she had composed. Gillian Thomas recited a very funny conversation which she had composed between the ghost of Lester B. Pearson and a person named Muriel Duckworth, on the occasion of the said person receiving the Lester B. Pearson Peace Medal, October 22, 1991. In the poem, Muriel refuses to approve of Pearson's decision to allow Bomarc missiles into Canada. Its closing lines read:

Betty Peterson

Muriel with Olive White, at Halifax celebration of Muriel having received the Pearson Peace Medal.

L.B.P.   Dear lady, I'm fading fast
            I've only got a visitor's pass.
            Tell me you understand
            How a man of my vision
            Could have made such a painful decision
            Give me that blessing in the name of peace.

M.D.   Lester B. This medal links you and me
            And I forgive you everything except—
            Remember what Martin Luther said
            "Here I stand. I can do no other"
            The Americans don't command our souls, my
            brother
            So get you back to the dead
            Mike Pearson
            With blessings on your head!

Birthday Parties

Muriel's birthday parties, held every five years, were festive events, real community celebrations. She loved a party, music, singing and dancing, and most of all introducing her friends to one another.

Eleanor and John hosted a wonderful party at John's house for Muriel's seventieth birthday on October 31, 1978. Muriel announced to great cheers that she was taking a six-month sabbatical. And she did! Muriel visited friends and family in California that winter. She spent a week alone enjoying San Francisco and stayed at the Friends' (Quaker) House. Her first day there she quite spontaneously participated in a non-violence training course that they were holding—a true "busdriver's holiday!" Muriel became increasingly interested in non-violence training as she grew older. On the upstairs hall wall in her cottage was a delightful poster saying, "Suppose they gave a war and nobody came."

Muriel wrote to her grandchildren about the celebration of her seventy-fifth birthday party:

> Dear Marya, Sylvia, Samantha, Tiffany, Danielle, Jacqueline, Nicholas,
>
> What a 75th Birthday I had! Did you all know that Danielle, Jacqueline and Martin were all here to celebrate with me and my friends? Did you ever go to a birthday party where there were seven birthday cakes? I guess they thought they couldn't get all the candles on one cake, and they couldn't bake one cake big enough that 150 people could each have a piece.
>
> It was such a lovely party, with candles, and balloons and decorations, and lots of good food, and the speeches by Martin, and Suellen Bradfield and me and singing. Danielle and Jacqueline and other children helped me blow out the candles and Martin made a movie at the party. That was Sunday evening. Danielle and Jacqueline and Martin left at 6:30 a.m. to fly to Ottawa on their way home to Montreal. So did Mr. Mureta, from Hiroshima, Japan, who was here for the showing of Martin's film "No More Hibakusha" on October 27. Mr. Mureta, who is in that film, thought my party was a lot of fun. So did I and I thank all the people who planned it and did all the work for it.

Betty Peterson

Muriel's 75th birthday party, Halifax, 1983.

> Yesterday, Halloween day, which was really my birthday—did you have fun? Did you dress up? Quite a few children came to our door. Oh—in the morning I planted a Japanese maple tree on the campus of Mount Saint Vincent University. That was a birthday present to me from my friends. And besides that, they gave over $1,500 to the Peace Fund which was set up in 1975 in memory of and in honour of your grampa. That was the most wonderful part of my birthday for me. I wish you could all have been here, though Danielle and Jacqueline and Martin were good representatives of the family.
>
> Lots of love, Grannie.[3]

Muriel's eightieth birthday was celebrated during the annual general meeting of the national Voice of Women, held that year in Halifax. The YWCA main hall was filled with women who feted Muriel with a long evening of stories, poems and songs, and messages and drawings on a "Muriel on the Wall." Many of the early Voices were there—Nora Toole, Kay Macpherson, Peggy Hope-Simpson and Dorothy Rosenberg—all with amusing tales about Muriel.

Muriel's friend Mickey Haase gave her a six-week trip to New Zealand for her eightieth birthday in 1988. Muriel had never been there and she knew no one personally. She wrote to a number of Quaker communities in New Zealand and to a few friends of friends and explained that she would be travelling alone and would enjoy meeting them and she mentioned her age. People were amazed to meet this vibrant woman who was so eager to see everything and who moved with impressive speed and grace. She had a wonderful time and made many new friends in the five areas she visited.

Alexa McDonough hosted Muriel's eighty-fifth birthday with an after-noon open house. Hundreds of Nova Scotians came to join in the celebration. Some of her favourite songs were sung by Yvonne White and everyone joined in a rollicking singsong with Chris Richards.[4]

The Spirit of Muriel

The night of Muriel's seventy-fifth birthday party I was driving home with Mary Cutler, an experienced nurse who had cared for many elderly persons. I asked Mary whether she thought Muriel was untypical of persons of her age or did one often find persons of such vitality at seventy-five. There was a long pause. Then Mary thoughtfully answered, "my first reaction was to say she is certainly untypical and then I remembered several others." "Is there anything they have in common?" I asked. "Their vulnerability," Mary instantly replied. "It's because they keep themselves so open to others, to pain and to joy, that's why Muriel and people like her remain so vital!"

Muriel's openness has meant she is undogmatic and tentative. Her own vulnerability makes her caring and sensitive to others. Mary O'Brien, a professor at Mount St. Vincent University, interviewed Muriel on spiritu-ality and ageing. To Muriel, spirituality is

> what links you with everything in the world and is related to creativity and caring and, in a sense, suffering along with the people who suffer.[5]

The awe she feels for life, the potential in a plant about to bloom, the potential for loving relationships between people—Muriel sees these as manifestations of the life force that some call spirituality. Even personal things which she cherishes have a relation to someone who is meaningful to her. She is reluctant to think of spirituality as "religion" or even as "God" because to her those concepts are often divisive. Muriel remains aware that her life experience and the way in which she was brought up are only small parts of a very big world and she does not want to foist on others her ideas of the origins of life or the nature of the life force, which she thinks of as only conjecture on her part. At the same time she values immensely Quaker practices such as meeting in silence, "holding one in the light," the struggle to arrive at "the sense of the meeting" and Quaker beliefs that you are guided by the light as you see it and you have an obligation to test it out and follow it, if it seems true. She believes in "that of God" in each person, though she might find it hard to love everybody. She feels at home in the Quaker community because it is a kind of outreach community that tries to figure out what it can do about specific problems as a part of the whole world community.

To Muriel, just as a seed is here to produce flowers, we are here to lead decent lives. She thinks we are born with a life force within us or a spirit that can move us towards good if we rely on it. As she sees it, without love people wither, and without goodness in their relationships they turn sour and sometimes violent. She agrees with Isabel Carter Heyward's thesis that evil is a break in relationship.[6] It is what keeps people apart. Reverence for nature and love of people is the essence of Muriel's spirituality.

One of the few tenets Muriel holds as an article of faith is that one should not think one is better than anyone else. This is what prompts her to see everyone as her neighbour and to be an activist for social justice. In the face of inequality she feels as children do when they say, "that's not fair!" As she explained:

> If you feel your link to all people, that other people matter as much as you do yourself and you matter a lot, then that link with people makes you do what you can so that other people should have a chance too.

She recognized the dilemma in her position as she went on to say:

> You feel it's one world and then you try to embrace the whole world and then you have to develop a way of living that makes it possible for you to go on living and accept the limits of yourself—an imperfect person, your own self-interests, your own wanting to be comfortable, acquisitive, recognizing that what you have is at the expense of other people . . . the fact that I have bananas on the table.

Yet in the face of perceived injustice, Muriel's passionate pacifism drives her into action because, as she puts it,

> I just can't stand the thought of that kind of treatment of human life and human possibility. I just can't stand it that people use their power to arrogantly destroy others.

And Muriel believes that women must take responsibility for resistance to war.

> Women can't bring back the spiritual unless they become fully recognized and they have to do that themselves, get themselves fully recognized as part of the world that you are trying to build. You can't do that with war. It can't be done by fighting it out, there have got to be other ways, got to be what you call "women's ways." We can't just have a world in which men can go out and do what they did in Iraq and what they did to Vietnam, just blindly kill everybody that comes in the way and go home and look like good fathers and good husbands. It's outrageous that we're in that state in the world now. We've got to get beyond that state and I think it's harder for men to see that. The leaders convince themselves that this war is a just war. I think we have to get rid of the notion that any war is a just war.

Facing Death

Perhaps it was because of Muriel's incredible vitality that her friends were shocked when she had a very sudden brush with death just before New Year's Day, 1994. Muriel spent over a month in hospital battling meningococcal meningitis and months afterward recovering at home. The fact that she survived at all was because her friend Pat Kipping got her to hospital so quickly. Immediately, Muriel's network sprang into action. Despite a bad snow storm, friends who lived within walking distance of the hospital were able to take over until her family could get there. They may have had tears running down their faces but they knew what to do. Donna Smyth and Gillian Thomas set about putting together a list of persons who would come at two-hour intervals around the clock. No one had to be asked twice. In short order they had one hundred people lined up whose chief function, besides being generally silent company for Muriel, was to do traffic control at her door. Visitors were asked to wait until she was better before coming to see her.

As before, it was many months before Muriel regained her strength. She did not know to what extent she might expect to recover. When she asked a nurse in the hospital what it would be like when she got over this particular event, the nurse briskly replied as she snapped a sheet over the bed, "I don't know! People of your age, when they get what you had, don't come here!" Muriel tried not to worry about it too much but rested and enjoyed the attention she received from everyone. She felt everybody should have such a convalescence!

As Muriel has learned more about her body through illness and operations, she marvels even more at the complexity of the body and how well it generally works. Having had two cataract operations she came to appreciate just how complicated the

Muriel with extended family, Austin, Thanksgiving, 1987.

eye is. When she had to have a pacemaker in early 1995, she was struck with amazement to find that the power that keeps the heart going is manufactured inside the body electrically, and that this can be replaced with a kind of a battery inside the chest, so that the heart can keep beating. She felt if she had even greater knowledge of how each part of her body functioned, that she would be in even greater awe of creation.

For a while it looked as though Muriel would finally have to slow down, but by the following year the spring was back in her step and her energetic voice could be heard on the other end of the telephone, inviting, exhorting, organizing. As she put it

> I don't think in terms of 'I'm being kept alive to do something' but rather, 'since I'm alive I should do something!'

For example, she agreed to chair a workshop at the International Education Centre in June 1995, at St. Mary's University during the P7, a mammoth community counter-conference to the G7 when the heads of state came to Halifax.

Muriel knows that she might have to face a time when she can no longer do what she wants to do and hopes she can at least in some way continue to support others. Just before her eighty-seventh birthday she came to terms with being old and with the recognition that her energy is limited. She has begun to inform people that she is "an old lady."

Preoccupied neither with life's beginnings nor with the afterlife, Muriel is content to take life as a mystery. Because she is so often surrounded by people, when she is alone she quite values her solitude and the chance to enjoy her apartment by herself. Whenever she reflects on people close to her who have died—Jack, her mother, her brothers and sisters—she ponders over their lives, and using her own experience for comparison, she has come to understand them better.

Remaining close to her family and friends and feeling her connection to her children, her grandchildren and her great grandchildren is very important to Muriel. She sees the ongoingness of relationships, going back into history and going on into the future.

Notes

1. Addresses given by M. Duckworth on the occasions of receiving honorary doctorates are to be found in PANS MG 1 Vol. 2933, No. 7.
2. Adrienne Rich, "Natural Resources," in *The Dream of a Common Language, Poems, 1974–77*. New York: Norton, 1978.
3. Letter from Muriel Duckworth to her grandchildren, 1 November 1983. Personal collection of M. Duckworth.
4. Yvonne White is a well known Black singer who gives the history of Black music in her recitals. Chris Richards is a young assistant in the Halifax school system. She belongs to a group of women singers who call themselves the Persisters.
5. Unpublished interview with M. Duckworth by Mary O'Brien, 26 May 1992. In the possession of Mary O'Brien, Mount St. Vincent University, Halifax, NS.
6. Isabel Carter Heyward, *The Redemption of God: A Theology of Mutual Relation.* Washington, DC: University Press of America, 1982.

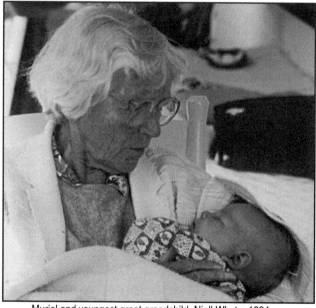

Muriel and youngest great grandchild, Niall Whyte, 1994.

Index

About the Author

*S*ocial worker, educator, community organizer, peace activist, Marion Kerans has lived and worked in Montreal, Vancouver, Toronto, Halifax and Pictou. She has six children and ten grandchildren.

Terri Nash

Muriel at her cottage, 1988.